THE EVERYTHING.
Private Investigation Book

Dear Reader,

About once a month, I receive an e-mail from someone offering his services as a private investigator, usually for free. Upon following up, I find that he has no training, no experience in the field, and hasn't even read a book about the subject. Needless to say, I can't use him. If I hired someone such as this—or even let him work for train-ing—his total lack of knowledge would be too distracting to another investigator. Someone like this wouldn't even be able to help; he would hinder an investigation.

Plus, if it takes two people to do one job, one of them isn't necessary. Read this book and others recommended in the text, check out the recommended Web sites (you can start with mine, *www.safersecurityinc.com*), get some training, and then call around to see if an agency can use a trainee. Have something of value to offer, and know how to articulate this value before you call an agency.

The second mistake potential investigators make is offering their services for free. You must realize that your abilities have monetary value; if you don't, no one else will. Also, it's a good idea to purchase your own basic equipment. With your own equipment, you'll never need to stand in line for what you need, and you'll be more attractive to an investigative agency.

As a former agent for the Bureau of Alcohol, Tobacco, Firearms and Explosives and licenced private investigator, I've learned that in this business you hold peoples' lives in your hands—sometimes literally, but more often figuratively. You'll have identifying information that, if misused, can wreck a life and a family. You'll be the keeper of secrets for people who trust and need you. Don't let them down; use your investigative powers for good and not evil. People enter the PI profession for different reasons. Some are interested in money: There's no doubt that money can be made, but there are other, better motives. I can't reiterate enough that the most rewarding motive is the knowledge that you've made a difference in the life of another human being, and that you will leave the planet a better place than you found it.

Sheila L. Stephens

Welcome to the EVERYTHING® Series!

These handy, accessible books give you all you need to tackle a difficult project, gain a new hobby, comprehend a fascinating topic, prepare for an exam, or even brush up on something you learned back in school but have since forgotten.

You can choose to read an *Everything*® book from cover to cover or just pick out the information you want from our four useful boxes: e-questions, e-facts, e-alerts, e-ssentials. We give you everything you need to know on the subject, but throw in a lot of fun stuff along the way, too.

We now have more than 400 *Everything*® books in print, spanning such wide-ranging categories as weddings, pregnancy, cooking, music instruction, foreign language, crafts, pets, New Age, and so much more. When you're done reading them all, you can finally say you know *Everything*®!

QUESTIONS?
Answers to common questions

FACTS
Important snippets of information

ALERTS!
Urgent warnings

ESSENTIALS
Quick handy tips

DIRECTOR OF INNOVATION Paula Munier

MANAGING EDITOR, EVERYTHING SERIES Lisa Laing

COPY CHIEF Casey Ebert

ACQUISITIONS EDITOR Lisa Laing

DEVELOPMENT EDITOR Elizabeth Kassab

Visit the entire Everything® series at *www.everything.com*

THE
EVERYTHING®
PRIVATE INVESTIGATION BOOK

Master the techniques of the pros to examine
evidence, track down people, and discover the truth

Sheila L. Stephens

adam

avon, massachusetts

To Don, with my love and gratitude.

An Everything® Series Book.
Everything® and everything.com® are registered trademarks of F+W Publications, Inc.

Published by Adams Media, an F+W Publications Company
57 Littlefield Street, Avon, MA 02322 U.S.A.
www.adamsmedia.com

ISBN 10: 1-59869-535-5
ISBN 13: 978-1-59869-535-9

Printed in the United States of America.

J   I   H   G   F   E   D   C   B   A

Library of Congress Cataloging-in-Publication Data
is available from the publisher.

This publication is designed to provide accurate and authoritative information with regard to the subject matter covered. It is sold with the understanding that the publisher is not engaged in rendering legal, accounting, or other professional advice. If legal advice or other expert assistance is required, the services of a competent professional person should be sought.

—From a *Declaration of Principles* jointly adopted by a Committee of the American Bar Association and a Committee of Publishers and Associations

Many of the designations used by manufacturers and sellers to distinguish their products are claimed as trademarks. Where those designations appear in this book and Adams Media was aware of a trademark claim, the designations have been printed with initial capital letters.

Photography copyright © 2008 by Steve Slocum.

*This book is available at quantity discounts for bulk purchases.
For information, please call 1-800-289-0963.*

Contents

Acknowledgments

For going on this trek with me, I'd like to thank my agent, Maura Kye-Casella, with Denise Marcil Literary Agency. Her guidance has been invaluable, and her encouragement motivating. I'd also like to thank the unflappable Lisa Laing, with Adams Media. Working with her has been energizing—and a pleasure. Thanks to my first writing teacher, Bonnie Hearn Hill.

I'd also like to thank my family and friends for their support and understanding. I've missed a lot of get-togethers over the course of writing this book, but they've been great about it. I especially thank my mom, Joyce Lenning, and my brother, Joe Lenning, for who they are and for their unwavering support. I also can't fail to acknowledge some of my best friends and supporters for getting me to this place: Victoria and Woodie Fritz and the entire staff at Dr. Lyman (Woodie) Fritz's Clinic, as well as author Lee Lofland.

Finally, thanks go out to all the readers of this book—from those who want to learn how to use one or two techniques presented here to those brave enough to jump into the profession of private investigation. To the latter, I pray that you use your newfound powers for good and not for evil.

Top Ten Items
Every PI Needs

1. Insurance—preferably errors and omissions—and a license

2. An up-to-date computer, preferably a laptop

3. A Web site

4. Professional business cards and brochures

5. A reliable vehicle of neutral-color and unremarkable appearance

6. Office space with secure storage for client and target information, and equipped with a computer, printer, and shredder

7. A low-lux video camcorder with image stabilization, zoom lens, and auto control

8. A variety of tripods

9. Communication equipment, radios, and a good cell phone

10. A wearable or portable covert camera

Introduction

▶ MANY BOOKS HAVE BEEN WRITTEN about private investigation. The authors of most of them state that investigation is about finding the truth. While this is not wrong, neither is it exactly right. Truth is a funny thing; it's often dependent upon perspective. Not to insinuate that there's no truth or lie, good or bad, black or white—but truth often hides in the areas between these concepts, where it's difficult to find. Sometimes, real problems arise when these areas become so murky that truth is impossible to determine with any real certainty. At this point, truth must often be determined in a court of law by someone other than the investigator. At some junctures of the investigative process, truth is actually irrelevant.

The only thing relevant at all times and at all stages of the investigative process is evidence. Investigators are looking for information that translates into evidence, not truth. Evidence can lead to what appears to be—but it is not always—the truth. Of course, everyone wants to uncover the truth, yet a successful investigation can be conducted even though truth remains in question. The investigator's job is to seek out, develop, and collect information, then deliver it in an understandable form that can be presented in court should this become necessary.

What is truth? Truth may seem to be fairly obvious. It may be presented in a document or public record that must be correct, right? Not always. What if that document, or part of it, has been forged or incorrectly recorded?

More "truth" may be presented in the form of video recordings. This type of evidence is guaranteed, isn't it? If it can be seen and heard, it has to be true, right? Wrong again. Recordings can be altered or edited, videos can be of such poor quality as to make identification questionable or impossible. Remember those grainy, blurry videos on the nightly news? Many surveillance cameras are not capable of doing the job for which they are installed. All video evidence must be verified.

This book does not presume to guide those looking for truth, but it will prepare anyone to find evidence. This is an overview of the field of private investigation, not an exhaustive examination of the subject, but there is something here for every reader. Everyone from the interested amateur to the seasoned professional will be able to glean nuggets of information that will make the reading of this book more than worthwhile. For the new investigator or one about to take the plunge, time and experience will add to the information contained here. Also, remember that laws, technology, and Internet resource links change, so check before you act.

The umbrella term "private investigation" covers a range of services. Some of these include divorce/infidelity; child custody; missing persons; insurance investigation; business/corporate security; and special investigations including legal and hidden camera investigation, bounty hunting, and cyber-sleuthing—all topics that this book will explore.

However, *The Everything® Private Investigation Book* is not just for readers at some stage of investigative experience; it's also an invaluable resource for journalists and novelists, students of criminal justice, those needing to do background checks on employees or tenants, and self-appointed armchair detectives. It's interesting reading for the knowledge-seekers of this world—those who just want to know how things, and people, work.

While the real-world practice of private investigation is not exactly what has been portrayed in novels and movies and shown on television, it's still one of the most rewarding and entertaining professions on the planet—but it can be dangerous. Anyone whose goal is to work as a private investigator must be sure that she has what it takes to do this job well, along with a willingness to cultivate the skills and knowledge necessary to do it safely. She must also be absolutely sure to use her investigative powers to make the world a better place.

CHAPTER 1

Do You Have the Right Stuff?

Investigators are not born with "the right stuff," though television and movies make this appear to be true. Investigative strengths are often spoken of as if they're genetically bestowed traits: Either you have them or you don't. In reality, nothing could be farther from the truth; these strengths are not present in one person's DNA and absent from the DNA of another. While it is true that some people may be better at certain things than others, everything can be learned, and everything learned can be improved upon.

Powers of Observation and Concentration

Observation and concentration are dependent upon one another and are related to something else—work. Investigators rarely fall across evidence as do television and movie PIs. Real investigators work for evidence using observation. Observation is work, and it is a product of concentration. Concentration—an act of will—is under the control of the person who wishes to concentrate. Thus, anyone willing to work can improve his concentration and observation skills.

Importance of Observation and Concentration

When you're sitting on surveillance, waiting for that one chance to snap a picture or film a few moments of your elusive target, losing focus can cause you to miss your chance—a chance that may not present itself again.

◄ PIs often have to sit on surveillance for long periods of time, waiting patiently for that "gotcha" moment. You must be able to stay alert and focused to get what you are looking for.

Federal agencies, large police departments, and large PI firms have an edge—available manpower—which makes surveillance much easier. Several investigators switch back and forth, sharing the task of watching the target. The Feds call this having the eyeball or having the eye. During any surveillance, someone must always have the eyeball—an uninterrupted focus on the target until the eye is passed to someone else.

This is the best way to keep a target under surveillance, yet it's not feasible for small police departments and PI firms, where the burden falls on one person, two or three at the most. Being the only person, or one of a few, responsible for having the eyeball can be tiring. It's hard work, but it's the only way to be sure you don't miss anything. If you do miss something, your client or supervisor will not be happy. Neither will you; for most investigators, getting the target is worth the discomfort experienced during an investigation.

A professional investigator may sit for hours in surveillance vehicles, crawl through wooded areas, and search through stacks of records to get what she needs. Nothing is quite like the "gotcha" moment, that instant when the investigator knows she's gotten the shot, the video, or the information necessary to crack the case, and she'll do what she must (legally) to get it.

In Chapter 18, the types of surveillance with which you must be familiar to achieve your own "gotcha" moments will be discussed.

Observation depends on one other element: prior knowledge. Without it, it's possible to look directly at evidence or facts and not appreciate their significance. What appears to one person as the idle scribbling of a bored teen is apparent to another as gang representation or messaging. What might be a mound of pale dirt to one person is known as "cheese," the newest threat in street drugs, to another. Possessing knowledge of the way criminals do their thing is as important as knowing how to do yours.

Because of knowledge, the object of your concentration makes sense, allowing you to process your observations. The more you concentrate and observe, the more knowledge you gain—and the more knowledge you gain, the better your concentration and observation skills. In fact, some experts argue that concentration is intelligence.

Improving Observation and Concentration

Although much is still unknown, research has shown that certain mental exercises add to the operating capacity of your brain, regardless of age, education, or experience. For example, view a picture you are not familiar with, then look away and record any details you remember. You'll be surprised at how much eludes you, even with the second or third attempt. This is normal. Continue practicing with different pictures and you'll improve.

Even with improved skills, take notes and pictures when on surveillance. These exercises utilize short-term memory, and though you may become so proficient that you can astound friends at parties, remember that short-term memory is limited and decays rapidly. Basically, your short-term memory only holds information until you can record it.

Several techniques that deliver information from your short-term bank to your long-term memory bank are:

- **Repetition:** memorization of poems or scripture
- **Consistent use of information:** complicated sequences of actions can be memorized by going through the sequences again and again
- **Grouping:** for instance, phone numbers are easier to remember when they are grouped between hyphens
- **Putting information to music:** most of us can still sing our ABCs
- **Mnemonics:** many techniques use imagery to link the familiar with the unfamiliar—linking an image to the information you want to remember

Besides exercises to improve overall function, several techniques can help your concentration while you sit on surveillance:

- **Breathing exercises.** Breathe deeply and slowly through the nose, then out through the mouth, pushing air from your lungs by sucking in your stomach.
- **Minimize distractions.** Do nothing that may divert attention from the target.
- **Comment aloud.** Many investigators talk to themselves as they watch. Describing the house, office, and grounds into a tape recorder may help you later when you write your report.
- **Snack.** Most investigators eat to stay alert.

If you use snacking, be aware that highly processed carbohydrates can make you sleepy, as can turkey and sugar products. Some experts write that there's not enough tryptophan in turkey to cause sleepiness, but others disagree—you'll know if it affects you. Instead, eating fruit, veggie sticks, cheese, nuts, or protein that can be eaten with your fingers will ensure a steady supply of fuel to your brain. Highly processed food will provide a quick, momentary pickup, then drop you just as quickly.

QUESTION?

Can concentration be improved?
The Web site Brainbuilder.com can help you focus. Recommended by neurologist and The Better Brain Book author Dr. David Perlmutter, this site provides the latest information about brain health, and exercises to improve function.

Observation and concentration are also related to motivation. Observant people are motivated by many things: curiosity, desire, pride, security, the desire to succeed, and more. Even fear can be a motivator—not stark raving fear, of course, which is paralyzing and counterproductive—but fear that you may miss your chance to get that shot of the target. A little of this type of fear pumps adrenaline through your body and sharpens your senses—but don't let fear drive you.

Communication Skills and the Ability to Listen

Communication is an important skill, particularly for the investigator. Networking depends on communication. To some, networking—a.k.a. schmoozing—is stained with negative connotations. One reason is that unscrupulous people have used it with dishonest intentions. The concept of networking has no such intent. The idea is to make contact with those who may need your services, and whose services you may need. It's a reciprocal relationship, not meant to satisfy the needs of, or provide gain for, one person.

Communication also helps the investigator in interviewing and interrogation. Therefore, learning this skill is a necessity. Yet, it's not about the ability to talk about anything at any time. It's about the ability to listen.

Communicating Effectively

Communication skills are the latch on the investigator's tool kit. They open the kit so that everything inside can be utilized. Spend time learning to communicate, especially if your skills are below par. Some suggestions follow:

- Look for the good in everyone; become genuinely interested in people
- Give sincere praise, but don't make something up; be honest
- Use names—but don't overdo it
- Don't argue; be flexible and willing to consider another point of view
- Ask questions—but don't accuse, don't condemn, and don't criticize
- Set up appropriate boundaries and respect the boundaries of others
- When you are wrong, admit it immediately; don't grovel, but make any appropriate amends
- Be willing to forgive when you've been wronged; holding a grudge hurts you more than anyone else
- Do more listening than talking; encourage the other person to talk about himself
- Don't talk behind anyone's back; once something's out of your mouth you lose control of it, so only say what you'd want others to know you've said

You may think there's nothing on this list that you don't know. The question is whether you act on what you know. Most people would like to behave honorably with others, but they don't always remember to do so. Place these principles where you'll see them—on your wall, your mirror, or in your car to remind you. Add your own principles and read the list daily. It will make a difference.

Even if you don't believe that you get back what you give, remember that relationships are vital to the investigator's success. You need people. If you cultivate relationships, people will tell you a lot. If you're abusive and surly, if you bark orders or ignore people, they won't be inclined to help.

Smile and speak respectfully; it will make the job of collecting information much more productive.

Listening Skills

Many people don't listen; they hear parts of what's said and then wait for opportunities to break into the speaker's conversation with responses they've formed while pretending to listen. The investigator has a particularly difficult time avoiding this trap. The answer? Have questions at the ready. Keep a pad in front of you to not only remind you of questions you've prepared, but to allow for jotting down new ones as the subject speaks. Be careful of losing consistent eye contact, however.

Listen to what's being said. Don't plan what you'll say next, don't point out discrepancies, and don't interrupt with questions. Law enforcement investigators who are trained in advanced interview/interrogation skills are taught to let the subject run through her entire testimony without interruption. Afterward, she's asked to go through it again—as many times as is necessary for the investigator to really hear what's being said.

Active listening is an effective tool for investigators. It's the practice of listening so closely that you're able to put what's been said into your own words and repeat it back to the speaker. One advantage is that if you've misunderstood or the speaker has misspoken, it can be cleared up immediately.

Gaining skill in active listening involves awareness and practice. Practice listening to friends and family. You'll be surprised at what you hear. You may also be surprised by the response. People love to be heard; it makes them feel as if they matter. Proficiency in listening may help not only your career, but your relationships as well.

The second advantage is crucial when interviewing victims: Active listening allows a victim to speak about what has happened to him and, more importantly, to know that he's been heard. Once again, you're not born with the ability to listen actively. You can learn, and if you already do something like it, you can improve. If you don't like the term, call it something else, but use it—it works.

To ensure that you don't miss anything during interrogation or interview, record the conversation, listen to it, and then listen again. It's amazing how, after listening until you think you can recite everything in your sleep, something important jumps out at you.

Perseverance, Patience, and Courage

These three attributes are interrelated, and again, they can be learned or improved upon. Certainly, personality effects acquisition of these attributes, as does willingness to exercise them. If you feel no inclination to improve, you may as well give up the idea of doing most investigative work. Investigation hinges on these three traits.

Patience, in particular, tends to be considered a trait you're born with. Investigations must be conducted with patience; investigators must sit in a surveillance vehicle until they get the shot or search through hours of records to find pertinent information. If you're only capable of sitting or searching until you're bored, you'll miss important facts. However, if you desire to find answers, solve cases, and unravel mysteries, you can increase your ability to exercise patience using another attribute—perseverance. Perseverance means that you don't give up when circumstances become difficult or your information source dries up. Desire is the key to patience, and it ignites the slow burn of perseverance. People are willing to persevere for what they really want. Decide whether you really want to do this kind of work; your answer will determine whether you have, or will want to develop, the patience and perseverance necessary to do so.

How does courage fit here? Courage is not the absence of fear, but the willingness to persevere in the face of fear. Emotional courage involves being willing to do the right thing even when challenged by pressure to do otherwise. Courage is not only a willingness to protect yourself and others, it's a willingness to ask the tough question of that high official you're interviewing—even in the face of anxiety.

Courage isn't foolhardiness. It doesn't involve taking unnecessary risks. It has nothing to do with proving that you're unafraid. Certainly, willingness to take necessary risks is an aspect of courage, but the wisdom to know when not to take risks is more important.

It's absolutely necessary for the investigator to be willing to go where others won't and to do what others fear—yet don't feel that you must do it alone. Take backup when you anticipate problems or work in dangerous areas. While it's true that you won't be able to do this job without courage, be smart about it.

Quick Thinking and Discretion

For the successful investigator, the benefits of being able to think several steps ahead cannot be measured. Neither can discretion—the ability to judge and make a decision regarding the relative importance of an event, statement, or item in relation to your investigation.

Quick Thinking

An investigator must be able to think on his feet and make judgments quickly—sometimes within seconds. The wrong judgment can endanger lives. For example, on a rolling surveillance, you may need to decide whether to squeak under that yellow light or stop and try to catch the target later. If others are in your caravan, this won't be a problem, but if you're alone, you have no good choices. You risk running the light or losing the eye. In this situation, there's only one choice—err on the side of safety. Tomorrow is another day, providing additional opportunities to follow the target. Alternatively, you may get lucky and pick up your target after the light changes.

Other situations will result in the need to make difficult choices, think on your feet, and remain aware of your environment. Experience helps, as does thinking ahead. Some experts believe that the best decisions are made within seconds, but only if the person making the decision is knowledgeable about the situation. This is the premise of Malcolm Gladwell's *Blink: The Power of Thinking Without Thinking*. Read Gladwell for more information on when and why these instant decisions are sometimes advantageous and other times disadvantageous.

Discretion

Discretion is dependent upon objectivity. The investigator will come into contact with people and situations that aren't always what they seem. She must objectively cut through pretense or misdirection to accurately judge what or who is before her.

Even clients provide misinformation. It's rare that clients intentionally deceive investigators, but it happens. More often, problems arise with the (not uncommon) practice of clients providing information that is a guess, a hope, or that cannot be verified. Therefore, launch every investigation within the framework of intelligent skepticism, never assuming that anyone has told the truth or that anything is as it seems. Verify all facts, no matter where you find them.

When on the witness stand, intentionally misrepresenting facts or leaving out pertinent information is called shaving testimony. It's perjury, and if proven, makes the perjurer subject to charges. Discover everything possible about your client and verify all information provided; don't let client misinformation or omissions cause you to appear to be shaving your own testimony.

Discretion will protect you from the client attempting to maneuver you into illegal activity for "a good cause." It will also protect you from those enamored of your profession. Television shows and movies have made the PI something of a celebrity. While you know there's nothing glamorous about the hard work you do, not everyone does. Occasionally, an emotionally needy or unbalanced soul may attempt to insinuate herself into your life or business. Don't let it happen. Trust your instincts. If you feel that something's wrong, it probably is. It's cleaner and kinder to discourage this person before she becomes attached (some have become dangerously attached) and feels entitled to your time and attention. Protect yourself by maintaining a polite distance from the outset.

A Good Memory

Memory is the storing of information in the brain over time. The three types of memory—sensory, short term, and long term—are all stored in different parts of the brain for different periods and using different methods. Long-term memory can be divided into different types as well. Many scientists believe that some types, more permanent than others, may weaken over time. At any rate, no matter how good your memory is, don't rely on it unless it's absolutely necessary. Keep a notebook and two pens with you. If you have trouble writing or if you're on a moving surveillance, take a small tape recorder. During those times when it's impossible to use either, memory comes into play.

Memory

Simple exercises help to improve memory. However, the very act of committing something to memory will strengthen your memory processes. Memorize poems, quotes, and passages from books or scripture. While you drive, memorize vehicle tags, phone numbers, and messages on signs. See how many strings of numbers you can hold in your mind at one time. This is short-term memory, but repetition delivers this information to your long-term memory bank.

The world is full of sights and sounds, so much stimuli that it's impossible to attend to all of it at once. You have learned to pay attention to what's important and disregard the rest, but memory is tricky on many levels. People attend to different aspects of situations for vastly different reasons. This explains how several witnesses can describe the same offender with such varying details they may as well be describing different people. Chapter 19 discusses memory as it relates to interviewing suspects, witnesses, and victims.

Memory may be affected by many things. Therefore, record as much as is feasible, not only because it fills in the blanks for attention, but also because it provides proof of case details. Increasingly, more police departments have outfitted patrol vehicles with cameras for this very reason. For years, federal agencies have recorded all aspects of raids and crime scenes. The technology is there; it makes sense to use it.

QUESTION?

How can exercise improve my memory?
A meta-analysis of eighteen studies showed exercise to be an effective tool for improvement of brain function, even in those over seventy years of age. As little as thirty to sixty minutes of fast walking several times weekly slows frontal cortex shrinkage and releases growth factors that increase connections between neurons. In this way, exercise is strongly related to increased memory and reduced dementia.

The following resources are a good place to start if you're interested in brain research:

- *Welcome to Your Brain: Why You Lose Your Car Keys but Never Forget How to Drive and Other Puzzles of Everyday Life,* by Sandra Aamodt and Sam Wang
- *Mind Wide Open: Your Brain and the Neuroscience of Everyday Life,* by Steven Johnson
- *The Better Brain Book,* by Dr. David Perlmutter and Carol Coleman

As you continue to research, stick to recognized sources. There's a lot of misinformation out there.

Note-taking

When you record an important fact, be sure to include the date, time, and place of occurrence. If others were present, note their names and phone numbers. If your case goes to trial, you may be asked to provide such information. Nothing causes a jury to view an investigator as lazy, incompetent, or uncaring more than hearing him answer "I don't know" too many times. Opposing counsel will use this to impugn credibility. It's all right to not know—occasionally. In fact, you absolutely must admit when you don't know—never try to wing it or pretend—but recording pertinent information will reduce "I don't know" answers and increase your credibility.

If you opt to use a tape recorder instead of a notebook, be sure that any essentials, such as batteries or chargers, are available. A recorder is great when you are on a moving surveillance, but keep a notebook for backup.

A notebook can be useful when you're on foot surveillance or when you're unable to speak sensitive case details into a recorder.

The best investigators record incidentals such as weather, temperature, and unusual details about the target or his environment. Develop this habit. Record the comings and goings of people and vehicles, not merely at the target residence or business, but in the surrounding area. This need not be included in your report unless proven relevant, but sometimes who or what is relevant won't be apparent until you have gathered more information, so record what you see and hear. These items are verifiable bits of information that create the perception of professionalism and boost the credibility of testimony.

When taking notes during interviews, write very little—jot only the main points, numbers, dates, etc. Pay more attention to your subject than to your notebook, but as soon as possible, supplement your notes so that they make sense; otherwise, they may appear unintelligible later.

Keeping Secrets

If you have trouble keeping secrets or delight in telling bits of information about others to anyone who will listen, you must learn to tame that tongue. Not only can revealing sensitive or secret information put your case at risk, it can put your safety at risk as well. When a client pays you, it's assumed that any information you discover is for her eyes only. In some states, a PI can be prosecuted for leaking client information. The likelihood of prosecution rises dramatically if the leaked information has been procured for an attorney or law enforcement agency. Even a casual remark to a friend can prove disastrous. Not only can you not control information once it's in another's possession, but you never know who may overhear.

If you spill the secrets of others to feel important, procure a confidante, gain notoriety, or obtain money, PI work is not for you. Secrets kept by investigators affect the lives of real people. If you have no understanding of this and no empathy for those whose secrets you hold, you're not investigator material.

Read the American Bar Association's Rule 1.6 of Client/Lawyer Relationship's guidelines regarding confidentiality. The main tenant of ABA regulations is that a client must give informed consent in order for the attorney to disclose information. An attorney is allowed to reveal client information only if she believes it necessary:

- To prevent reasonably certain death or substantial bodily harm
- To prevent the client from committing a crime or fraud that will result in substantial injury to the financial interests or property of another (meaning the client has used or is using attorney's services in furtherance of this crime)
- To prevent, mitigate or rectify substantial injury to the financial interests or property of others that will result from the client's criminal act (meaning the client has used or is using attorney's services in furtherance of this crime)
- To obtain legal advice concerning how the attorney should comply with these Rules
- To establish a defense on behalf of the attorney; to establish a defense to a criminal charge against the attorney based on client conduct; or respond to allegations regarding the attorney's representation of the client
- To comply with another law or court order

These are reasonable guidelines for investigators. In fact, several private investigative organizations have used ABA Rules as a basis for their own guidelines.

Writing Skills

Without some skill in writing, reports will appear unprofessional. The good news is that writing skills can be improved. Check with learning centers, universities, community colleges, or continuing education centers if you want to brush up on your skills. The fees are low, and you can find courses that concentrate on business writing. Libraries in some cities have set up adult education programs, as have nonprofit organizations. Of course, you can always go back to school. Online schools, such as the University of Phoenix, have classes designed to teach writing, not necessarily leading to a degree. However, should you want a degree, an online program provides flexibility for the working professional.

If you have a learning disability or an aversion to writing, hire someone to make sense of your reports. Nothing turns a client away faster than slipshod report writing. How can anyone know whether unseen aspects of your business are professional if the part that is visible, your report, is weak, unorganized, sloppy, or full of misspellings?

Investigative report writing consists of the six basics taught in school: who, what, where, when, why, and how. Your investigation answers these questions. If you can't articulate who you investigated, what you found, where, when, and how you found it, and why it's important to your case, your investigative efforts are of little use to any client.

Today's private investigator can't throw a case together and rush to the next. Because information is his business, he must be capable of relaying that information in a clear manner. Professionally written communication, or the lack of it, can directly determine the size of fees that clients are willing to pay.

Organizational and Analytical Skills

If your goal is to build a firm of investigators, organizational and analytical skills are essential. Even as a one-person operation, you may deal with more than one case at a time, and unless you have some ability to organize and prioritize, you may become overwhelmed and inefficient. Analytical skills make sense of case information.

Organizational Skills

Suppose your note-taking skills are excellent and your case notes extensive. This won't matter if you can't find them. Paperwork and filing isn't exciting, but if you don't do it, you'll end up with piles of paper. The longer you let those piles grow, the longer it will take to separate paperwork for quick access. Investigators have been known to scoop accumulated paper into boxes for storage, and years later spend hours digging through them because a case finally made it to court or to appeal. Touch paperwork as little as possible. Experts agree that the more times you touch a piece of paper, the more time you waste.

Make files for each case. When you have a piece of paper in hand, file it. When you remove a videotape or CD from your camcorder, put it with the case file. Organizational skills are about providing a place for everything and keeping everything in its place so you won't waste time searching for things.

Planning is a skill that allows you to focus on what's important, and helps you set aside interruptions that steal your day. List tomorrow's tasks in order of importance, then use this list to plan your time. Let the minutia go, or delegate if you have employees. If this seems impossible, keep an interruption log for a week, recording every crisis or interruption. At week's end, evaluate the log to determine which incidences could have been avoided, which could have been put off or delegated, and which should never be avoided. Plan to deal with such things in the future to recapture much-needed time. In the investigative world, time really is money, so plan your day and work your plan.

Using an intern can help keep you organized. Many community colleges and high schools have internship programs. Tapping into these can provide several hours of free help each week. Delegating tasks to the student intern will provide experience for her and freedom for you to concentrate on the priorities of your daily to-do lists.

For more information on organization, see these resources:

- University of Illinois Counseling Center: *www.couns.uiuc.edu/brochures/time.htm*
- Harold Taylor Time Consultants: *www.taylorintime.com*
- Dr. Donald E. Wetmore's Productivity Institute: *www.balancetime.com*
- Franklin Covey: *www.franklincovey.com*
- Day-Timer: *www.daytimer.com*

- Entrepreneur.com: *www.entrepreneur.com/worklifebalance/time management/archive115694.html*
- *The 7 Habits of Highly Effective People,* by Stephen Covey
- *How to Get Control of Your Time and Your Life,* by Dr. Alan Lakeins

Analytical Skills

Working a case will often result in a mass of seemingly unrelated facts. Making sense of it requires the consideration of all possible problems and solutions using analytical or problem-solving skills. Traditionally, investigators have used deductive reasoning when solving cases. Logicians no longer consider the view of deduction proceeding from the general to the specific to be correct. It is correct, however, to say that deduction is based on a premise or premises. If a premise is incorrect, then the conclusion may be incorrect.

In a simplified example, if you begin with the premise that a man is having an affair yet you have no evidence aside from client suspicion, subsequent information may appear to lead to the truth of the premise. Essentially, the premise may color the way evidence is viewed. At the very least, beginning with the husband-is-untrue premise can cause the investigation to go down the wrong road long before finding the right road.

It's safer to begin with a broader premise, such as: the husband is doing something to cause his wife's suspicions. Working from this premise allows for gathered information to lead you where it will. The accumulated evidence may tell you that he is indeed having an affair or it may lead in a different direction. The husband may be working overtime, he may be hiding an unsavory habit such as drinking or gambling, or he may have another issue unrelated to infidelity.

FACT

Charts and graphs help in analyzing data. Software such as Inspiration can be an invaluable tool, allowing the investigator to chart relationships between people and information. Seeing facts on paper can reveal previously unrealized associations. With Inspiration, charts can be saved and new associations explored without losing the originals.

The MindTools Web site, (*www.mindtools.com*) suggests a concept called "drilling down" as a means of breaking complex problems into smaller components. See this site for a discussion of this tool that can help investigators unravel complicated cases. MindTools also recommends a technique it calls the "Five Whys": begin at the end result or problem and work backwards, asking why. When each question is answered, ask why again, until the root problem is revealed. If this doesn't happen fairly quickly, you might be going down the wrong trail.

This chapter has outlined many of the skills necessary for conducting investigations. Hopefully, you've gained confidence that you have the right stuff for success as a PI. If you are established in a different field, maybe you've learned that you have what it takes to complete your own investigations or choose an investigator. Perhaps seeking knowledge for knowledge's sake, you merely enjoyed the read. No matter how you intend to use this information, remember that anything can be learned, and anything learned can be improved upon.

CHAPTER 2

Education and Training

Earning a degree in criminal justice or a related area is not a requirement for becoming a PI. However, not only does a degree speed up the learning curve, it broadens opportunities in the field. A degree provides a platform that no amount of experience can match. Degrees boost resumes and confer legitimacy. In other words, clients like to see credentials, and while a degree is not absolutely necessary, it's beneficial in many ways. However, should you decide to travel a different route toward the private investigation profession, there are several ways to do this.

Schools and Universities

It's possible to find criminal justice programs that fit your goals and schedule, no matter how far along you are in your educational goals. Online universities offer training courses in private investigation, and even traditional universities have added online courses and diploma programs for the distance learner. For those who must work a day job, the online format is fantastic for the student is able to view lectures and study when his schedule allows. Accredited online programs may be flexible, but they aren't easy. The workload can be heavy and it takes a great deal of self-discipline to complete an online course. The payoff is in the end; alumni report that they've been adequately prepared to enter their field.

◀ There are many ways to get an educational foundation in private investigation. If you decide to pursue a formal education in private investigation, make sure the school you choose is an accredited institution.

Find the online school that's right for you. Look into some of the many sites which point to accredited schools, particularly those offering criminal justice and related programs. The following are popular, informative sites:

- *www.elearners.com/online-degrees/criminal-justice.htm*
- *www.allcriminaljusticeschools.com*
- *www.directoryofonlineschools.com*
- *www.collegeanduniversity.net/colleges-programs-states*
- *www.legal-criminal-justice-schools.com*
- *www.univsource.com/cj.htm*
- *www.directoryofschools.com/Criminal-Justice-Degrees.htm*
- *graduate-programs.net*

Many online programs offer a full menu from which to choose. Some schools allow work experience to be transferred into credits that count toward degree programs. Be careful of this practice, however, as accredited institutions allow very few credits to be applied in this way, and unscrupulous schools have used it as a means of "selling" worthless diplomas.

ALERT!

Whether you have a criminal justice degree or law enforcement (LE) experience, remember that PI and LE investigators operate very differently. LE investigators have information systems and police powers that are not available to PIs. The LE detective who enters private investigation must learn to locate people and information without these advantages.

Even traditional colleges and universities have gotten into the distance education business. Boston University offers a highly rated online criminal justice program, as do the University of Michigan, the University of Cincinnati, and several others. These programs are identical to their highly rated on-site programs. Because of demand from mid-career professionals and new students alike, more online options are added to brick and mortar programs all the time.

PI Organizations

When you do an online search for private investigation schools, private investigation courses, private investigation training, and other key phrases, the number of hits returned is amazing. It's easy to find training; the problem lies in finding good training. Myriad nonaccredited agencies, schools, and even individuals offer training. While these programs do not lead to a degree, many, such as PI organizations, offer certificates of completion, some of which can be completed entirely online. Choose carefully. Do extensive research before you join an association so you can determine the right fit for your business.

The novice may find it difficult to differentiate between legitimate training centers and fraudulent ones that give students little or nothing of value in return for their money. Most states have PI associations, which can help you find legitimate programs. Organizations are a good place to begin the search for training.

National Association of Investigative Specialists (NAIS)

NAIS is a Texas-based PI association that serves as a resource center for private investigators across the nation. NAIS began with four investigators in the 1970s and has grown steadily since. Membership in NAIS provides many benefits, such as a membership directory that offers national and international exposure and an online library of downloadable books, resources, and training aids. Free graphics files, Web page set up and marketing aids are also available, as well as investigative forms and checklists. NAIS also has a PI museum, and provides information about equipment and accessories. A great organization headed by Ralph Thomas is at *www .pimall.com/nais/nais.j.html.*

National Association of Legal Investigators (NALI)

NALI provides certified legal investigator status to those who complete its educational and experience requirements. Applicants must pass oral and written exams and continuing education units. Investigators with NALI certification are highly sought by corporate and legal employers. The organization provides oversight for its members, who must pledge to abide by a code of ethics. Its Web site, *www.nalionline.org,* provides links to more than 3,000 investigative resources.

United States Association of Professional Investigators (USAPI)

USAPI is an organization whose mission is to upgrade the standards of private investigation. Its board of directors has developed an extensive training program and a comprehensive certification program toward this goal. USAPI's unique board is composed of such luminaries as Dr. Henry Lee, celebrated author of numerous books and articles on forensic science; Jimmie N. Mesis, owner of *PI Magazine*; and Vernon Geberth, retired lieutenant-commander of the New York City Police Department.

Another unique aspect of USAPI is that it offers membership to all professional investigators, not only PIs. One of the benefits of expanded membership is the opportunity for networking and learning from those in all fields of investigation. For full membership, the association requires proof of one year's investigative employment in any area—law enforcement, military, or the private sector—although other levels of membership are available. Member benefits include reduced insurance rates, discounted car rental rates, deals on dining and entertainment, and other perks. USAPI offers the Board Certified Professional Investigator (BCPI) training program that leads to accreditation. Find USAPI information at *www.usapi.org*. See Chapters 13, 15, and 16 for more information concerning legal investigators, requirements for certification, and business opportunities.

World Association of Professional Investigators (WAPI)

WAPI is an organization dedicated to promoting the profession of private investigation and security companies of all types in the public and private sector. Its Web site, *www.wapi.com*, provides a member directory that includes investigators around the globe. WAPI requires members to abide by a code of ethics. Membership benefits include international networking opportunities; interagency assignment opportunities and support; a newsletter; and professional indemnity insurance. It's another high-quality association for the newbie and experienced investigator alike.

PI Magazine

This excellent magazine, available at *www.pimagazine.com*, lists state, national, and international associations. The PI Directory and PI Classifieds allow investigators to advertise on a well-visited site where clients can find services and investigators can find each other. Articles by world-famous investigators are well worth the subscription, and there's always information concerning training, conferences, and seminars.

The magazine also has a link to an online store, *www.pigear.com*, with an extensive choice of equipment, books, and accessories that are useful to the private investigator. It includes an RSS feed that can be downloaded onto your computer, providing a steady stream of up-to-date information about the profession.

Internships/On-the-Job Training

Internships are available from many police departments and federal agencies. Some offer internships for high-school students. These programs offer limited training and ride-alongs with police officers. They teach the qualities and skills necessary for entering the police academy upon graduation or upon reaching a minimum age. In fact, many high-school students apply and are sworn into the departments in which they intern. Most federal agencies offer internships to college students. Each agency has its own requirements, so research the position before applying.

It's also possible to obtain an internship from an established PI company. Companies train investigators in different ways. Some have classes that new employees must attend while others pair the newbie with an experienced investigator for a time. Requirements vary from company to company, but the practice of on-the-job training isn't unusual. One-person operations or small firms may work with other investigators or firms they trust. In this way, a small company isn't forced to turn down jobs that require more manpower than it possesses. These companies may be willing to take on a trainee as a contract worker. Contracting also saves money; small firms can't afford to keep investigators on a payroll while they wait for clients.

When you start your own business, incoming cases can be sporadic. One month there may be very little work, but the next could bring more cases than you can handle. Networking with other agency investigators and budgeting for a steady cash flow can be the difference between success and failure.

Working with an accountant can be a type of on-the-job training. Most people with no accounting experience can find themselves in trouble by not understanding bookkeeping and tax requirements. Therefore, the smart business owner will hire professionals to handle these things, but she will also become a student of all that she does not know. While the investigator is better served by doing the work she is familiar with, she must also protect herself from being taken advantage of by others. Pay professionals to do what they do best, but learn all you can in order to provide oversight.

State and Local Requirements

Most states require a license specifically for conducting private investigations. However, as of this publication, the following states do not:

- Alabama (PI license required by Birmingham and Mobile; business license required for all)
- Alaska (PI license required by several cities; business license required for all)
- Colorado
- Idaho
- Mississippi
- Missouri (license required by several cities)
- South Dakota (business license required through Department of Revenue)
- Wyoming (regulated by local jurisdictions)

Although these states do not regulate private investigators like other states, they may require some type of license, usually a business license. The reasons these states don't regulate PIs differ, but the general argument for this absence of oversight is that regulation—and the fees accompanying it—may force the small investigator out of business or prevent would-be investigators from entering the field. State licensure is seen as an unnecessary and burdensome expense. Though no overall requirements for licensure in these states exist, individual cities may have PI license requirements, but in most cases, this practice amounts to little more than a means for generating revenue; typically, no regulations accompany the licenses.

The reason for putting regulations and licensing in place is to protect the public from unscrupulous and incompetent investigators. Regulations provide guidelines within which investigators must operate. Fingerprinting and background checks are common, further protecting the public by revealing an applicant's past and weeding out those with criminal histories. Without a license, it is anyone's guess whether the investigator's claims of education and experience are correct. Corruption often flourishes in the absence of operational guidelines.

In an attempt to counter this, most states have created Web sites where PI licenses can be verified. Some provide information concerning client complaints and disciplinary actions against PIs and agencies. In states where oversight exists, boards typically have the power to enforce attendance at training academies and continuing education classes as well. Boards can also discipline agencies or individual investigators for actions such as:

- Invasion of privacy through trespass, eavesdropping, illegal surveillance, or other means
- Assault and related offenses
- Violation of search and seizure laws
- Violation of laws concerning weapon use and concealed weapon carry laws
- Violation of federal and state constitutional laws and principles
- Violation of state ethics laws
- Violation of additional state criminal laws and procedures pertaining to investigations

Another area that can be sanctioned by oversight agencies is that of padding fees, although it's difficult to prove. Most investigators are careful to steer clear of this violation, but there are always the few who take advantage when they see an opportunity.

ALERT!

Research your state's requirements before operating. Some states not only require a license, but class time and a passing exam grade that proves the investigator's knowledge of the field. The Web site *www.crime time.com/licensing.htm* provides licensing information for each state. Don't cut corners! Operating within compliance is essential for success.

Operating within compliance also means compliance with state and local tax authorities. Contact an accountant or your state tax department. The Web site *www.taxsites.com/agencies.html* provides links to each state's tax agency.

Diploma Mills

In recent years, there has been a proliferation of so-called checkbook credentialing agencies and diploma mills. Widespread use of the Internet, coupled with low-cost computer software and hardware, has brewed a recipe for deceit. In other words, unscrupulous individuals and companies stand ready to "sell" credentials over the Net.

Selling of Credentials

Using the newest software, with printers capable of intricate reproduction, people craft phony diplomas that are almost impossible to differentiate from the real thing. Operators of diploma mills are inventive and know how to market bogus products. They appeal to greed and the desire to obtain something without working for it, and they attempt to nullify the purchaser's conscience.

Only a few blatantly acknowledge that they sell credentials, but the market is large enough to keep even these types in business. Many sellers move headquarters and change names on a regular basis to avoid prosecution. Others make justifications guaranteed to appeal to those with little time or inclination for investigating their product and accreditation. These fake schools also appeal to those who rationalize that because they know so much about the field, it's not really fraudulent to buy a degree.

Those who are willing to buy their credentials are satisfied with being required to pass a simple test or take a short class—or perhaps buy a pamphlet or a book advertised to cover material for their degree or certificate. Not only is this throwing away money, it can lead to sacrificing reputation and dignity—maybe even freedom.

There exists an even more insidious seller of credentials: the one advertising his diplomas as novelty items. On almost any day, these diplomas can be purchased on eBay. For example, eBay listings advertise diplomas that can be created to "look exactly like the real thing" and configured with any name and any degree the buyer chooses. Some sellers even include a transcript with each purchase. Despite the sellers' protests that the product is a novelty item, this type of imitation is intended to deceive.

The Importance of Accreditation

In education, there are only three words that matter: accreditation, accreditation, accreditation. Many diploma mills list accreditation from superior-sounding bodies, but these bodies are either nonexistent, created by the mills themselves, or have no power to provide the accreditation that is claimed. This isn't meant to insinuate that all legitimate private investigation programs are associated only with universities, nor that they're accredited only by the same bodies that accredit colleges and universities. This warning is directed at those wishing to acquire degrees in criminal justice-related areas.

In the wake of the September 11 terrorist attacks, schools around the nation have experienced increased enrollment in criminal justice and associated degree programs. Forensic science degrees are especially in demand. Increased demand has led to many legitimate schools rushing to acquire criminal justice or forensic degree programs in order to get their share of this market. Critics claim that some of these hastily constructed programs don't prepare students adequately for the workforce.

A related problem is that no nationally recognized standards for forensic science programs exist. Forensic science is not the only program faced with this problem, but it's a good example. Even well-meaning schools can produce a curriculum that falls short of preparing students for competing in the real world. In short, schools may be accredited, but not on the level that will allow their students to transfer credits to other schools or universities, receive federal financial aid, and qualify for prime positions in the workplace.

A further, more prevalent problem is that the university may be accredited at an acceptable level, but one or more programs within that university may not be. Therefore, it's important to be vigilant in checking out any program. In the case of forensic science, the nonprofit American Academy of Forensic Sciences (AAFS) has created standards for accreditation. A number of schools across the nation have voluntarily applied for and received this accreditation.

If you want a degree in criminal justice or a related field, let the search for a good school be your first investigative assignment. Check watchdog agencies such as the Diploma Mill Police at *www.geteducated.com/services/ diplomamillpolice.asp* and the AAFS at *www.aafs.org* for forensic science programs that have been granted the association's full or conditional accreditation.

Diploma mills are no longer hidden, backdoor operations. Because of the Internet, they sit out in the open, hawking their illicit wares with incredible boldness. Yet more often than not, they appear legitimate. While recognizing them is more difficult than ever, you should be suspicious of any organization that will allow you to purchase a diploma or certificate or earn a degree quickly with little or no coursework.

During a two-year investigation of diploma mills, Senator Susan Collins received bogus degrees in medical technology and biology. One of the first to officially document the ease of gaining false credentials, Senator Collins is responsible for encouraging the Department of Education to develop a Web site informing students of the accreditation level held by colleges and universities. This site can be accessed at *www.ope.ed.gov/accreditation.* Developers warn that a school that does not appear on the list is not necessarily a diploma mill. However, you should exercise serious caution and perform further research on any school that's not listed.

FACT

Check out Dr. Zoe D. Katz, PhD at *www.dreichel.com/Articles/Dr_Zoe .htm.* Dr. Katz is a cat. Her owner, Dr. Steve K.D. Eichel, PhD., ABPP, credentialed Zoe to prove that more oversight of credentialing bodies is needed. His success in providing Zoe with a certification by three major hypnotherapy associations and a diploma in psychotherapy proves his point about the proliferation of "pseudo-credentialing."

While it's true that a degree is helpful, it's not necessary for private investigation. Education helps any profession, but many successful investigators have no degree. The decision to obtain one should be made on an individual basis, dependent on long-term goals and plans.

Continuing Education

Many of the same concerns apply when obtaining continuing education units (CEUs). Even though criminal justice programs and private investigation courses may not require CEUs, anyone desiring success will stay up to date. These fields are dependent on continually changing technology. Career suicide can result from ignoring these changes. Technology changes so quickly these days, it can be in use before most people realize it's even available.

Therefore, it's advisable to study the craft continually. Join organizations that assimilate information to members and network with others in the field. Another means of staying current is subscribing to PI and legal RSS feeds. Feeds can deliver current information to your computer regarding legal news, court cases, pending litigation, court rulings, and research tools. They can provide access to legal blogs. They're essential for the legal investigator and anyone who wants to stay current.

RSS represents Really Simple Syndication, the type of technology used to create feeds. Most feeds deliver text such as news or blog information, but they can also deliver podcasts. Examples of a few sites from which feeds can be obtained include:

- Detective.com: *private-investigator-detective.com/RSSFeedDirectory .aspx*
- New York Times: feeds of articles about private investigation, technology, science, law, and other subjects at *www.nytimes.com/ services/xml/rss/index.html*
- PI Buzz: the official blog of PI Magazine at *pibuzz.com/feed*
- Law.com: *www.law.com/service/rss.shtml*
- University of Pittsburgh School of Law: *http://jurist.law.pitt.edu/ paperchase/feeds.php*
- American Bar Association: *www.abanet.org/tax.rss*

These sites may also have newsletters and blogs to which the investigator can subscribe. Newsletters provide current information and links to training, products, and sometimes, other investigators. Remember the importance of networking. Cultivating relationships with reliable investigators can save time and money.

This section can be summed up in three words: Never stop learning. The world is full of more things than human beings can comprehend in one lifetime. Even an experienced investigator can ask, "Is there a better way to do this?" and "How can I improve that?"

CHAPTER 3

Ethics—The Good, the Bad, and the Ugly

No one is unethical. Even Tony Soprano and Michael Corleone exercised ethics of sorts. Ethics are a code of morality, a system of moral principles that govern appropriate conduct. Simply put, ethics are taught, caught, and accepted. They're taught in childhood by family or a social circle. Later, they're caught by exposure to differing standards of behavior from teachers, peers, and workmates. However, they're not yours until they are accepted and internalized. It's never too late to inventory your personal ethics and alter whatever's lacking.

Ethics Overview

The word "ethics" has roots in the Greek word *ethos*, meaning character, and the Latin word *mores*, meaning customs. The combination refers to the internal standards and customs that guide the choices people make when interacting with each other. From a philosophical perspective, ethics defines that which is beneficial for individuals and society and puts forth the idea that people owe each other duties in a civilized society.

The intersection of law and ethics is another issue. While laws are often derived from ethical or community values, all values and mores aren't reflected in the law. For example, there are no laws against lying (except lying to investigators), betraying a friend's trust, or repeating a confidence. However, these things are widely condemned by most people. Therefore, law cannot be the only measurement of ethics since it ignores much important behavior governing human interaction. While they are not illegal, these behaviors are critical to a civilized world. In some instances, good ethical behavior can prevent illegal behavior, just as bad behavior can escalate to the point of illegal behavior. In many ways, ethics is related to courtesy.

For instance, allowing someone in front of your vehicle in heavy traffic isn't something you must do. Yet performing this courtesy with a smile can soften another driver's ruffled feelings and avert the escalation of anger. Conversely, preventing that driver from pushing in front of you (though you may feel justified) is discourteous. It may get you yelled at, or waved at with a special finger.

Ethics governs the behavior that makes societies civilized. The act of treating others the way you'd want to be treated is the glue holding civilization together. When this is absent, chaos ensues, leading to lawbreaking. Imagine the highways and interstates full of people cutting in front of each other, tailgating at high speeds: It would be chaos. The following Web sites are helpful resources on ethics: DePaul Institute for Business and Professional Ethics, *http://commerce.depaul.edu/ethics*; and LegalEthics.com, *www.legalethics.com*.

It's obvious that good ethical behavior is important for you as a PI, but knowing the parameters of your own personal ethics is even more important. Before you face certain ethical situations, decide how you will deal with them. What will you do when it seems that the only way to get video of your subject is to crawl through her property and record her through a window? Decide that you will not jeopardize your case by breaking the law. Decide that you can be creative enough to conceive of a way to get her out of the house in order to film her. Decide now so that when the temptation is greatest, you know where your limits are.

What will you do when faced with leftover money after winding up your investigation? You'll have the choice of returning your client's money or padding your bill to make it seem that these funds have been used. Decide now which course you'll take. Decide from the outset that you'll return the unused funds. Don't think for a minute that it doesn't matter—and don't fall into the trap of believing that the client won't know the difference.

Ethics: The Good

Good ethical behavior is crucial for PIs, yet ethics as a code of behavior is defined individually. In light of this, how can good ethical behavior as a whole be defined? As there is no universally accepted code to which PIs can look for guidance, it's prudent to look to guidelines set up by various professional organizations.

National Association of Legal Investigators

NALI requires its Certified Legal Investigators® to follow a strict code of ethics. Training for certification includes an education in the ethics of private investigation. It stresses that the integrity of the profession hinges on personal investigators who adhere to the code and gain the trust of their clients.

FACT

The NALI member pledge states that the private investigator is required to uphold the honor of the profession and devote her talents to her client unless she is asked to do something unethical. The private investigator is bound to protect the interests of other PIs, but must always tell the truth, even if it means revealing the unethical practices of another PI.

The NALI code of ethics covers the relationships of private investigators with clients, the public, and each other. The code condemns bribery and other unethical practices. In addition, it stipulates that private investigators will:

- cooperate with law enforcement, other investigators, and related professions so long as a client's rights are not compromised
- conduct themselves with integrity; investigators will not misrepresent themselves or their abilities
- advocate for the private investigation profession and explain to the public the services the profession provides
- truthfully report facts and make recommendations based on fact, regardless of personal opinions
- respect clients' and employers' confidence
- respect the law
- assist other private investigators in attaining further experience and education
- provide appropriate compensation for other private investigators
- refrain from publicly criticizing other private investigators

In addition, the code prohibits investigators from participating in entrapment. Entrapment is any act by law enforcement or its agents that is intended to induce or persuade someone to commit a crime that he had no intention of committing prior to law enforcement intervention. Investigators are also responsible for ensuring that their methods do not place anyone in danger.

The American Bar Association

The ABA's Center for Professional Responsibility outlines the ethical rules it expects its members to abide by. The ABA Center for Professional Responsibility has compiled eight rules and sub-rules under Model Rules for Professional Conduct. The entire list of rules can be found at *www .abanet.org/cpr/mrpc/mrpc_toc.html.*

These rules cover a broad range of areas, but investigators should take note of the areas concerning client/lawyer relationships. Investigators should treat their clients as lawyers do theirs. Basically, the ABA's policy states that clients should be informed of all relevant details, apprised of how the lawyer will meet their objectives, and receive prompt answers to queries.

The National Association of Legal Investigators has modeled its code after the ABA's. See more about NALI in Chapter 2.

Association of British Investigators

The Association of British Investigators has developed a code of ethics to which all members must abide. This body's mission is to promote quality training and ethical standards for professional UK investigators. Members pledge to uphold the privacy of their clients, respect the law, divulge all facts uncovered during an investigation, and "to perform all professional duties in accordance with the highest moral principles and never be guilty of conduct which will bring reproach upon the profession of the private investigator."

Creating a Code of Conduct

Ethical guidelines provide a framework for making choices. Common sense dictates that you make these choices according to established laws, community mores, concern for fairness, and attention to the needs and safety of those around you. Choices should also be made with respect for everyone involved, including yourself. Never behave toward others in ways that are demeaning. Never use techniques to acquire information that may result in the violation of your own ideas of right and wrong. Don't allow the fervor to "get your man" drive you to compromise integrity.

Devise your own code of ethics before facing a questionable situation. By deciding where you'll draw the line between right and wrong, you can navigate the gray areas in between and meet the challenges of investigative work with the tools needed for making difficult decisions.

The Bad

Tony Soprano and Michael Corleone's ethics might fit here. Their criminal enterprises were labeled "just business." In the beginning of the Godfather saga, a line was drawn between acceptable crimes—prostitution, gambling, etc.—and unacceptable crimes—selling drugs, especially to children. However, this line is far beyond mainstream society's line, which is to avoid committing these crimes at all. Before Tony Soprano whacked one of his friends for breaching some part of their ethics, he assured him it was nothing personal. And, oddly, the friend agreed that it must be done—for the sake of business.

The ethics of criminal gangs also fits under the bad category, at least from the perspective of mainstream ethics. Gang members have rationalized that their lifestyle and behavior is necessary for survival, yet this doesn't hold up to scrutiny. They want what they want so they take it, and they do what they want regardless of the health and safety of others. Gangs make up their own creeds with little regard for the law and no concern for those they victimize. Many gangs have a counterculture of mores that their members follow strictly; however, it includes rules that sanction certain crimes for the good of the group and condemn those who would tell the truth (or snitch) to law enforcement authorities. These rules are for the gang itself, and they run counter to larger society. Other fringe groups such as cults, white supremacists, and terrorist groups have a similar counterculture of ethics to which they are devoted, ethics that infringe on the rights and safety of others. As such, their ethics are bad.

What does this mean for the PI? She must uphold a professional code of ethics, including obeying the law, respecting clients' rights, and performing with honesty and integrity. The interpretation of honesty and integrity leaves some wiggle room, but PIs must think beyond themselves and focus on the fraternity of private investigators as a whole. NALI provides a good framework, but if you are ever uncertain, it's always wise to err on the side of caution.

Rule 8.4, Misconduct specifies what the American Bar Association defines as bad ethical behavior. It can be found at: *http://www.abanet.org/cpr/mrpc/rule_8_4.html.*

It is professional misconduct for a lawyer to:

(a) violate or attempt to violate the Rules of Professional Conduct, knowingly assist or induce another to do so, or do so through the acts of another;

(b) commit a criminal act that reflects adversely on the lawyer's honesty, trustworthiness or fitness as a lawyer in other respects;

(c) engage in conduct involving dishonesty, fraud, deceit or misrepresentation;

(d) engage in conduct that is prejudicial to the administration of justice;

(e) state or imply an ability to influence improperly a government agency or official or to achieve results by means that violate the Rules of Professional Conduct or other law; or

(f) knowingly assist a judge or judicial officer in conduct that is a violation of applicable rules of judicial conduct or other law

Can you as an investigator draw upon these guidelines for misconduct? Yes. They are applicable to this profession as well as the profession of law.

The Ugly

Taking advantage of people at their lowest is ugly. Whether it's done intentionally or not, when an investigator pledges to provide services to someone in need, takes money for these services, then doesn't honor that pledge, the result is ugly. Depending on the situation, it can also be criminal.

The Switch

One ploy unscrupulous investigators use is to accept a job from one person, locate or film incriminating evidence, then offer to sell that evidence to the target instead of delivering it to the client. The investigator tells the client that he hasn't located any hard evidence. In this way, he obtains payment twice; many times, the target is willing to pay even more than the client has paid. This happens most often in divorce and child custody cases where outcomes are so important to each party. To protect himself, the con artist attempts to gain the discretion of the purchaser and, more often than not, his duplicity is never discovered.

Innocent people are hurt by this con. There is more at stake than the obvious loss of client funds. Lifestyles and even children's lives are at risk. The con artist doesn't care who will be shafted because of his actions, nor does he care who the better parent is. However, at the worst, his actions could condemn a child to life with an abusive parent. He has taken the decision out of the hands of the court and has determined the outcome of the case.

ALERT!

Because of heightened emotions during divorce and child custody cases, the target is often unable to resist informing the client that he now has information for which she paid. The client usually goes directly to the police, and investigators who are caught turning evidence over to their targets are subject to several criminal charges—among them, extortion and fraud.

There are times when a client is so embarrassed at having been duped that she does nothing. This isn't likely when children are involved, but it happens. If she does report the crime, however, an investigator may spend time in prison. More often than not, the PI closes up shop and reopens somewhere else under a new business name—and perhaps a new personal identity. In states without PI oversight, this can be a real problem.

The Cowboy

This type of investigator thinks he's John Wayne or Clint Eastwood as Dirty Harry. He brandishes weapons in most inappropriate ways. He roughs up suspects for information. He talks at length about law enforcement subjects that he knows very little about. He bluffs his way through everything. If his responsibilities weren't so serious, he would be humorous—think of Barney Fife with bullets in his gun. This investigator is also about as capable as Barney, blundering his way through investigations and stomping through people's lives with just as much finesse and bravado.

The Shyster

The shyster looks for ways to take advantage of clients. She pads bills with hours she hasn't worked and mileage she hasn't driven. She spends unnecessary nights in hotel rooms charging meals and incidentals when she's close enough to drive home. She drags the case out, providing bits and pieces of information as long as money is forthcoming. When the money stops, she moves on, usually leaving clients with very little information. This type of investigator has been known to charge for several investigators when only one actually works the case—and sometimes the case isn't worked at all, but the shyster collects her money.

The Mouse

This investigator is afraid of everything. He's afraid of offending suspects and witnesses. He's afraid of being burned, afraid the target will see that he's surveilling or following her. He's so afraid that his behavior is altered to the point that he appears suspicious. His fear produces the very situation he's afraid of encountering.

Because of this, whether he's been burned or not, he doesn't get video of the target because he believes he can no longer follow her. He tends to invest in wigs and makeup in order to change his appearance. While this is not always a bad idea, it doesn't do him any good because he still feels burned. Incomplete disguises can backfire: What if you see the same person in different parts of town, wearing different hats or wigs? Disguise is an art; don't try it unless you can really pull it off.

The Poorly Informed

This investigator thinks she has a natural talent for investigation and doesn't need training. She reads PI and mystery books and always knows the ending before reaching it. She's followed her boyfriend and kept up with him fairly well, so she hangs out her shingle, buys some equipment, and goes to work. She usually doesn't last. Unless this investigator obtains professional training, she tends to fade out of the business—and she should.

The Corner Cutter

This investigator defrauds the client. Giving anything less than the best is defrauding. The corner cutter is lazy, always looking for shortcuts. She becomes tired of sitting on surveillance and leaves too soon. Other times, she falls asleep or decides to do errands, returning only to find that the target has left and she's missed her chance. She doesn't take the time to record pertinent details, so she turns in reports that aren't sufficient for use in court. This investigator knows the right way to investigate, but she doesn't put forth the effort.

The Spy Master

This investigator thinks he's in a James Bond movie. He sees conspiracies and hidden meanings in every situation. He's in love with the idea of being an investigator, but not crazy about the day-to-day work. He longs for a glamorous, exciting lifestyle and tries to create it amidst the humdrum of his normal life. In other words, he lives in a fantasy. He's no good to his client; he's likely to string the client along, claiming that something is just out of reach, and may actually manufacture evidence in support of his claims. However, he cannot produce real evidence no matter how much he wants to. His reports are likely to be as colorful as any fairy tale.

Ethics and Privacy

Technology is a double-edged sword. Its growth has benefited society in multiple ways, but it has also opened new avenues for bad ethical behavior, especially the misuse of information. Because personal and business information can be attained, stored, and reproduced so quickly and easily, the danger that it may fall into the wrong hands is greater than ever. Many safeguards have been put in place to protect the public, but those implementing these safeguards are invariably behind the curve due to the proliferation of new technology. Therefore, an individual is on her own and must protect her information. As an investigator, she must safeguard the information of her clients.

Ethics and Technology

Cell phones are convenient and provide a feeling of safety. Users typically feel strange without one. Yet these conveniences have become one of the greatest risks to identity and information theft in recent years. One reason is that people using cell phones are everywhere—so much so that they've become almost invisible. No one pays attention to anyone taking out a phone (kind of like that car alarm that's barely noticed as it blares away down the street). However, a person with a cell phone could snap pictures of your credit card, driver's license, or personal checks. Even clerks have been known to do this. Because you wouldn't do this, don't be naïve about the number of people who will.

Additionally, you must make sure you safeguard your clients' information just as carefully as you do your own. The following recommended actions from the Federal Trade Commission will help you accomplish this:

- Inventory personal and sensitive client/employee information and its location.
- Determine how this information puts you or your clients at risk—for example, who has access to information and what checks and balances are in place. If the safeguards are insufficient, strengthen them.
- Lock personal and business data away from other files.
- Limit keys to this locked room or cabinet and keep track of who has them.
- Train employees to never let sensitive info out of their sight—not even for short breaks. It only takes a moment to steal information.
- Never leave mail in the box, locked or unlocked, overnight.
- Shred credit card offers and anything that may contain personal information.
- Keep sensitive client information only so long as you have a legitimate business reason for using it.
- If you must use this information, develop a written record retention policy that justifies keeping sensitive client and employee information. Record why you keep it, how long you'll keep it, and when and how you'll dispose of it.
- Receipts must include only the last five numbers of a credit card, not the entire number.

One strategy is to invest in a hidden camera system to help with employee and customer/client accountability. Employees should be trained to handle client/customer information as if it were their own. Many times data goes missing due to carelessness; employee education can reduce these errors.

Hidden cameras may disclose employee ineptitude, noncompliance with training, or even duplicitous or illegal acts. If you're squeamish about watching employees who don't know they're being watched, have them sign an agreement upon being hired which informs them that they may be subject to periodic surveillance of their duties. Be sure to include that this is for the purpose of quality control and any needed retraining. Then follow through and either record them periodically (cameras can be rented for this purpose) or have a covert system installed.

Once you've given fair warning, if his performance is still under par or if he steals from you, you have a serious problem in this employee. Yet you'll be surprised at how often this proves to be the case. Over time, people tend to forget they're being recorded, even when they are under visible surveillance, and will revert to their normal behavior. See Chapter 17 to find out why visible cameras aren't recommended for this purpose.

FACT

Federal laws such as the Federal Trade Commission, the Fair Credit Reporting Act, and the Gramm-Leach-Bliley Act require businesses to keep sensitive client information in a safe manner. Check into your state and local laws concerning the security of client information. In many cases, there are slight, but important, differences. See *www.ftc.gov/privacy/ privacyinitiatives/safeguards_lr.html* and *www.ftc.gov/privacy/privacy initiatives/safeguards_educ.html.*

The FTC protects public privacy using the authority of two very important acts: The Fair Credit Reporting Act and the Children's Online Protection Act. See Chapter 12 for more information about privacy issues and laws and Chapter 17 for audio/video laws.

Ethics and Obtaining Evidence

Illegally obtained information is of no more use to the PI than it is to the law enforcement investigator. However, a fine line exists between legal and illegal and between good and bad ethics. In those rare moments when nothing but conscience is available to guide her, the investigator should always lean toward the legal and choose the good. By doing so, she not only protects the evidence and the client, she protects herself as well.

You'll need to cultivate contacts with all types of people. People possess information you need, and getting it can be dicey. You must make choices as to how close to the line you can walk without crossing it. Some investigators have cultivated relationships with people who have access to prohibited information. For instance, they have bribed phone company employees to get unlisted phone numbers and protected addresses; in some cases, unethical investigators have persuaded phone company employees to let them listen in on private conversations. Dispatchers and even police officers have been bribed to run NCIC reports that can only legally be run by law enforcement officers—and then only for official purposes or open cases. Gangs and organized criminal groups have put their own people inside phone companies, courthouses, and police departments to obtain information. Information is big business.

This is a lazy and dangerous method of investigation. The information you gain is not worth throwing away your career. If you are caught, you may lose not only your reputation and your business, but your freedom as well. Legal means are available for discovering information. Don't try to circumvent the law. When you are found out, don't expect your contacts—or accomplices—not to roll over on you to save themselves.

Ethical guidelines provide a framework for making choices. Make these choices according to established laws, but also according to community mores and concern for respect, fairness, and the safety of others. Never behave toward others in a demeaning manner. Never use techniques that result in the violation of your own idea of right and wrong, and never allow the fervor to "get your man" drive you to compromise your integrity.

If you're caught breaking and entering with your new lock-pick set, or pretending to be a police officer or utilities worker in order to gain access somewhere—or any of the many ploys used by television and film investigators—it won't matter that you're a PI. You'll go to jail. It may sound simplistic, but you can never go wrong if you just do the right thing.

CHAPTER 4

Setting Up Your PI Business

Starting a business can be exciting; being your own boss is liberating. You answer to no one, right? Well, not exactly. In the real world, everyone answers to someone. When you sit at the top of your business, you'll find that all kinds of people expect you to be accountable to them. Local, state, and federal tax agents expect timely compliance. Creditors and investors expect payment. Employees also hold expectations, as do clients. In fact, when you take a client's money, you work for him. Essentially, you walk a fine line when you deal with people.

Business Models

There are many business models from which to choose, but if you're a new-bie, it's safest to go with an established type. An overview of the most-used models may help you choose the one that best fits your needs.

Sole Proprietorship

One owner is responsible for the entire operation and for all business debt. She takes the risks, and she reaps the benefits. Yet being a sole proprietor doesn't mean that the owner is in business all alone. She may employ many people, but hasn't created any formal structure such as a corporation or LLC.

One disadvantage of a sole proprietorship is that personal assets aren't protected from litigation or creditors. Another is that the owner must pay taxes on all profit as income, whether or not she pays herself a salary. For example, when business expenses are deducted from the total business income, whatever remains is assessed as income to the owner. On top of this, the owner is subject to self-employment tax on all income, a tax shared between employee and business under a corporation. A sole propri-etor pays her share and the business's share. However, the sole proprietor-ship is a simple operation with very little structure and regulation, so some business owners prefer it to other business models.

Partnership

A partnership is much like a sole proprietorship, except that more than one person shares responsibility for business operations. As with sole pro-prietorship, no formal structure is necessary. Partners share profits and losses and are personally responsible for business debt. The downside is that if your partner skips town, you're responsible for the entire business debt, not merely your half.

C Corporation

This model protects your personal assets from business liabilities and losses, particularly from lawsuits and creditors. The corporation becomes a legal entity that is created through the state, which can open bank accounts, enter into legal contracts, and issue shares of ownership. If one person forms a corporation, he holds 100 percent of its shares and holds all offices—president, vice president, secretary, and others. He also pays taxes on profits as well as on dividends from shares. If multiple owners exist, their liability and profit is determined according to numbers of shares; a board of directors, elected by shareholders, appoints officers.

A major advantage of corporations is that they've been operational a very long time. Therefore, with years of case law behind it, the corporation model is stable and not likely to be affected by major alterations, unlike LLCs, which are comparatively new.

In regard to taxes, the occupation of private investigation is labeled as personal service. In simplified terms, any profit remaining after payment of the owner's salary (the investigator is a salaried employee of his corporation) is usually taxed at a higher rate than for a sole proprietorship or partnership. The alternative is to take every bit of profit as salary, which is not good business, or shift money to take advantage of lower tax brackets. Without an in-house accountant, this can be expensive and time consuming. The solution may be the S Corporation.

S Corporation

The S Corp also protects personal assets from business liabilities. The main difference between S and C is that the S Corp is a "pass-through" tax entity. As such, it passes income and loss through the corporation to the individual owner(s). Some describe this as paying taxes once, as opposed to paying twice with a C Corp. This is not entirely accurate, but in simple terms, the same profit subject to self-employment tax under the C Corp is not assessed under the S Corp. It's only assessed, or taxed, under personal income, not personal and corporate income.

In addition, S Corps are restricted to 100 shareholders, shareholders must be U.S. citizens or an estate or trust of citizens, and only one class of stock may be issued; no preferred stock is allowed. Additionally, S Corps are required to use the calendar year as fiscal year, while C Corps aren't.

Limited Liability Company (LLC)

This model provides the protections afforded the corporation without the massive amounts of paperwork. The owner isn't required to hold lengthy meetings nor keep minutes, which saves time, paperwork, and possibly employee costs. Another plus is that the owner is spared some restrictions of the corporation but is granted the same ability to deduct operational losses against income.

Tax options are flexible in that owners can choose to pay taxes as do C Corps or become pass-through entities such as S Corps. C Corps pay what is sometimes called double taxation, providing increased flexibility. Using income shifting, they're allowed to move money around to take advantage of lower tax brackets, thus reducing tax liability. LLCs aren't allowed this flexibility (neither are S Corps).

FACT

In the case of either corporation type, some circumstances can be judged to "pierce the corporate veil," allowing creditors or lawsuits to hold owners personally responsible for debts and liabilities. Examples include the owner's personal guarantee of debt; failure to pay taxes; failure to provide adequate insurance; and defrauding customers, employees, or others.

One disadvantage, that only time will cure, is that LLCs haven't been operational nearly as long as other business formations; therefore, credit may not be extended as readily. In fact, several states restrict the operation of LLCs in minor ways. Yet operational requirements are simple compared to corporations, and there's no denying that LLCs are growing in popularity.

DBA

DBA stands for Doing Business As. DBA is also called assumed name, fictitious name, or trade name. It doesn't protect your business name or lend liability protection, but registering a DBA, according to your state's requirements, allows you to open bank accounts and legally operate under a name that's different from your legal name.

Other types of business entities include nonprofits, limited liability partnerships, and limited partnerships. There are some exceptions to the examples provided, so find a good accountant to help you decide which business formation is best for you.

Pros and Cons of Business Ownership

Owning and operating a business can be lucrative, but it's not for everyone. The numbers of businesses that go under each year attests to this fact. Yet sometimes, everything works together to cause a specific product or service, offered at the right time, in the right place, and in the right manner, to capture public attention and meet public need. This is not accidental, however; it takes a lot of work. Know the risks and benefits before you begin.

Negative Aspects

While many businesses are formed each year, unfortunately, many have short shelf lives. The Small Business Administration (SBA) reports that 50 percent of all small businesses fail within five years of opening their doors.

SMALL BUSINESS OPENINGS AND CLOSINGS—2002–2006

Category	2002	2003	2004	2005	2006
New Firms	569,750	612,296	528,917	653,100*	649,700*
Closures	586,890	540,658	541,047	543,700*	564,900*
Bankruptcies	38,540	35,037	34,317	39,201	19,695

*Estimate

U.S. Dept. of Commerce, Bureau of the Census; Administrative Office of the U.S. Courts; U.S. Dept. of Labor, Employment and Training Administration (2005).

The myriad reasons businesses fail include poor financial management, lack of experience, poor location, intense competition, personal use of business funds, poor inventory management, unexpected growth, and low sales. The owner is responsible for making sure the business doesn't succumb to these pressures. How can you protect your business from these inadequacies and mistakes? First, assess your business. Is the problem lack of experience? Study your craft and work with seasoned investigators. Worried about location? If you are opening in a public location, study area demographics and check with your chamber of commerce.

The point is that the owner has more responsibility for success or failure than is usually admitted. Certainly she can't control whether the competition possesses more operating capital, but she can control whether she scopes out the other guys before deciding to compete against them. She can also look for ways to perform better and advertise this improvement to the public.

Get the idea? When you start a business, it's what you make it. Accept this, and do all you can with the areas that are under your control, so that areas not under your control—a natural disaster or economic slowdown— are less likely to wipe you out. Is starting a business risky? Yes, but it has numerous rewards.

Positive Aspects of Business Ownership

Looking at statistics with a "glass is half full" attitude, realize that although half of small businesses fail within five years, half of them suc- ceed. Some advantages of owning a small business include:

- Flexibility of schedule—though you may work more hours, you decide when
- Freedom to choose jobs you want and refuse ones you don't want
- Freedom to perform your work your way
- Freedom to outsource the boring stuff and concentrate on creative business building
- Opportunity to better meet specialty client needs and requests
- Opportunity for increased earning capacity and decreased tax liability
- Opportunity, using the Internet, to look and perform big without big business costs
- Opportunity to love what you do and do what you love

Remember that ending up with a successful business entity will depend on how much preparation you're willing to expend at the beginning.

Is smaller better than bigger? Perhaps—at least in some ways. Small firms contribute much to the economy and are responsible for employ- ing a huge portion of American workers. According to the U.S. Depart- ment of Commerce, Bureau of the Census, small firms have the following characteristics:

- Represent 99.7 percent of all employer firms
- Employ about half of all private sector employees
- Pay more than 45 percent of total U.S. private payroll
- Generated 60–80 percent of net new jobs annually over the last decade
- Created more than half of nonfarm private gross domestic product (GDP)
- Hired 40 percent of high tech workers (scientists, engineers, computer workers)
- Made up 97 percent of identified exporters in FY 2004
- Produced 28.6 percent of known export value in FY 2004
- Supplied 22.8 percent of the total value of federal prime contracts in FY 2006

According to these statistics, the American economy is dependent upon small business, yet there is no denying that owning one is risky, at least for the first five years and quite possibly after. However, this section will outline means of reducing the risk and optimizing possible gains. If you want to start your own business, the first step is to create a business plan.

FACT

Small business is the backbone of the U.S. economy. According to the U.S. Department of Commerce, U.S. Bureau of the Census, half of all American workers are employed by small businesses. It also reports that, over the past ten years, small businesses created 60–70 percent of all new jobs. For more information, see *www.sba.gov/advo/research*.

Business Plan

The business plan is not just a piece of paper your banker or creditor requires before you can borrow capital. It's a roadmap for reaching your destination, a blueprint for construction of your business. The last section discussed reasons for business failures, revealing that the overwhelming majority can be traced to poor management. The business plan is your management tool for prevention of failure; to state this in positive terms, it's your management tool for success.

Accounting software such as QuickBooks Pro and Premier, Peachtree, and others have sections on creating business plans. Standalone software, such as Business Plan Pro, Individual Business PlanMaker Professional, and Business Plan Writer, can be purchased as well. You can also find Internet sites such as *www.businessplan.com*, which advertises easy-to-use templates with charts, and *www.bizfilings.com/products/ubp.asp*, which advertises a wizard for use with QuickBooks information. There are many more, but if you don't want to create your plan, you can pay someone to do it for you. However, be careful if you choose to do this because a plan is designed to help you think about where your business will go.

Entire books have been written about business plans, illustrating how complex the process can become. However, it needn't be overwhelming. Your new business won't require an elaborate plan, just one with the flexibility to handle alterations and additions as you grow. Should you desire a very simple plan, begin with the one below.

Business and Owner History

Whether you are applying for expansion capital for an existing business or planning for a new one, you must convey your history. If your business is a startup, provide details regarding the skills you have gained from past experience.

The bank or investor uses this section, but completing the personal inventory benefits you as well. Seeing your qualifications profile in print accomplishes two things. It reveals the strengths on which you can capitalize and areas of weakness you must strengthen.

Summary of Business

Sometimes called executive summary, this step includes business description, location, and description of principle products and services.

Business Description

Include the name and particulars of your business: address, phone numbers, Web site, and other relevant information. Consider these points when you decide on a name. Let your name advertise for you. Right now, you need a name that tells the public who you are and what services you offer. Smith & Associates sounds professional, but professional what? With Smith, you'll spend more advertising money than with a name such as Security Associates.

It's true that some successful PI firms have not adhered to this advice. They argue that Smith & Associates provides the impression of an upscale firm—they're willing to expend additional advertising monies in order to continue that perception. Make your own decision.

In your business description, provide an overview of your services. Do you specialize in one area, such as missing persons and skip tracing, or do you offer other services? List them all.

Business Location

Describe your potential client and the location that will draw him to your business. Will you seek the high-end client? Attorneys and professionals? If so, take a walk through their offices to get a feel for the atmosphere that says success to them. If you can afford it, create this atmosphere in your office.

Principal Services or Products

Describe the services that you've listed earlier. Be specific. Will you perform the services yourself, or will some require skills you don't possess? Will you purchase special equipment in order to offer these services? If you sell products, describe them, along with any restrictions on their use or special storage and/or display requirements.

Market and Competition for Services or Products

Who is your market? Where are they located? Why are they a possible market for your products or services? Note who your competitors are, how they conduct business, and what their fees are.

Do a little reconnaissance to determine the competition's marketing scheme, line of products, services, pricing, and fees. Be careful, however; don't waltz in and openly take notes or ask too many questions. No one likes reconnaissance, but PIs are especially secretive. A better method of reconnaissance is to speak into a small tape recorder—discretely.

Available Management and Resource Personnel

Who will work with you and what are their strengths? What are their backgrounds and skills? Profile your accountant, attorney, and any associates or investors. Do the same with consultants, but remember that this plan is for you. Allow it to show you where the holes exist in your management team so they can be filled with competent employees, consultants, or resource personnel.

Business Goals and Timeline

In this section, be specific as to how you intend to grow the business. Specify how much you plan to gross in six months, one year, three years, five years, and so forth. If you plan to add products or services, identify each one and discuss when and how you'll purchase and introduce them. List vendors or possible vendors. Want to add investigators, a secretary, vehicles, or specialized equipment? Add the specifics. Want to add a second office in another part of town or in a different city? It all goes here.

Of course, you don't have to plan for the life of your business right now, but think as far ahead as possible, and use these suggestions to help with setting goals. Use your business plan as your roadmap, and watch it grow and morph in any direction you desire.

Financial Needs Summary

State your financial start-up needs. This involves pricing everything you'll need, from paper clips to surveillance equipment to furniture. It takes time, but is the only way to ensure that you'll have enough money to generate the healthiest possible start. Include monthly expenses as the beginnings of your budget, and add at least six months operating costs to provide a cushion.

Projections of Earnings and Investor Returns

Provide a description of how you'll return any investor earnings. Work with an accountant to ensure accuracy and feasibility.

Target Market Description

Specialists recommend that new owners identify and focus on the prospective client who possesses the highest potential for monetary return as the target market. This doesn't mean that your market should be entirely limited to this client group, but resources spent gaining these clients are likely to be returned along with profit. This long-held theory has undergone some criticism in recent years, however. One reason is that many investigators insist that they can't compete in today's market by putting most of their eggs in the target market's basket. They prefer to offer a large menu of services to a larger market. They believe clients expect it. You must decide which theory is best for you.

Comparison of Company Services to Competitor Services

Describe your competition's products and services in detail. In what way are you better than your competition? How do you do your specialty better than anyone else? Why would a client choose you rather than the competition? Can you discover areas for improvement; if so, how will you implement improvements?

Marketing and Sales

Startups tend to underprice the competition. This is not a good idea. Don't spend time gathering clients whose only concern is low prices when you must eventually raise yours to stay in business. When you raise them, you'll have to go after new clients who will pay your new prices.

Don't undervalue your worth. Perception is key. Don't tell the world that you aren't worth the price everyone else charges. Of course, if a few agencies hold a monopoly in your area and have priced their services egregiously high according to areas with more competition, you may want to rethink this issue.

Advertising Venues

Advertising is a large part of your business plan. This is the section in which you indicate the type of advertising you intend to use. Describe the medium in which you'll advertise, how much it will cost, and how you'll pay for it. If you want to increase advertising as you grow, specify how and when.

Policy for Credit, Returns, and Rentals

Determine your policies for returns and rentals. What will your return policy for clients who become dissatisfied entail? You'd better know before that irate client complains about your investigator's expense charges. In fact, this policy should be included in the client agreement or provided at the time the agreement is signed. If it is provided in a separate document, leave space for the client's signature acknowledging receipt. Many investigators refuse to return money that has been legitimately used no matter the complaint. Others provide an unconditional money-back guarantee as to their services. Study the policies that others have set up and put together one that fits your needs. Better yet, speak with an attorney.

Work Place—Home Office Versus Public Office

Successful PI firms use many different location models. There is no one right or best model, so choose the one that's right for you—home, public, or virtual office.

Home Office

Benefits abound for those who enjoy working from home. Low overhead and tax benefits allow the investigator to retain more profit while finding time to be closer to family. Many who work from home boast of doing some of their work in pajamas. The Small Business Administration reports a record number of business owners working from home, along with employees of larger businesses.

◀ You can establish an office with all the resources you need wherever you feel most comfortable.

Disadvantages are not absent, however. Your home is an inconvenient place for meeting clients and lacks the professional atmosphere of an office. Besides, some clients will not be as fond of your children and pets as you are. A distinct disadvantage of the home office is distraction. Everywhere the business owner looks, he's reminded that he's also the homeowner. A pile of laundry screams for attention, neighbors and delivery people ring the bell. If he has children, interruptions can be constant.

ALERT!

If you work from home, never allow clients access to your address and phone number, and don't make private information publicly available. While most clients are everyday people, this profession will eventually draw the crazy, the frenzied, or the person working off of his last nerve and perhaps his last brain cell. Domestic cases particularly may bring you in contact with this person. Protect yourself and your family.

There's also the irritating fact that friends and family feel at liberty to impose. Many home workers have heard, "Since you're free, can you pick up Tommy?" or some other request from seemingly busier persons. Well, you're not free—you're working, but it can take a while to convince others that you expect to be afforded the same respect for your time as others are at their day jobs. Ultimately, for those who can manage distractions and attend to business, home is a great place to be based.

Public Office

Locate near your target clients or in a location frequented by them. If you are in a shopping area, a center with a large anchor store such as Target or high-end department stores will draw customers who will see your business.

Check foot and vehicle traffic around the area before choosing a location. Walk-by or drive-by traffic is a gift to retailers. It provides many eyes to view your signage and decreases the need for heavy advertising. If you sell products or provide home security in any manner, a retail location may be a good choice.

Parking is another consideration, especially for retail locations. Clients will go elsewhere if getting into or out of your location is too difficult or time-consuming. Consider a location with parking in the rear for clients who are wary of being seen around a private investigation office. This is not a must, as you won't encounter shy clients as often as you might expect, and you can always arrange to meet elsewhere.

Also, consider that many public locations require a build-out, meaning that you are provided a shell and will need to build any inner walls or offices you need. You'll also be responsible for the costs of flooring, counters, and security systems, and less often, for air conditioning systems, lighting, wiring, plumbing, and other essentials. Many times, skillful negotiation will keep some of these costs in the landlord's pocket and out of yours. Read your contract carefully before signing.

Contact your Business Development Office. Inquire about restrictions in your potential location. Ask about whether the commercial area has rules that aren't immediately apparent, such as limitations on signage, parking, and décor. Other restrictions might be the number of business types allowed to operate, a limit on the hours you're permitted to remain open to the public, or even a certain number of hours you must remain open.

Locating your public office may take some research. While it's true that retailers benefit from a high-traffic site, investigators may not need so much. When you offer only services, a lower overhead location may be preferable. With the savings, you could add or improve services or save your clients some money. Yet if you decide to go the lower-priced route, you must still locate in a convenient, clean, well-lit, well-maintained section of town. Importantly, check out the area's history of break-ins, robberies, and vandalism. Don't neglect this aspect of location research for the protection and safety of clients and employees.

If you have very little startup capital, you may decide to offer investigative work to an attorney or another owner whose business is compatible with yours, with the qualification that you be allowed to use part of his space. Investigators have gotten started this way; however, you must be sure that a written, signed agreement outlines the responsibilities of both parties. Include the number and type of work hours required for your use of space. Otherwise, the agreement can become confusing.

Before deciding on your public location, return to your business plan and the demographics of your target market. If you don't intend to specialize, this may not matter, but if you plan to work with attorneys, for example, look at their income, age, and lifestyle before determining your location. Be sure that you'll be in the right place to attract and service them. Attorneys' offices tend to cluster in or near urban areas because of the proximity to courthouses, police departments, jails, and centers for records. Yet this depends on the type of law the attorneys practice. You may also find them in small commercial and even residential areas.

ALERT!

Before locating your public office, be sure that the population of your target market is adequate to support your business, or is at least large enough for profitable specialization. Equally important is the need for a stable or rising area economic base. Don't get stuck with a lease that traps you in an area where businesses are floundering or dying.

Look for good schools, clean and well-maintained property, adequate transportation, and convenient services. New commercial or residential construction is a good sign, as is the movement of large companies into an area. You can also look into incentives for business development in disadvantaged areas. Some cities offer this as part of inner-city revitalization plans, often with lucrative incentives. If this is attractive to you, be sure that the businesses who will locate near you are to your liking. Look hard at restrictions, transportation, parking, lighting, security, maintenance, and convenience. If it's all up to par and you can handle the risk, go for it; many businesses have been successful doing so. Just be sure the area is truly in revitalization.

Virtual Office

Somewhat on the order of executive suites, virtual offices are set up to fit the needs of those who cannot or will not expend the cost of regular office space. Executive suites provide short-term leases complete with a telephone and receptionist, common area privileges (bathroom, kitchen, conference room), and mail service. Copy/fax machines and other services are available for a fee. Executive suites are attractive to those who require services sporadically, paying only for what they need when they need it.

Virtual offices are fairly new arrivals on the scene. A virtual office isn't physical space. The purpose is to provide everything the business owner needs while saving the costs of space. This allows the small business owner to be based at home or in an inexpensive space but still show an upscale address to his clients. Services can be added according to the owner's budget or preferences, but the basic virtual office is an address in a prestigious area, with mail receipt and forwarding, discounts on supplies and couriers, and low-priced leasing of offices and meeting rooms for short periods of time. Other features, such as a telephone receptionist, a fax and phone redirection service, and more, can be added. While you work affordably from home, no one will ever know, because you schedule meetings in this sumptuous conference room.

Virtual Assistants

A virtual office assistant works much as a regular assistant—only from her home. She answers your phone, takes messages, types reports, and if you want, acts as the face of your business. However, if you only need an assistant for certain hours or certain days, she's there for you. While there will be no office space in which to meet clients, your virtual assistant will provide the image of an office setting. Many clients look for this.

Office Equipment and Furnishings

Don't break the bank furnishing your office, no matter where you decide to locate. It's true that you should match location and décor to the type of client you want to attract, as discussed earlier in this chapter. However, even if you are blessed with deep pockets or a willing investor, be careful of overspending in this area.

Appearing professional and successful need not cost a fortune. Be creative. Look for going out of business sales, scratch and dent stores, and wholesale warehouses. Check the paper for yard and estate sales in influential neighborhoods, and search flea markets and antique dealers. You may be surprised at what you find. Depending on available time and motivation, you can find solid wooden pieces at unfinished furniture stores just waiting to be stained and finished. Remember, besides furnishing a nice office, if you seek the high-income client, you must locate where she is. Don't expect this client to meet you in a dingy third-floor walkup with poor lighting and shabby furniture.

One small aside regarding the use of antiques to furnish your office: As office furniture, they will depreciate, but as antiques, they will grow in value, providing the benefits of tax deductions and increased capital worth in one package. Why do you think those attorney's and doctor's offices are full of these pieces?

Have your flea market antique appraised to be sure of its age, then refinish it or use it as is. A debate rages as to which process protects the value best, refinishing it or leaving a piece in its purchased condition. No matter which you choose, furnishing your business with certified antiques will provide the aforementioned benefits—and with very little expense if you "find" them.

CHAPTER 5

Marketing and Money Matters

This section will discuss startup issues such as capital, insurance, taxes, fees, and getting paid, as well as one of the most important aspects of startup—marketing. Marketing involves making the public aware that your business exists and promoting the services you provide.

Startup Capital

In large cities, you'll find a great deal of competition for PI work. Don't let this be a deterrent. A good investigator is always in demand, and private investigation is a wide field, offering employment in many areas. If you're not interested in owning a business, alternatives abound. You may have an interest in:

- Insurance-claims investigation
- Process service
- Background/pre-employment investigation
- Bill collection and repossession
- Business security/loss prevention
- Hotel security
- Financial/corporate investigation
- Executive protection
- Legal investigation
- Bounty hunting

◀ A loan is one way to obtain the startup capital you need to get your business up and running.

Although you can work for others doing these things, each of these services can also be offered on a contract basis to other businesses. Capital won't be a concern if you opt for a salaried position, but it is of primary concern when you start your own business.

Even if you work from home, you must consider the costs of equipment, supplies, advertising, and other essentials before you open for business. If you operate from a public location, the costs will be higher. If possible, visit a PI office and take silent inventory or ask an investigator. Realize that some of them will help you, but some are secretive or unaware of the benefits of networking.

You may consider borrowing money for startup or expansion, but be sure you have means of repayment. Include it in your business plan. Be especially careful of easily available high interest loans—this type of money will overburden your budget, and the interest rises like a rocket. Instead, consider investors.

FACT

Angel investors may be a good place to begin your search for startup or expansion capital. Angels are out there, but they aren't easy to find. Angel networks provide capital for entrepreneurs. Inc. Magazine compiled a list of angel networks worth investigating in 2005. You can find more information at *www.inc.com/articles/2001/09/23461.html*, complete with links to investors in eight U.S. geographic locations.

Business Bank Account Versus Client Trust Account

When a client pays his retainer, it's not yours until you complete the work for which you received it. Because of this, it can't be deposited into your regular business account. Doing this is called comingling of funds, and it is prohibited. The solution is to open a separate account where the retainer is held in trust for the client. Once you have worked the retainer, you're permitted to transfer funds from the trust account to your business account. Any unused portion must be returned.

When you comingle a retainer with regular funds, the possibility of spending it is very real. If the client decides to close the case or it's completed before the retainer has been expended, you may be unable to return the unused portion. Nothing will destroy your reputation more. Some states have laws specifying what must be done with interest earned on a trust account, so check with your state. Even if you don't reside in a state that regulates PIs, use trust accounts anyway. They are a mark of professionalism.

Investigators often try to bypass the costs of these accounts, but the results can be more costly than the minimal fees charged. You may have the same inclination. You look at the well-dressed professional client writing the check and cannot imagine being stiffed, but it happens. When you deposit that check at the conclusion of the investigation, insufficient funds or a stop payment may have rendered it useless. The myriad excuses given by clients for refusing to honor these checks, even after receiving excellent service, boggle the mind. Although it doesn't happen often, don't allow anyone to put you in the position of shelling out attorney and court fees in order to be paid.

Getting Paid

People will pay for something they want or need. After it's delivered, they're much less eager to remit. Therefore, collect your fees up front.

Individuals as Clients

Get paid first! Require a retainer and a signed agreement. Perform casework until the money is expended or the case has been completed. Return any remaining funds. If the case remains unresolved and the client wants to continue, accept another retainer. It's just good policy; stories of nonpayment are numerous.

When people desperately want to find someone or need information or surveillance, they're likely to commission work far beyond their ability to pay. While client motivations may not be malicious, the result is still disastrous for everyone. It can be easily prevented by operating with funds up front. Not only does a retainer keep your business in the black, it prevents the client from overextending himself when he is in an emotional state and prevents ugly collection situations. This doesn't mean that investigators don't perform pro bono work—many do—but only when they choose the cause and can afford to give away the hours. Protect your business first, and you'll be capable of helping those who really need your help. Always require a signed client agreement. See Chapter 13 for more information about working with clients and client agreements.

Business Clients

If possible, collect retainers from business clients. This is more difficult than collecting from individuals. Businesses are not accustomed to remitting payment in this manner and some view the request for retainer as an affront. However, if you're successful in making this arrangement with a business, be explicit about how and when you'll be paid. A written contract protects you both, so don't hesitate to pull one out and fill it in—then get a signature. Without it, there can be problems.

Don't let payment become an issue. If you must write letters and make phone calls for payment, you've probably lost your client. Avoid such uncomfortable situations by using a prearranged, written, and signed agreement. Of course, the only real way to prevent the necessity of hounding your client for payment is to receive a retainer before beginning work.

For example, after receiving the initial retainer, if you haven't specified in writing that you'll continue to work according to monies retained, you might have to settle for the remainder of your fee after the job is complete. Doing this places you in a negative position from the outset because expenses must be paid during the investigation. Attorneys understand retainers and should be willing to hire you as a contract employee according to these terms. After all, they require retainers in much the same way.

You'll almost certainly run into the business client who won't pay up front. Before deciding whether to accept the case, ask agencies in your area about their policies. If the climate is conducive toward billing business clients (risk assessment companies particularly like to be billed), you might decide to take the job, but be sure to ask about the payment timeframe. Insurance risk assessment companies are accustomed to being presented with investigator information, so don't hesitate to present your qualification to them. Many will take a chance on you, especially if they're unhappy with their present investigator.

If you decide to bill, set up a regular billing date. Be aware that many firms pay bills once a month, and almost none pay upon receipt of invoice. Furthermore, large firms often take longer than small firms to pay. The most common reason for this is that invoices must pass through several hands before the person with authority to cut your check is authorized to do so.

However, you need your money. You've expended time, gas, and perhaps travel expenses for hotels and meals, and your monthly overhead just keeps coming due whether your large company has paid or not. You may have also paid investigators.

To receive payment quickly, offer a small reduction from the invoice amount. For the client, even if it's not company policy to take advantage of a reduction, it's an attractive incentive. Introduce a 2–5 percent reduction for payment within a reasonable timeframe, perhaps fifteen days. Most businesses will oblige. This reduces your income slightly, but it greatly increases your cash flow, which is at the heart of keeping your doors open. Never forget that thriving businesses have been forced to close because of cash flow problems.

◀ As a private investigator, you will have a large number of receipts and bills you need to keep track of.

Work with an accountant to determine which billing method is best for you. Also, ensure that invoices and everything you send to the client appears professional. Microsoft Word, WordPerfect, and many business software programs such as QuickBooks provide invoice templates that can be customized. QuickBooks does the math for you and keeps up with income and expenditures. If you sell products on the Internet, QuickBooks will integrate with some Webhosting firms. Preprinted forms can also be purchased at most specialty stores such as Target, Best Buy, Staples, Office Depot, and Office Max. You can also find them online.

ALERT!

Keep your fees equitable. Don't raise your regular fee 5 percent for Mr. Large Corporation only so you can offer to reduce his bill by 5 percent on the invoice. People talk. Keep your reputation untarnished by charging everyone a fair fee—the same fee. Should you decide to offer such an incentive to every client, figure it into your regular charges beforehand.

Collecting Payment

Most investigators prefer to deliver the bill in person for several reasons. The first reason is that this business is all about relationships. You want to touch base with your client, visit a short time (don't waste her time, nor yours), and cement your relationship. The second reason is for you to leave with your fee in hand. It's difficult for a client to put you off when you're standing in front of her. Many things can delay your payment if you mail the bill, including winding up in the "to be paid" pile and subject to someone else's payment schedule. Cash flow is extremely important in this business, so you don't want this to happen.

One more point about the bill: Itemize it. Don't expect a client to be satisfied with a large lump sum. Explain where his money was spent—gas, other investigators, phone calls, and any unusual expenses. Also, don't pad your bill. Treat your clients as you would like to be treated. Clients often discover padded bills, so don't take the chance.

Licenses and Taxes

This subject isn't nearly as exciting as surveillance or undercover work, but it may be even more important. Without compliance with local, state, and federal requirements, you won't operate any business for long. Protect your investment and your future by obtaining all required licenses and permits. Most states have business license divisions, so check out the Small Business Administration's (SBA) Web site for links to business licenses nationwide at *www.sba.gov/hotlist/license.html*. The SBA site is overflowing with resources for business owners and would-be owners.

Compliance is also important as a barometer of integrity. If you're trustworthy with small things, the perception is that you can be trusted with large ones. There mustn't be a hint of illegal or improper behavior attached to you or your firm, and it's both improper and illegal to operate without a license and without paying taxes. If you don't think this is important, you need to take inventory of your ethics. Besides, information about noncompliance gets around. See Chapter 3 for more information concerning ethics.

As a private investigator, you are a keeper of secrets. Regardless of your skills or experience, you sell something more than services. You sell your reputation. Keep it sparkling so that clients know they can trust you. When faced with temptations to cross the line of good ethical behavior, don't do it; next time, it'll be easier to stay on the right side of that line.

If you're not good with paperwork or really hate doing it, hire someone to do it for you. The tax authorities are powerful. Even Al Capone was finally taken down by the IRS when law enforcement couldn't make charges for his more violent crimes stick. See Chapter 2 for information concerning each state's regulations for business licenses.

Insurance

Insurance will be a large chunk of your operating budget, but is essential to your business. States differ in their requirements as to type and amount, so check with yours before acquiring a policy. Some states will also require that you be bonded. Shop around; companies that specialize in PI firms don't usually charge as much as those who don't. If you sell products, there will probably be a separate policy requirement with additional costs.

Types of Insurance

Liability insurance to include errors and omissions is required by most states that license investigators. Even when it is not required, errors and omissions insurance is the only real protection for a PI. This is because there are many areas where mistakes can be made in this business, as well as gray areas that have not yet been defined by case law. Electronic surveillance is one such area.

You may be following the current law for electronic surveillance in your state, yet if the client or target challenges this in court, you may find yourself on the wrong side of the judge's decision. Errors and omissions will cover this as long as you were acting under the law as you knew it to be. If information acquired concerning a target turns out to be wrong—a misprint, someone else's information or even missing information—you can be sued. With only liability insurance, you won't be fully covered. While these examples are unusual, they do happen, as do other mistakes that may be beyond your immediate control but can be held to your account.

QUESTION?

Is one insurance policy as good as another?
Carriers and policies differ. Be sure your protection continues after retirement or business closure. Some policies won't cover claims made even one day after the date of dissolution. If coverage is $2 million (the minimum amount that today's business clients like to see), be sure you know whether that's a cap for the entire year or whether you're covered for $2 million per claim. Also, be aware of the maximum number of claims that will be covered per year.

A Hypothetical

Take this hypothetical example. You're filming a worker's compensation target living in a rural area. You pull a map of his property at the courthouse, set up your vehicle, and film on the public road down from his house. You aren't trespassing and you aren't violating surveillance laws, but the map is incorrect. You have no way of knowing it, but the road you are using is not public at all; it's the target's recently purchased private road. Oops! If this case never goes to court and no one challenges your mistake, then you're all right. If you are challenged, it can be expensive to prove that you were acting in good faith according to a faulty map. If it goes to court, you'll probably be exonerated—probably—but you can never know what a judge or jury will decide. Don't take the chance—protect yourself with errors and omissions insurance. Besides, even if you are exonerated, the cost of paying an attorney through the process of trial dates, postponements, and more trial dates can be enough to bankrupt a small business, no matter the outcome.

Large firms keep attorneys on retainer, but small firms must bear hourly costs. Most investigators spend an entire career without being sued, but in this litigious society, it only makes sense to guard against the possibility. Besides, clients are more comfortable with firms that are fully insured, realizing that it prevents them from becoming embroiled in a lawsuit against you.

The Bottom Line

If you are in business for yourself, don't neglect insurance on vehicles, equipment, and business premises. Large investigative firms provide employee insurance as well. You won't be able to offer this until you build up regular clients and a stable monthly income, but you can compensate your contract investigators with a few extra dollars per hour. Keep competent investigators by treating them well. Don't try to build your business at their expense.

The Yergey Insurance Agency (*www.yergeyins.com*) has developed a true errors and omissions program for PIs at a much lower cost than other insurance companies. This policy extends for a period beyond close of business, so coverage is available if you're sued after your business closes.

Marketing and Promotion

The purpose of marketing is to ensure that the pricing and packaging of your services and/or products creates demand and makes people eager to purchase from you. Advertising today is very different than it was as recently as ten years ago. While this book provides insufficient space for completely covering this subject, it will offer a solid overview and direct you to sources for further research.

FACT

Unless you specialize in a super narrow area, you meet potential clients every day—standing in line at the bank, sitting in your vet's office, or riding in an elevator. The secret to connecting with people—even strangers—lies in asking questions. Let the other person speak, and respond with appropriate questions reflecting your interest in what they've said.

Advertising for Name and Logo Recognition

This type of advertising differs from sales advertising in that it doesn't seek to convince the viewer or reader to purchase anything. While products or services may be used in ads, the focus is on the company. The ads make the business name and/or logo linger in consumers' minds and usually elicit positive emotions and leave the audience feeling good.

This kind of advertising is expensive—think of the millions of dollars companies pay for a few minutes of airtime at the Super Bowl. You can use this type of advertising in a smaller way by creating a professional logo. Graphic artists can do this for you. Simple services are also available at stores such as Wal-Mart and Office Depot. Online companies such as VistaPrint.com have pages of logos from which to choose. You may decide on one of these prepackaged logos for a very reasonable price, but VistaPrint will also create logos to your specifications, as will many online and on-site companies. Spend available funds up front on the creation of a logo; it's your main recognition tool.

Are logos really important?
Yes! Name and logo recognition, or branding, builds trust in your company. People trust what they recognize and distrust what they don't. Place your logo on business cards, stationery, brochures, pens, and anything that ends up in the hands of prospective clients.

Many people will advise you never to put money into a logo that will need to be updated later at additional cost. This is good advice—if you have the funds to have your logo professionally created at startup. It's pricey to do so, and all companies update them periodically to show a fresh "now" look. This leads to the other school of thought: Lacking the means to do anything else, create your own logo, or have it done with minimal cost in order to get your business up and running. Of course, if you have no talent for this, don't do it yourself. You know if something looks professional; if you can't create this look, forget it.

Advertising to Specific Audiences for Specific Sales

Unlike advertising for name recognition—which spreads information over a large area—sales advertising focuses on specifics. It can be aimed at target markets using specific products or at target markets using your general product line. This is an oversimplified explanation, of course.

If you want, work with a consultant, although as the owner you know more about your business than anyone else. Professional consultant Suze Orman (*www.suzeorman.com*) offers tips to help you manage advertising for your business. Also, many nonprofits, such as SCORE (*www.score.org*) and the Acadia Center for Social and Business Entrepreneurship (*www.acsbe.com*) stand ready to assist you.

Print Advertising

A professional business card is absolutely necessary for building contacts and name recognition. Brochures, while more expensive, can be invaluable in providing potential clients with an overview of your business. If you have the time and inclination, you may want to create your own. You may be familiar with VistaPrint and PaperDirect, but there are others that have features that may appeal to you.

Many marketing experts recommend a press kit over brochures alone. The press kit is useful when targeting a particular client or business. You can purchase plain pocket folders or customized folders with your name, logo, address, and phone numbers and a slot for your business card. Inside, place a letter of introduction with an invitation to learn more about your services by viewing the contents of the kit. The next page should detail how you're different from the competition. If you can get clients to write a short recommendation, include those blurbs on a separate page or two. This can be tricky in private investigation; clients may not want to talk about their cases, but some—especially businesses—may be willing to give a generic bit of praise.

A third page should provide your history and the history of the business—who you are, how and why you started it all, and what your mission and purpose are. Put it in story form and personalize it by writing in first person. Another page should detail your services. If you've created a brochure of services, use that instead. If you have copies of press releases (which should be provided to newspapers at startup), include them. Any promotional materials such as pens or sticky notes with your name and logo can be included, and be sure your Web site is referenced. In the introduction letter, suggest that you'll give the client a call within a specified period of time to answer any questions.

Other advertising vehicles include magnetic signs for your automobile, billboards, trade shows, radio and television ads and spots, magazine ads, and Internet blog sites. You can also volunteer to write a security piece (if your writing is strong) in local newspapers or magazines—even your church bulletin. Think creatively and other ideas will present themselves. Choose the venue that matches your budget.

Networking

Many networking groups meet regularly. Some charge one-time fees for membership, others charge monthly fees, and still others don't charge at all. Some have monthly lunch or breakfast meetings. Most require members to provide leads for each other. Meetings are usually mandatory, and members are only allowed to miss a certain number of them. Should you join one of these groups, distribute plenty of business cards, and do your part in providing leads. Offer to speak to the group on some issue of security. In fact, preparing a speech on a security topic of general interest will prepare you to present your skills anywhere at a moment's notice. Business Networking International is one of the largest networking groups. See its Web site at *www.bni.com* for more information.

Speaking

Businesses and organizations look for fresh speakers. Make yourself available to the Rotary, Lions, Kiwanis, and other service organizations. Join one if you're interested in community service, which can be rewarding, but also goes a long way in establishing good will with other business owners. Don't use these organizations as a way to get new clients, however. Members will spot this type of motivation in no time. Join because you want to give back to your community, and think of any work that arises from this as icing on the cake. For speaking engagements, check with your Better Business Bureau and Chamber of Commerce. It may keep a listing of speakers according to subject or profession.

Creating a Web Site

No marketing tool is more recommended than a business Web site. You may still want to use the Yellow Pages or something like it, but do not neglect securing a presence on the Web. When asked, many business owners report searching the Web first for products and services, and many never reference the phone book at all. If you know nothing about using the Internet, now is a good time to learn. Colleges offer low-cost community programs that teach computer and Internet basics. Online programs are also available, as well as educational software.

Web Site Basics

If your aversion to learning this technology is strong, you can pay someone to create, maintain, and operate your site. If you do, set up some means of employee oversight to be sure you haven't put a shyster in charge of the house; do a background check for past reported offenses. If you can budget the funds, hire a good Web site designer who has a track record with other businesses. Unfortunately, whenever there's a demand for any service, fraudulent and incompetent companies spring up to fill it like toadstools after rain. Many will put out their shingle and advertise that they design a great site. Be sure to check them out before deciding on one.

When you look at different designers, make a list of characteristics you'd like your site to have. Ask each candidate to supply a portfolio of links to live sites they have designed. Go to each site and note whether the designs look professional and the sites are easy to navigate. Be sure that your designer doesn't crowd Web pages with too much text bunched up in one long paragraph. Breaking text up with space and pictures makes it more attractive and readable. Be careful with inexperienced designers, but don't write them off immediately. They may be able to give you a great Web site for a low price; just ask to see examples of other projects and be very detailed with your questions.

After you choose your designer, obtain a written contract of exactly what has been agreed upon—down to colors, number of pages, and any flash or specialty features. To avoid being duped, require a breakdown of costs that can be readily understood. Put charges and fees in writing as well. Communicating by e-mail provides a record of your transactions from the outset.

QUESTION?

Now that I have a site, can I sit back and wait for phone calls?
No, although many people think you can. Publishing your site doesn't guarantee that anyone will ever see it. Once it's operational, you must inform the world that it exists. You must drive business to your site with effective marketing.

If you have less money than time, you can put together a simple but effective Web site yourself. Many companies host do-it-yourself sites and provide support. Prices vary, so search thoroughly before deciding on your host. The following sites have received favorable reports:

- *www.homestead.com*
- *www.econgo.com*
- *smallbusiness.yahoo.com/ecommerce*
- *www.atlasinfo.com*
- *www.godaddy.com*

Ready-made or template sites such as these don't offer the flexibility that custom-built sites provide. However, for the price and limited time required to launch them, ready-made sites are functional and attractive. Flash and special features can also be added. When you choose a site, decide which features you absolutely must have, then work with that list and your budget to find the right hosting company.

Marketing Your Web Site

If you do an Internet search for Web site marketing, you'll find a lot of information on one important marketing tool: search engine optimization, a method for having your site appear higher on an Internet searcher's key word search results page. In other words, when a client enters a search for "private investigators your city, your state" into any search engine, many pages will be returned. You don't want your site to be listed on page fifty, as most people don't search past page three. Optimization can improve your standing on the list. However, don't believe any claims that guarantee you'll appear on the first page or within the first ten sites returned. At the present stage of technology, no one can guarantee this. All anyone can promise you is to improve your ranking.

ALERT!

Ever wonder how all those ads appear as sponsored links on your Google search results page? They're delivered according to key words that relate to your search. The advertiser pays no fee unless you choose the ad and visit his site. Check Google's AdWords and AdSense at *www.google .com/intl/en/ads* to see if this advertising method is for you.

Other factors affect your position on search engines. Key words help with your site's ranking, but there's a lot of misinformation about this subject. Learn much more at *www.webmarketingnow.com/tips/meta-tags-uncovered.html.* You can also sign up for free marketing newsletters delivered to your inbox, but be aware that, because they're free, most will include advertisements.

If you are looking for extreme Internet marketing, C. J. Bronstrup may be your man. A former private investigator, he claims to obtain better results with nontraditional marketing methods than with traditional techniques. Bronstrup warns that marketing information can be deceptive. For example, when someone advises that additional sites linking to yours will allow your site to be more available to search engines, be careful. This is only half true, according to Bronstrup. In order for any site to pull yours up by merely linking to it, that site must already have a ranking much higher than yours. A link from CNN or Fox News to your site can pull you up, but a link from a two- or three-person operation will have little effect. See his main site at *www.atlasinfo.com.*

One of the newest marketing techniques is called viral marketing. This type seeks to encourage the voluntary passing of ads through social networking sites and e-mail. Promotional messages are embedded into sites such as MySpace and YouTube, using cute or funny video clips, interactive games, and text messages. Promoters use the networking function of these sites to pass their message along—one person may send it to four people, who each send it to four more, and so on. In this way, it multiplies quickly through the online community like a virus. Large corporations with resources for creating eye-catching messages, especially video clips, are using viral marketing in a big way. However, the real power of these sites is evidenced by the number of viral clips that are made by an ordinary person with a camera.

This section is meant to provide a starting place for your research of marketing information—there's a lot more out there—but be careful. If you're unsure of the veracity of a site or a marketing technique, don't use it. The Internet is difficult to police. It's a cyber no-man's-land where the legitimate and illegitimate exist side by side, but it also offers the small business owner an opportunity to present a large presence.

Creating Professional Reports

The final report is as important as any other part of your investigation. It must appear professional; if it doesn't have the earmarks of professionalism, all your efforts won't matter much to your client. People are influenced by what they see, and a professionally typed and formatted report that is easy to read and free of typos and grammatical errors lends credibility to your investigation and its results. To some degree, this may be simple perception. The ability to write a good report may, in reality, not reflect on your investigative skills one bit, but only you will be aware of that. If you can't write a good report, hire someone to do it for you; it's that important. A report has several sections: title page, introduction, body, conclusion, and additional information.

Remember that this is highly sensitive information concerning another person. Because you're responsible for keeping this confidential, store it in a safe location. Most investigators lock their case files away. Even other investigators who are not involved in a particular case have no right to view that information.

Title Page

This page begins with your agency name as the heading. Put the client's name, address, and phone number below that. Next, add the title of the investigation, such as "Smith/Norris Child Custody Case." Some investigators put the period of time that they worked the case. You can put what you want on this page, but this information seems to fit appropriately.

Introduction

Page 1 is titled "Introduction" or "Summary." Organize the case into a very short summation. Some PIs like to put only the introduction on page 1, while others begin the body of the report on this page. Your summary could begin with something like: "On October 27, 2008, Mr. Dan Smith retained this office for the purpose of a child custody investigation regarding his ex-wife, Candice Norris, and her male friend, Michael Peters." The introduction shouldn't be more than one page—ideally it should be about half a page—and should read something like a book jacket summary of a novel.

Body of Report

This can be written in several formats. Some investigators write the report as a day-by-day recounting of the events, many times in paragraph form. The format that seems to be most readable is that of incident-by-incident reporting. In other words, the top of the page shows the day and date. The highlights of the day are reported in first-person or third-person narrative.

October 27, 2008
6:00 A.M. Investigator left his residence.
6:30 A.M. Arrived at target residence and set up surveillance.
7:00 A.M. Ms. Norris exited residence with two children.

Conclusion

At the end of this play-by-play description, you may elect to write several paragraphs detailing your observations and drawing conclusions. Any recommendations can be included here.

List of Additional Information

In this section, you'll add any sketches, pictures, itemization and location of DVDs, interviews or background check information, official records, and the like.

Polishing the Report

The report must be typed. Use your spell check and grammar check; if you're still uneasy, have someone else proof it for you.

CHAPTER 6

Missing Persons: Skip Tracing, Adoption Searches, and Genealogy

Investigations of missing persons are usually known as domestic cases, although some missing persons have nothing to do with domestic situations. However, overlap of these investigations is common and investigative techniques are similar, so they have been included here together. This section outlines skip tracing, an investigative specialty that is about locating people who've skipped out on something or someone. Skip tracing is used in divorce cases, child custody cases, missing persons cases, adoption searches, and genealogy traces, both of which are discussed in this chapter.

Overview of Skip Tracing

Skip tracing is the art of locating people who have gone missing. The name arose from the idea that one has "skipped" town or "skipped" out on bail. Many PIs call missing people "skips," whether they are missing intentionally or not. Skip tracing can yield a good income for those who specialize in it, especially if investigators cultivate relationships with attorneys, insurance companies, and bail bonding and loan companies. Yet it's time and work intensive, and can be dangerous.

◀ There are many resources you can use to help you find a missing person.

FACT

The great majority of missing persons aren't lost or abducted. They're missing because they want to be. Some are in hiding from creditors, families, or spouses. Some are escaping something unbearable in their world. Others disappear due to psychological problems, or are running from a mistake. Many of these skips return or are located. Only a minority of missing persons cases require professional investigative techniques.

Numbers concerning reported missing persons are staggering, especially considering that not all those missing are reported. Consider the following U.S. statistics provided by the FBI's NCIC:

- The number of people reported missing in the U.S. increased 468 percent from 1987 to 2000.
- Reports of missing persons increased from 154,341 in 1987 to 876,213 in 2000.
- Of those missing in 2000, 152,265 were categorized as endangered or missing involuntarily.
- Of the 876,213 reported missing in 2000, 85–90 percent were juveniles.
- The number of reported missing persons is estimated at an alarming 2,100 people per day.

Some adults walk out of their homes or workplaces and never return. If no physical or emotional illness is present, and no suspicion of wrongdoing surrounds their departure, it may not be reported. Those close to these skips either search for them or let them go. The disappearance of society's marginalized—the homeless, drug addicted, and the physically, emotionally, or psychologically challenged—may go unnoticed and unreported as well. With children, it's a very different story. Children do not possess the same means of supporting and protecting themselves as adults do, so they are more vulnerable to harm and exploitation. Therefore, when they're missing, it's everybody's business.

These cases require immediate attention, whether the child has been abducted or has run away. In recent years, law enforcement authorities have put policies in place to increase response time in cases involving children. This change in attitude and policy has also resulted in the police taking missing persons cases more seriously than in the past. In many cases, child protective organizations and public outcry have pushed the changes.

ALERT!

Even when an abductor poses no obvious danger to a child, many experts feel that psychological damage can result from years of hiding and lying. Some abductors say they run from a spouse who is harmful to their child but has been able to weight the judicial scale in their favor through influence or other resources. True or not, these abductors are acting unlawfully.

Many children are abducted by noncustodial parents or caretakers, but just because they've been taken by someone they know doesn't mean they aren't in danger. The public may see these abductions as less than urgent because the child is with a relative or someone who cares for her. Yet there may have been a grievous reason that a parent or caretaker was denied custody—drug use, physical or sexual abuse, neglect, or other offenses that place the child in harm's way. See Chapter 9 for more information about child abuse and the way in which pedophiles differ from other abusers.

Types of Skips

There are two basic skip types: the intentionally missing person and the unintentionally missing person. A third skip is difficult to categorize and lies somewhere in between. This is the person who has walked away from something—a relationship, marriage, or creditors—but isn't necessarily hiding. The abducted missing person will be discussed in the next chapter.

Person Not Intentionally Missing

The first type of missing person is the one who doesn't know anyone is looking for her. Although this person is usually not hiding, the connection between the searcher and the one sought is usually so tenuous, and the knowledge one has about the other so limited, that some investigators classify this search as more difficult than others. Unintentional skips could be any of the following:

- An old love or friend
- A birthparent, birth sibling, or birth child
- Runaway children or adolescents with little or neglectful family
- An unclaimed property owner or one owed some kind of payment
- A life insurance policy holder—person may not know they're named as beneficiary
- A missing heir—person has no knowledge of being named in someone's will
- A missing witness—this skip could be intentional or unintentional

- A person of interest or witness to a crime—also could be intentional or unintentional
- Those needed for genealogy or genetics history purposes

Person Intentionally Missing

This skip is in hiding and determined to stay missing. As such, he poses a challenge. It's not unusual for the PI to receive these cases after someone else has searched unsuccessfully for a long time. Often, there's a good deal of paperwork to review before beginning the search, and past mistakes have been detrimental to the investigation. Because of this, some investigators charge more for cases that have been worked by others. Some types of intentionally missing persons follow:

- Bail bond skips
- Collection skips—judgments, credit card payments, loans (including repossessions)
- Runaway children or adolescents
- Tenant skips—commercial and residential
- Rental or lease skips—appliances, furniture, and electronics are frequently rented today
- Witnesses to a crime or persons of interest—intentional or unintentional
- Persons wanted for the purpose of bringing a civil lawsuit or some other legal action
- Alimony and child support skips

Skip tracing is an easy means of making money. It's a difficult investigative specialty at which you can spend years becoming proficient. However, it can be lucrative, especially if you develop a reputation for finding the unfindable. If you are successful, the rewards are great—not only monetarily, but emotionally as well. Although skip tracing often involves locating people who have committed crimes or hurt others, it's also a business of returning people to those who love them; when the missing ones are no longer alive, it's a business providing peace of mind and closure by returning the remains to the family for burial and consecration.

The Distant Skip

This third skip is difficult to categorize. It lies somewhere between the intentional and unintentional. This is the person who has walked away from something; however, although he's never reconnected with those he abandoned nor paid the debt he left, he's not actually hiding in that he hasn't changed his name or credentials. He's counting on distance to separate himself from whatever obligations lie behind him. Therefore, he's easier to locate than other skips—usually.

Skip Tracing and the Internet

If you're picturing an investigator sitting at a computer all day, finding everything he needs to locate skips, you're wrong. The Internet is a wonderful tool for skip tracers, but it won't give you everything you need all the time. There are still many records that aren't online or show information only for recent years. Some types of information may never be collected and distributed in an online database. Therefore, you must know where to look.

Where to Search

With all the sophisticated tools available, don't forget that, depending on the type of skip, it could actually take less time to use old-fashioned techniques. After having narrowed your search to a specific area, look in the phone book; you may find your skip there. For example, as you use your profile information to interview everyone the skip knew, someone may mention, "Yeah, I think I heard him say that he was moving to Minneapolis." Look in the Minneapolis phone book first. Not every skip is a master at hiding. Another method of narrowing your search is to send your skip a letter at his last-known address. If you write "address requested" on the envelope, the post office will send the letter back to you with the skip's new address if he has forwarding service. Of course, a hardcore skip isn't likely to do this, but you never know who will. Even people who use everything they can think of to erase their steps still make mistakes.

If you have a phone number without an address or vice versa, you may not have to use a reverse-lookup site. Many times, it's quicker and easier to call the phone company, provide them a phone number, and obtain the address. This won't work if the number is unlisted, but you'll be surprised at how many people don't have unlisted numbers.

While it's possible to do an Internet search to obtain information about the skip, it's not likely to yield any results. As anyone who has employed this technique knows, the information can be there one day and gone the next. Why this happens is complicated, but basically, if your skip hasn't been listed somewhere on the Internet recently, you're not likely to find her this way.

Of course, you can search in pay databases, as listed in Appendix A, but many free sources exist that may provide what you need. Among these are property appraiser's Web sites, including *www.whitepages.com*, *www.msn.com*, *www.argali.com*, and others.

The Social Security Death Index (SSDI) is a database of most people with a social security number who have died since 1963 and who have been reported as deceased to the social security administration. You can find it, free, from many genealogy Web sites such as Ancestry.com. It's also included on the better search engine sites. However, a large number of sites will try to charge you for the information. Many times, checking the index will tell you whether a skip is using a deceased person's social security number and identity. This happens more than anyone may realize. However, mistakes have been found in the index, so double-check your information.

Be aware that the death index isn't the Social Security Administration's master death file, which is available to the public under the Freedom of Information Act. If you're relying on information from the master file, get it directly from Social Security. Otherwise you can't be sure the information is up to date.

The People Connection

When you've searched for the skip and have found no indication that he's anywhere on the planet, you may become discouraged. Many investigators stop at this point. Don't be one of them. You're looking to gain a reputation for finding the unfindable, so you must persevere. If your skip is so deeply hidden he doesn't even cause a blip on the radar screen, look for someone close to him instead.

Maybe his wife, girlfriend, or even his child is easily located. In the case that he isn't living with any of them, he may make contact or even visit eventually. Setting up surveillance at the most likely party's home or business is time-consuming and costly, but it may be your last resort—if your client has the resources.

At the point you hit a dead end, you'll be very happy you've created a skip profile and have asked all those tedious questions about family members, friends, and associates. If you haven't asked enough questions, go back to the client and ask more. Soon you'll have a feel for the types of questions that are essential and will help later.

Call or interview profile people in person. Many times, they either know where the skip is hiding or provide leads which can help you locate her. If they know her location, don't expect them to divulge it, unless you're lucky enough to be searching for someone who has left a path of scorched earth and angry people in her wake. Even if she hasn't, and her associates and relatives remain close-mouthed, there may still be clues. For example, it's not unusual for an investigator to spot something in the relative's or associate's house or location (once again, thanks to the profile) that tells him the skip is staying there or has been there.

In some cases, the skip is actually on the premises. Often, those hiding him aren't aware of the hints they give out, such as being unable to stop glancing nervously in the direction of his hiding place or attempting to cover something belonging to him. It's less usual that the skip has answered the phone when the PI called or opened the door to her knock. Because of this, it's good policy to take another investigator with you. You can never know how a skip will react to finding you at his door.

If no relatives or known associates can be found or will talk, canvas the areas where the skip was last known to be. Check with her landlord (if she rented) and with neighbors. Neighbors will often know where the subject has moved—maybe not an exact address, but enough information to aid in locating her. Also, check with former coworkers and bosses. You might present yourself as an old high school friend, but if you do, be sure you have enough details to pull it off.

Using Cell Phone Records

Unless you're working on a case with law enforcement or an attorney, don't attempt to gain access to your skip's phone records; it's now illegal without a subpoena. In the past, investigators were notorious for obtaining these records by developing relationships with phone company personnel and paying them for these private records. Another technique was masquerading as the skip and requesting that phone records be sent to a new address (usually a P.O. Box). Investigators lumped these actions under the heading of pretexting. Yet, there's a right and a wrong way to pretext, and this is the wrong way. You don't need to lie or steal other people's property in order to get the information you need.

If you are working with law enforcement or an attorney, have the skip's cell phone records subpoenaed. These records may reflect the subject's new billing address. If he's erasing his tracks, he'll probably have changed service providers; however, the records may reveal phone numbers of people who are new to you. Call them; you may get lucky.

Many believe that cell phones are untraceable. Not only is this untrue, but prepaid phone cards can also be traced. Phone Validator (*www.phone validator.com*) is a free service to help you find whether a number belongs to a landline or a cell phone. It provides reverse lookup (crisscross) and other services.

In the case of professional skips, finding their paper trail is more challenging. However, it's almost impossible for people to exist without leaving some kind of paper trail. Even those who guard against putting anything in their names can forget something and leave a trail—or they may make their trail using the names of others.

You may also find your skip through public records, which keep files of payment for things that most people cannot avoid using, such as gas, water, power, or other utility bills. Many skips forget that cable television bills identify their location. Ownership of homes or vehicles, possession and use of credit cards, and voting records leave a paper trail that can be picked up and followed.

Chapter 10 provides a description of the profile that should be created before you begin your search for a skip. Ignore this step at your peril. Profiling your subject at the outset of a case can save hours and even days of searching. Your client is the first source of info, of course, but you'll find that the subject's friends, associates and co-workers can often provide information of which the client is ignorant or has incorrect or incomplete knowledge.

Knowing as much as possible about your skip will help you find his trail. Does he need medicine or a specific type of medical treatment or rehab? Does he collect government assistance, workers compensation, unemployment, or food stamps? What are his hobbies, likes, and dislikes? Checking records, you may find that he's been arrested, spent time in jail, or checked into a rehab program. Checking newspapers (some of the better search databases have news searches now) may reveal an article about him winning a blue ribbon at the annual rose growers association in Wheresit, Arizona. Any of these things may also turn up information about someone close to him. The more you know about him and those around him, the more you'll know where to look.

The Missing Birth Parent or Birth Child

It's not unusual for people to look for a child they placed for adoption. Neither is it unusual for a child who has been adopted to search for birth parents. This type of investigation is the most challenging, except, perhaps, for abandoned infant cases. Complicating the fact that years have passed between the adoption and the search is that one party may not want contact with the other. Further complications can include lost or misplaced records when departments relocate; records destroyed by fire, water damage, or even mold or mildew from sitting in a damp basement; and attorneys who have moved or died. Records may have been placed on microfilm or microfiche and moved to libraries or storage facilities.

Again, go to people. Ask around to find out who worked in the records office during the time of the adoption. Many people will help if you're pleasant and respectful. Although some states have enacted laws enabling adoption information to be accessed, most have not. Furthermore, adoptions aren't handled the same way in every state—and the process is different depending on whether the adoption was private or processed through an agency. Therefore, the first step should be to research the state's adoption process and laws. The most common types are:

- **Open adoption:** adoption is arranged between the birth mother and the adoptive parents
- **Agency adoption:** performed by an adoption agency, a state or local governmental agency, a religious organization, or some other non-profit entity
- **Private adoption:** arranged by an attorney or another individual, and the only monies allowed to change hands are to cover medical and certain related expenses; not all states allow private adoptions
- **Black market adoption:** basically the buying and selling of babies, illegal in every state; it's one of the most difficult investigations to crack, but it's not totally impossible
- **Adoption of the abandoned child:** the most difficult of all; it's not impossible, but don't raise your client's hopes too high as the odds are against finding the child's origins

Laws protecting adoptions originated years ago, when the stigma of unwed mothers was great. States that have changed adoption information laws to allow access to records reflect the lessening of that stigma in U.S. society, and give hope that more states will follow suit. Several documents begin an adopted child's paper trail. Some of them follow:

- **Original birth certificate** issued by the hospital where the baby was born (if born in a hospital)
- **Record of birth filed** (along with birth certificate) with the health department and state office of vital statistics or records
- **Amended birth certificate** issued by the court when a baby is adopted (original is sealed)

- **Docket appearance or log book recording the adoption procedure,** court appearances, etc. (if adoption is legal); usually performed in the courthouse of the county where the adoptive parents reside
- In some states, courts require **social worker home visits and reports** detailing the fitness of the adoptive parents
- **Hospital records** (if hospital is known)
- If private adoption, **information from the attorney or individual who facilitated it** (if known or found)
- **Notice of petition for adoption** may be printed in local newspaper(s); sometimes these notices provide names of some of the people involved

Many times, adoptive parents know the birth mother's name, but more often than not—especially in agency adoptions—they don't. In this case, finding the child's original name can be the biggest hurdle to overcome. However, over the years, many adoption registry sites have emerged on the Internet. Make your client aware that adding his information to as many registries as possible may help locate the missing birth relative. If that person is also looking and registers on the same site, they may find each other. See Chapter 6 for information on finding birth names and locating registry sites.

FACT

After the adoption is final, the child's original birth certificate is sealed. In states that don't allow access to records, a judge can rule that they be opened. This is rare and usually contingent upon a serious issue such as a medical problem or an equally weighty need. Gaining access to records is still difficult in most states.

After the birth relative is located, it's never a good idea for one party to contact the other without permission. Even when the other has also been searching, his feelings, privacy, and schedule must be respected. Some states have passed laws requiring that a third party meet with both birth relatives before introducing them to each other.

Genealogy Searches

Some people do genealogy research in order to locate living relatives. Others want to know from which branch of the world tree (or haplogroup) they originated and whether there are any famous (or infamous) people in their ancient line. Having an X and a Y chromosome, men can identify the haplogroup of both their maternal and paternal lines and trace paternal surnames. Women can only trace their maternal line. Yet, with a DNA sample from a close male relative—a brother or father—they can trace the paternal haplogroup. This becomes increasingly difficult with more distant relatives.

In simplified terms, human cells contain organelles, or mitochondria, which contain identifying DNA. This mitochondrial DNA, or mtDNA, tells the story of your ancestry. As groups of humans travelled away from their origin, the DNA of each haplogroup mutated over time, creating markers that you carry today. These markers identify your haplogroup's travels, linking it to a specific time and place. Markers of individuals are then compared in order to identify and link specific relatives.

QUESTION?

How close can genealogy sites come to my family origins?
Reputable genealogy research sites don't promise to use DNA results to pinpoint your haplogroup to the exact spot, region, or even the country from which your family originated. Instead, they can reliably provide information of a wider nature, such as to which one of several dozen ancient groups you belong and the general time and course of your group's migration.

As DNA testing becomes more affordable and easily collected (swabs are generally used for these tests), more results will be available for comparison. You may even find that someone of note lies along your family tree. Many famous people, living and dead, have been tested—Katie Couric, Marie Antoinette, Czar Nicholas, and Jesse James to name a few.

- Ancestry.com (*www.ancestry.com*)
- National Geographic.com (*www.nationalgeographic.com/ genographic/index.html*)

- Genetic Genealogy (*www.dnaancestryproject.com*)
- Myfamily.com (*www.myfamily.com*)
- One Great Family.com (*www.onegreatfamily.com*)
- Rootsweb.com (*www.rootsweb.com*)
- Geni.com (*www.geni.com*)

Other sites are available, but be very careful which ones you use. As with anything on the Internet, be sure of a site's reputation and reliability before you provide identifying information. Also, remember that many records aren't available online. A great deal of information, especially older information, hasn't been digitized or even entered onto microfiche. In these cases, you'll have to travel to wherever the records are held to do some digging.

CHAPTER 7

Divorce, Infidelity, and Child Custody Investigations

Emotions in domestic incidences and investigations are volatile, and they can change in a moment. Ask an officer how often a spouse has called the police for help and then attacked the responding officer for arresting the abuser. It's common. Ask an attorney which type of law is most likely to result in the attorney being shot. She'll tell you that it's family law. People in these situations are highly emotional, so if you decide to work these cases be prepared for anything.

Clueing In on Infidelity

Humans have an amazing early warning system—intuition—yet most people ignore it. Why? It's because they aren't always sure from where their feelings or suspicions arise. If there's no concrete evidence to point to, people tend to discount what they intuitively know to be true. Yet intuition is hardwired within you. Cultivate and use it. Law enforcement investigators who have interviewed many victims will tell you that most victims reported some type of early warning intuition that they failed to heed.

Without knowing that an attacker was inside, more than one woman has reported that the hair stood up on her neck or she felt something was wrong when entering her home. Others felt it when getting on an elevator with a soon-to-be attacker, when walking through a parking lot prior to an attack, or when walking by a car before being pulled inside. They knew something was wrong, but they ignored the signals from this "other" sense because their physical senses didn't pick up anything.

The intuition of married people is astounding, but usually, it is acknowledged only in retrospect. The client may tell you he remembers answering increasing numbers of hangup calls; recalls his spouse hurriedly hanging up upon his approach; and remembers long, unexplained, or poorly explained absences, all of which he noticed but dismissed. At the same time, he felt his wife pulling away or losing interest and knew that something was different (conversely, some clients report that the spouse is more attentive).

He may have noticed that her appearance changed. Maybe she began to work out, diet, or overdress for a trip to the grocery store. This was his early warning system in action—and ignored. Eventually, the client admits that he wasn't imagining things and comes to you for confirmation. He's in a terrible state, alternating between guilt at thinking badly of his spouse and hurt and anger at what he believes to be true.

By the time someone finds lipstick on a shirt, a never-received jewelry or lingerie item charged on the credit card, or is told that the spouse has been seen in a suspicious situation with someone, infidelity is a probability. At this point, the investigator is not asked to verify suspicions, but to obtain evidence of the infidelity. Even then, however, the investigator shouldn't make a determination, but should maintain an open mind and let the evidence take her where it will.

Divorce and Infidelity Investigations

Divorce cases can come from the public or from attorneys. Attorneys in small firms rarely keep investigators on payroll and will contract out investigative needs. If the attorney contacts you, he's your client and the one who will sign your client agreement. The complainant is his client. Be sure that this is understood so that everyone knows how—and by whom—your fees will be paid. Cultivate relationships with these attorneys and you'll have a steady stream of cases.

◄ A private investigator will often be asked to provide proof that a spouse is cheating.

Many times, the client or attorney needs to prove that the target has been guilty of infidelity, is unfit to care for children, or is in possession of hidden assets. Some PIs won't work these cases; they feel it entails digging up dirt and they aren't comfortable doing it. Yet others make a career of it. If done right, it won't be a dirt-digging project, but a means of helping families in need. Not every case will end in divorce; sometimes people reconcile. If your client expresses the desire to work through her marriage, however, don't try to be her counselor; refer her to a licensed counselor or psychologist.

When working these cases, you'll attempt to obtain video on the target, documenting his comings and goings, associates, and possible infidelities. Gather as much information as you can beforehand. Obtain a picture of all players. Question the client as to the spouse's work, habits, hobbies, and interests. Get the make, model, tag number, and description of all vehicles.

Perform a background check. Do a dry run by the spouse's home, workplace, and any areas he frequents (such as a bar, golf course, country club, and possible girlfriend's home and work).

QUESTION?

What is the U.S. divorce rate?
Divorce statistics can be misleading—look to the oft-cited divorce rate of 50 percent. That number is reached by dividing the number of marriages by the number of divorces in any given year. Experts argue this is misleading because the couples who got married are not the same as those who filed for divorce. Experts maintain that the divorce rate in the U.S. has never exceeded 41 percent.

Video is often the defining evidence in these cases. Because evidence is on screen for all to see, most he said/she said arguments are eliminated. To protect your evidence, use a new, clean tape or DVD every time. Never record over existing information or you may be accused of altering your video. This won't be an issue with the new digital recorders—just download the information to your computer and burn it to a clean, new disc or DVD.

While it's difficult to argue with video, some targets will say, "That looks like me, but it's not." Let the attorneys deal with this problem, but you can help by obtaining corroborating witness information. Interviewing bartenders, hotel managers, even friends and coworkers after you have your video can substantiate video evidence. Witness testimony isn't easy to come by, but it is worth seeking. Although it is considered the least reliable type of evidence, a preponderance of witnesses testifying to the same information can sway jurors.

ESSENTIAL

At the point infidelity is proven, encourage your client to retain an attorney, especially if divorce is impending. Deliver recordings and information proving infidelity to the attorney's office for the client to view in his presence. A therapist or friend may also be present. Provide adequate support; some clients have killed spouses, spouses' lovers, and even themselves after viewing this information.

Premarital and Infidelity Investigations

It's no longer only the wealthy who are concerned with the background of future mates. Premarital investigations have become popular in recent years as con artists increasingly prey on those with comfortable resources and generous or lonely hearts. Many an unscrupulous man or woman has latched onto someone with a steady income, good credit, and a need for companionship—then cleaned out their victim en route to the next mark.

FACT

It's easy for someone to hide her true history and identity today. Our mobile society, where even neighbors are strangers, lends the con artist anonymity. Anonymity can lead to ease of deception. If the client has any doubt, the person she suspects should be checked out.

A simple background check will usually reveal the proverbial skeletons in the closets of these leeches. Some of the better database services check newspaper articles during specified periods of time, turning up information on those who've been suspected of crimes but never charged or imprisoned. Bad press about someone doesn't prove anything, but it's a clue that may lead you to new information. When doing background checks, don't neglect searching arrest records as well as convictions; although not proof of wrongdoing, arrests for crimes certainly suggests that things may not be as they seem and that further investigation is warranted.

Many women suspect that the man they're dating may be married or may not actually be the person he represents himself to be, especially if he lives at a distance or travels. This has traditionally been a woman's concern, but the number of men checking out their girlfriends or fiancés has increased in recent years. See Chapter 16 for background check resources.

While there may be many reasons to commission a background check on someone close to you, this list details the most often reported reasons:

- Provides little information about himself
- Is not available on most weekends and holidays
- Provides only a cell phone number, usually doesn't answer, and returns calls much later
- Receives a number of phone calls that he prefers to keep private
- Won't frequent certain sections of town or specific businesses or restaurants with her
- Runs into people to whom he "forgets" to introduce her
- Never asks her to his home or lives in a bare apartment even though he possesses a good job

If several of these reasons are present, a background check may be in order. It's alarming how many times a check will reveal either a home and a wife or husband of which the client is totally unaware, or the harsh reality that the client's loved one has left his genuine, often tarnished, identity behind and presented a false one to her. See Appendix A for information on the paper trail and its significance in determining someone's background and identity.

Check Your Mate: Hidden Camera Stings

The practice of baiting a spouse or partner who is suspected of being a serial philanderer is a controversial type of investigation. The service provides pictures of trained investigators, and the client chooses one he believes to be the target's "type." The chosen bait wears a hidden camera and goes to an area the target is known to frequent. He may not approach the target, but may be receptive to her approaches.

The Sting

If the encounter takes place in a bar, he may sit a few stools or tables from her and order a drink. If she approaches, he's allowed to respond in a natural manner without enticement. After a certain amount of time with no response, he may make eye contact and smile. If she doesn't approach or act seductively toward the bait, she has passed the test. If she does respond, every word, action, and expression are recorded for the client to view. This type of investigation began with men as targets, but it has quickly expanded to women targets as well.

The controversy here is that some see this as a setup. They feel it's unfair to present targets with an attractive, available person and then film their natural response. This might be true if the undercover operative were allowed to seduce the target, although many would argue that people are presented with opportunities to cheat on their spouses or significant others all the time. This investigation is merely a means of putting to rest any suspicion that the target is inclined to cheat, or alternatively, obtain evidence that he is cheating. Still, being a controversial and sometimes messy business, many investigators steer clear of these investigations. Others make a living doing them.

ALERT!

Should you decide to have your mate investigated for infidelity, be sure your operative knows the difference between being available and being seductive. If she doesn't, it can ruin your entire case. Remember, everything—her tone of voice and any suggestive statements or actions—will be recorded by the camera and picked up by audio. The target must initiate all contact and action.

Audio Recording Laws

If the investigation takes place in a two-party consent state, meaning that both parties to the conversation must be aware of its recording, turn off the audio—especially if you intend to use the recording in court. Some investigators record audio if the video is for the client's eyes only. This is playing with fire, however, as penalties in many states are high. As to workers' compensation surveillance, most risk management companies require the audio be turned off, even in one-party consent states.

Never believe that your client won't spill the beans to the target about audio recording. Often, emotions are so high the client can't keep himself from throwing the details in the target's face, in which case she or her attorney will realize that she was recorded without her knowledge. If he does this, it all falls back on your shoulders. If you're operating in a two-party consent state, you're in trouble. If you're in a one-party consent state, only one party in the conversation must be aware of the recording. That party is your operative, so you can legally record audio. See Chapters 17 and 18 for more information concerning audio and video surveillance and Chapter 12 for working within the law.

The Missing Parent

Parents who leave their children without paying court-ordered child support or who reach a certain amount of arrearage in payments are colloquially referred to as deadbeat parents. Official terms used to refer to those who don't pay are not so harsh—usually some form of noncompliance.

A Contentious Issue

The term deadbeat is offensive to many, who argue that the term itself is punishment because it leads to the often incorrect assumption that everyone who doesn't pay child support does so out of irresponsibility and lack of caring for their child. They site other reasons for noncompliance, including (but not limited to) the following:

- Illness or disability
- Loss of employment or a cut in pay or benefits
- A return to school in order to keep or advance employment
- Support has been used to alienate a child's affection
- Support has been used as a weapon for revenge in the hands of a bitter ex-spouse
- Support is higher than is reasonable in relation to income
- The ex-spouse spends child support on non-child-related expenses

Proponents see the laws concerning child support as just and necessary for the welfare of children. Measures such as garnishing of wages, revocation of driver's licenses, and even prison sentences are seen as punishment for nonpayment and as deterrence.

Father's Rights (*www.fathersrightsinc.com*), Father's Rights Foundation (*www.fathers-rights.com*), Men's Rights (*www.mens-rights.net)*, and other advocacy groups have been formed to change the current laws concerning child support. Women's groups have also organized around the issue of child support, many promising to search out the deadbeat dad for collection of support or to send him to prison.

The PI's Role

No matter which side of this issue you stand on, provide the same professionalism as you would any other. If you can't do this, don't take these cases. Refusing a case about which you feel ambivalent won't hurt your income, but accepting one to which you're unable to give your all can't help your integrity and can hurt your reputation.

Police departments don't have the manpower or the time to search indefinitely for parents who leave their spouses and children without paying support. When the trail becomes cold, they must usually direct their efforts toward other cases. At this point, the remaining spouse may contact a PI in order to continue the search.

These cases must be worked with the same diligence as any missing persons case, but they are more difficult. Begin by creating a profile and determining motivation. One reason is that not only does the parent not want to be found, but he also doesn't want any evidence of his workplace or the amount of money he makes to pop up on anyone's radar screen.

The first and best place to start looking for a missing parent is with those who last saw the parent or those with whom the parent will likely stay in touch—his own parents, family members, friends, or adult children. If these people won't talk, they can be kept under surveillance.

Child Custody

Child custody is most often associated with divorce, but divorce is not the only circumstance that brings up the need for custody investigations. Today, for many reasons, grandparents and other family members regularly petition the courts for custody of minor children. Even friends of the family have been known to get involved and go to an investigator. As with divorce, these cases can be messy. Motives are not always pure, and emotions can be volatile on all sides.

Setting Up the Investigation

Because motives can be murky in child custody cases, until you get into the investigation, you can't be sure whether your client is actually the better parent. It's not your job to decide who should have custody. Just as with attorneys, if you take money for services, you must deliver those services whether you believe your client to be in the right or not. However, you are at liberty to return that money and bow out of a situation where you believe your client has done wrong or is capable of doing wrong to the child in question—unless your state has a specific law against it. Most do not. Your state may also have a law requiring you to report your suspicions, especially if you've uncovered any real evidence.

Interview neighbors, teachers, friends, grandparents, and anyone with information about the treatment of the child. If the parents still live in the same house, hidden cameras can be installed to view the parent when he is alone with the child. Many times, this more than reveals the nature of treatment that the child receives at the hand of this parent. Put all these observations together into your report and let the evidence tell the story. Surveillance and videotaping will show the manner in which the child is being cared for.

If you are conducting an investigation after a child has been taken by a parent who does not have sole custody, treat the case much as you would a missing parent case. Begin with those who last had contact with the parent who took this child.

Clients want different things from these investigations. Some are looking for documentation of the target behaving in an unsafe manner with or around their children. Some behaviors normally documented in these cases are:

- Failure to safely strap a child into a car seat or seatbelt
- Taking child somewhere—a park or zoo—then paying little or no attention to their safety
- Using alcohol or doing drugs in the child's presence
- Driving erratically with child in a car or behaving erratically around child
- Throwing raucous parties with child in the home
- Leaving child alone in a home, apartment, or car while they run out for something
- Leaving child in an obviously unwashed, undiapered, or unattended condition for long periods
- Allowing child to play with toys inappropriate for his age, toys with small pieces that can cause choking, toys with sharp, dangerous parts, or objects such as knives and scissors

Be prepared for the disturbing fact that your client may not be in the right. Your client may have motives for hurting the target, getting revenge, or soliciting money, and there may be no evidence of unfit behavior for you to document. Never stretch or manufacture evidence in any case, but be particularly careful here.

Interviewing Children

If a child returns with stories that seem made up or imaginary, be open to the fact that they may be true. This is especially hard for the child's parent or caretaker. No spouse wants to think that they've married someone who could abuse or allow someone else to abuse a child. Some people are so pained by the thought of their child being hurt they can't bear to believe it happened. Some want to believe that the child misinterpreted an innocent action. Others are reminded of their own abuse, something they've tried to forget, so they dismiss what's right in front of them. Still others believe that children are fanciful and imaginative, and that their testimony is not as trustworthy as that of adults. The little-known truth is that children's testimony, if not contaminated or tampered with, is quite reliable. Some experts believe it's more reliable than any adult testimony. Children stay in the moment more than adults. They're not thinking about what to fix for supper or how to pay the phone bill. They're present and aware most of the time. See Chapter 19 for more information on interviewing witnesses, including child witnesses.

FACT

Clients often place hidden cameras or voice recorders in the lining of their child's bag or in a favorite doll or stuffed animal in order to discover what happens on visiting day with a parent or grandparent. This can backfire: If the materials are discovered, your case may be over. The target will always be suspicious that she's being watched and alter her behavior accordingly—at least until the settlement is over.

Investigators should survey the target and record anything questionable about his treatment of the child. In some cases, the client should also buy or rent a camera. If the child persists in her stories, the client may need to record her spontaneous remarks, but they must be unsolicited and made with the child unaware of the recording. Have the client set up a camera and discreetly turn it on when the child begins to speak of suspicious incidents. The child can be asked to repeat what's been said but cannot be prompted or asked leading questions.

Leading questions are those that direct someone to answer in a predetermined manner. For example, "You don't like going to Daddy's house, do you, sweetheart?" is a leading question. Most children will know exactly how you mean for them to answer. Better: "Do you like visiting your daddy?" This is an open-ended question with no pressure to answer either way, as long as no disparaging tone of voice or facial grimaces accompanies it. Recording questions such as these will go a long way for your side if the case goes to court. It may also encourage the court to provide some counseling for the child.

Children have returned from a visit with a parent, grandparent, relative, or babysitter with stories of being shut up in locked rooms or closets, of being hungry or left alone for hours, and of physical abuse. Parents would much rather believe that stories such as these are tall tales or dreams, but the horrible truth is that these things—and worse—actually happen.

Counsel your client to never accuse her child of lying when he tells stories such as these. Help your client find the truth before making judgments.

QUESTION?

Do children ever lie about abuse?

Children have lied about being abused. However, it's not the norm. The act of abuse is so heinous and the effects so far reaching, it is incumbent upon society and those closest to the child to investigate an abuse allegation thoroughly, rather than dismiss it because a few cases have been proven to be false. Fear of not being believed is one of the reasons that children don't report abuse.

Men aren't the only abusers of children. Statistics reveal that 25 percent of reported abusers are women. Many boys have reported that they were confused when an older woman initiated sexual relations with them, mainly because they believed the myth that males should enjoy sex with anyone at any time. Later in life, many feel the need to seek counseling or to explore their feelings about what happened. Abuse of a minor is still abuse, whether the minor is a male or female, and the ill effects can be equally damaging upon either sex.

CHAPTER 8

Missing Children and Adolescents

The police have primary responsibility for missing children, but families and attorneys often hire PIs to supplement and intensify the search. For many reasons, children are most vulnerable, and the motives for harming children vary widely. Some predators are motivated by the money they can make by selling or prostituting children. Others take a sexual or romantic interest in children, and some are intent upon torturing and killing their victims.

The Missing or Abducted Child

Many predators are attracted to under-aged children and hunt them as prey, but some use a slower, grooming method for gaining control over children. So far, a means of curing or stopping predators is unknown, so it's imperative to find missing children quickly.

Stranger Versus Known Abductor

Most investigators who search for abducted children no longer make a great distinction between the stranger abductor and the known abductor. One reason is that children—and even parents—have difficulty making that distinction. Who is the stranger? Is it the neighbor who walks his dog in front of the house every day? Is the landscape worker or housekeeper a stranger? Is the clerk at the local store? The insurance salesman? The maintenance man?

Yes and no. They may not be the family's closest friends, but neither are they total strangers to parent or child. Some call this type the acquaintance abductor. These familiar fixtures in the lives of families aren't likely to appear sinister. People feel that they know someone who is often around, yet behind the smiling dog walker's exterior could beat the heart of a predator. Furthermore, statistics show that these—and persons even closer to families—are the most likely abductors of children. Doctors, teachers, scout leaders, school bus drivers, preachers, priests, coaches—even baby-sitters, friends, and relatives abuse children. What's worse, abusers often choose a profession that brings them close to under-aged children.

ALERT!

Stranger abduction of children, while always a horrible possibility, isn't the most likely scenario. When it does happen, however, research reveals that it's most likely to end badly; victims of stranger abduction are most at risk of sexual assault, injury, or death.

Because the abuser can be anyone in a child's life, experts no longer recommend that parents stress "stranger danger" as much as in the past. A different approach must be taken to prepare children for anyone who treats them in ways that invade their personal space, cause them fear, or require them to do things they don't want to do.

Missing Child Timeline

Most of the time, missing children return home or are located. It's the ones who don't return, children who aren't found—or are found too late—that haunt those who search for them. Statistics differ as to how long a child is likely to live after being abducted, and all of them are disheartening. Because there's no way of knowing the abductor's ultimate goal in taking a child, the worst outcome must be assumed from the outset, with every search proceeding as if the child has very little time to live.

Twelve-year-old Polly Klaas was abducted at knifepoint from a slumber party in her California home in 1993. She was found dead sixty-five days later. Her father, Marc Klaas, formed KlaasKids (*www.klaaskids.org*) to help prevent abduction and locate missing children.

One of the first steps to take when a child is missing is to check the whereabouts of registered sex offenders within a specified distance of the child's home or place of abduction. When located, they're interviewed, and any alibis for the child's estimated time of disappearance or death are checked. The problem is that many sex offenders have never registered. Others provide bogus addresses or move frequently without reregistering. There's also the offender who is yet to be caught—the one who has never been charged and no record exists. He's out there but no one knows who, or where, he is.

Federal and State Responses

One of the most expedient measures put in place in recent years is the Amber Alert. In 1996, nine-year-old Amber Hagerman was abducted from her Arlington, Texas, neighborhood while riding her bicycle. Her body was found four days later in a drainage ditch, four miles from her home. Though a neighbor provided a description of the driver who pulled Amber off her bike and into his truck, her killer has never been found. Despite her grief, Amber's mother fought for a change in the law. Because of her efforts, an early warning system is now in place in most states for missing children.

For more information, go to the U.S. Department of Justice's Amber Alert Web site at *www.amberalert.gov* or the National Center for Missing and Exploited Children's Web site at *www.ncmec.org*. You can also find information about the FBI's Child Abduction Rapid Deployment (CARD) teams at *www.fbi.gov/card*. These specially trained teams of four to six agents respond when a child is missing. CARD teams help by providing investigative assistance and technical resources to state and local officers, primarily in the case of nonparental abductions or child ransom.

FACT

In 2006, special agents from the Federal Bureau of Investigation's (FBI's) Crimes Against Children Task Force warned that, according to recent statistics, 74 percent of all abducted children who are murdered are killed within the first three hours. These staggering numbers punctuate the reason that expedient measures must be taken when a child goes missing.

Individual states are trying to establish measures to protect children from dangerous predators. In 2003, nine-year-old Jessica Lunsford was kidnapped, raped, and murdered by a convicted but unregistered sex offender. In response to public outcry, thirty-three states passed some form of Jessica's Law, which proposed stricter sentencing guidelines for first-time sexual offenders.

The Missing Adolescent

Adolescents are neither children nor adults. They inhabit a world in between the two, a world filled with hormones, lack of experience, curiosity, and feelings of immortality. It's a difficult time for parents who seek to protect them and prevent impulsive mistakes.

The Involuntarily Missing Adolescent

Adolescents go missing for numerous reasons, but recent years have seen an increase in adolescents who leave after meeting someone they have made contact with on the Internet. These adolescents don't always intend to leave home permanently, but when they find that their online buddy is suspicious, it's usually too late. Some adolescents have been sold or kept as sex slaves, some are released after differing stages of abuse, and some are never seen alive again.

Cyber-sleuths from the FBI's computer forensics division are called in to help solve computer-related crimes. They analyze hard drives and recover information about chat rooms, e-mails, social networking sites, and instant messaging. Young people are inquisitive and can be drawn into online activities without being able to recognize the danger, and without the resources to protect themselves. They just don't see that the kid on their computer screen, the one who understands them and all their problems, could be a big hairy guy waiting to make his move.

FACT

The Peachtree City, California, police department has a secret weapon—Heather Lackey, Internet undercover officer. She enters chat rooms as a thirteen-year-old girl and reports that she consistently attracts predators within minutes. The first thing she's asked is whether anyone is around. Predators try to ensure that parents aren't around to view what they say to children. Therefore, parents must maintain the family computer in the family room—never in an area where the child or adolescent can use it alone. Additionally, investigators must be vigilant in finding new methods of catching these cyber-predators.

The world holds many dangers. Today's youth see a culture of alcohol, drugs, violence, risk-taking, and criminal behavior as not only desirable but preferable to the seemingly staid, boring lifestyle of their parents. This culture's faux glitter can lure unsuspecting teens to a place where predators lie in wait. Regardless of whether they have a happy home life, teens can be drawn into this fake world looking for excitement, love, money, or whatever they feel is lacking in their lives. It takes skill, determination, and grit to search for these children, and those who do it consider it a mission. Private investigators with a talent for computers may decide to specialize in these cases. The Internet has opened a dark new world to inquisitive children and is a continual threat to their safety. Investigators willing to enter this world may rescue some of these kids or prevent others from being sucked into it. Chapter 16 has more information on computer crime investigation and cyber-sleuths.

The Voluntarily Missing or Runaway Adolescent

Sometimes, information regarding a missing adolescent's motivation and clues as to her destination can be found online. Kids post material to such sites as MySpace, Facebook, and YouTube. Whether from immaturity or an unrealistic expectation of privacy, they write things on these sites as if no one but friends will see them.

Because of this, law enforcement officers routinely monitor these social networking sites, and although some members have wised up and are using code, critical information is still available. If the runaway has a Web page, it may provide the investigator with clues to his motivation for running, which can lead to his location. The Urban Dictionary (*www.urbandict ionary.com*) attempts to stay up to date with code that adolescents use, both in person and on the Internet. With this info, when you stand behind your child as she types "POS" to some unknown person, you'll know that she is communicating "Parent Over Shoulder." In other words, "my mom or dad is looking at my computer screen."

Registering Children for Future Identification

Registering children is a controversial issue. Some are concerned about privacy issues. Others see the collection of this information as a necessary protection from real evils.

Fingerprinting Children

In your investigation, you must discover if the parents have had the child fingerprinted. This is especially important in cases of very young children whose appearance will change, sometimes drastically, as they grow.

Note that fingerprinting isn't important only for finding and identifying a body—live children have been identified through fingerprints.

QUESTION?

Is fingerprinting children an overreaction to the possibility of their abduction?
Most experts recognize that the small effort involved in fingerprinting a child may provide huge gains if the unthinkable happens and the child goes missing.

If the child was abducted before she could talk, fingerprints are vital to identifying her later, especially if she does not have any birthmarks or unique identifiers. Even older children may be unable to aid in their own identification, having little memory of their life prior to being abducted. Not every parent has a child fingerprinted, however. Some are a bit superstitious, saying they don't want to tempt fate. Others don't even like to think about the possibility. Still others have fingerprinting on their list of things to accomplish, but never get around to it.

◀ Having your child's fingerprints on record can be very useful if your child ever goes missing.

There is a very small group that is afraid of fingerprinting children due to privacy concerns. These people fear that the government will gain control of any database, which may fall into the wrong hands and be used against their children in the future. Others feel that the likelihood of their child being abducted is so low that they do not need to have their child fingerprinted.

Age Enhancing or Age Progression Photos

If your case involves a child who's been missing for years, ask whether a photo was ever taken of the child for age enhancement purposes. Pictures taken for age-progression purposes should show the full face at a specified distance from the camera, and in front of a specified background, usually solid blue. While age progression can almost always be accomplished whether or not a picture such as this exists, taking one with these specifications provides the best possible outcome. If age enhancement hasn't been done, have the client deliver a photo to someone with the technological skill to progress the child to his present age. Some police departments and federal agencies do this, as do some private organizations. Age progression software can help bridge the gap between a child who has been missing for years and her present, altered appearance. The photo can continue to be aged if the search goes on for years. Flyers of age-enhanced photos have led to children being recognized and returned to ecstatic families.

Age-progressed photos can be hand-drawn or computer generated. Artists who do them have studied how bone structure, hair, and skin change during the aging process. Using this knowledge, they can guess how a child's appearance has changed over the years with amazing accuracy. Experienced artists also use pictures of family members to age a child in the same way his family members have aged. However, very few artists can do this. Check with local government agencies such as the FBI. They either have an artist or can inform you of the location of the nearest artist. The following sites may help:

- Forensic Artist, *www.forensicartist.com/agepro.html*
- Crime Library, *www.crimelibrary.com/criminal_mind/forensics/art/6.html*
- Dr. D'Lynn Waldron, *www.dlwaldron.com/ageprogression.html*

- Charlaine Michaelis, *www.doenetwork.org/media/news61.html* and *www.forensicartist.ca*
- Court TV, *www.courttv.com/news/hiddentraces/boyinthebox/recon_side1.html*
- Sketch-Artist.com, *www.sketch-artist.com/AP-services.html*

You can also find computer programs such as FACES, FACETTE or FaceID and SuspectID that are used by law enforcement agencies. APRIL Age Progression Online is available for progressing your own photographs. However, if you decide to use this site, remember that you won't have the capabilities of trained artists who utilize knowledge of the manner in which skin, bone, hair, and other features change over time.

Gathering and Storing DNA

Parents can now store their child's DNA in the event that the worst occurs. Controversy concerning this issue is similar to the privacy issues discussed under fingerprinting. Some people fear DNA collection even more than fingerprinting.

There are many sources for DNA collection, but one excellent source is the Amber Stick, provided through the Amber Code Project (*www.code amber.org/idkits.html*). Working with DNAPrint Genomics, the Amber Code Project sells an Amber Stick; proceeds support the project. The Amber Stick is the first fully portable child identification device. Compatible with any Windows-based computer, the stick is a small USB flash drive that comes with built-in software to hold identifying information. Version 2 allows all DNA analysis information to be uploaded in PDF format.

The information is encrypted, and the stick is secured by a password. It's inexpensive and comes with free shipping and a three-year warranty. See all the other benefits provided:

- Instantly creates automatic missing persons flyers ready for printing
- Automatically creates a file to be imported into a law enforcement computer
- Is password protected and encrypted for privacy and peace of mind
- Holds information about your entire family and your pets, all on one stick

If a child goes missing, parents can give the Amber Stick to a law enforcement officer, provide the password, and let them transfer the information and file a report. Minutes count when a child is missing, and the Amber Stick reduces reporting time. As a private investigator, making the public aware of this product and service is a means of giving back to your community.

Abduction Prevention

It's impossible to prevent all cases of abduction, but experts agree that it is possible to decrease the number of abductions through several measures. One is for parents to be aware of sex offenders in the surrounding area. Another is to teach children to respond correctly to those around them. Known and parental abductions are the most difficult to prevent for obvious reasons—parents, family members, and babysitters have legitimate access to the child and it may not be immediately known that they've abducted him.

Sex Offender Registries

There are many ways to check whether someone has been convicted of a sexual crime. The federal sex offender registry is maintained by the FBI at *www.fbi.gov/hq/cid/cac/registry.htm*. It provides links to all fifty state registries and known sex offenders. You can search by state or across multiple states at the federal site. Remember that states have different parameters as far as type and severity of offenses posted for public notification.

Other sites do it differently. FamilyWatchdog.us (*www.familywatchdog.us*) is a site that allows the user to search by name or location. A map of areas surrounding the entered address (five miles to begin with) is returned, along with the number of and colored boxes denoting the residences or workplaces of registered sex offenders. Clicking on each offender box pulls up their name, address, offenses, and picture. FamilyWatchdog.us provides the source of its information and statistics, usually the state sex offender registry.

Be aware that other sites have taken this name or a form of it. They attempt to imitate the service and redirect new users to themselves. However, most charge for their service and are questionable by virtue of this misdirection. In fact, opportunists have hijacked the addresses of many legitimate sites. Be sure to thoroughly research these types of sites before trusting them.

Educational Resources

Many good programs are available to teach children to be safe. Because of space limitations, only a few will be discussed here. One of the most influential and far-reaching resources is the site concerning Megan's Law, *www.registeredoffenderslist.org/megans-law.htm.* Megan's Law arose from the 1994 abduction, rape, and murder of seven–year-old Megan Kanka by a two-time registered sex offender living across the street from her family.

No one in the community knew of Jesse Timmendequas's crimes. Neither did they know that he lived with two other sex offenders he'd met in prison. He lured Megan into his home with the promise of a puppy. Megan's Law dictates that sex offenders must register their addresses with officials so that neighbors can know if an offender lives close by. The site outlines other stipulations of the law.

Should you register, with a $10 activation fee and a $4.95 monthly membership fee, you'll receive access to the National Registry Alert offender registry. Enter your zip code and receive reports on each registered offender in your area, plus maps, addresses, photos, and conviction information. You'll also receive an ID kit and updates when sex offenders move in and out of your community. This site also offers rules to help keep children safe.

More Missing Child Organizations and Resources

The National Center for Missing and Exploited Children (NCMEC) is possibly the best-known organization of its kind. Established in 1984, NCMEC has dealt with more than 519,000 leads. Its CyberTipline, 1-800-THE-LOST, is a 24-hour phone number for reporting missing child cases and sightings.

For more information on the commercial exploitation of children, see the National Institute of Justice's Web site, *www.ojp.usdoj.gov/nij*, and search for CSEC or Commercial Sexual Exploitation of Children. You'll be given articles and resources to learn about this subject—from the many aspects of child exploitation and those who exploit them to the newest means of detection and prevention.

ALERT!

NCMEC's research leads to the estimation that one in five females and one in ten males are sexually assaulted or abused before reaching adulthood. Unfortunately, data—while incomplete—indicates that less than 35 percent of these cases are reported to any authority.

Almost 300,000 tips regarding the sexual exploitation of children were reported through NCMEC's CyberTipline between 1998 and 2004. Tips increased tremendously in those six years, from 4,578 in 1998 to 112,017 in 2004. NCMEC reports the recovery of more than 118,700 children to date.

Abuse Investigations: Child, Spousal, and Elder

9

Abuse often has nothing to do with the reason some-one is missing, but in some cases it's a direct factor. Also, because many missing children are abused by their abductors or leave home because of abuse, these categories are discussed together. Any abuse is reprehensible, but child and elder abuse are especially repugnant. These populations are vulnerable targets and must be protected by those responsible for their care.

Child Abuse Investigations

Demand for investigating abuse cases, especially child abuse cases, has grown in recent years. Theories abound as to whether abuse has increased or is simply being more widely reported. Victims have historically been ashamed of revealing abuse because they felt they were somehow to blame, but that is changing. Many experts feel that the media has been influential in uncovering the scope of abuse, but critics argue that they have been responsible for creating an unwarranted nationwide fear of abusers, causing the public to see them behind every tree. An uncomfortable truth is that law enforcement personnel who work these cases are astounded at the numbers of abusers encountered in a single operation. They don't feel that the media or anyone else is overstating the danger, and they urge that more media awareness and community education is warranted. Further time and research may reveal the truth of this, but for now, it is incumbent upon everyone to be aware of these abusers and be knowledgeable of the best means for protecting children from them.

Families or their attorneys usually hire PIs to investigate suspected child abuse—and usually do so before any suspicions have been reported to the police. Not only do most people deny it until they no longer can, but they hesitate to report suspicions of abuse without concrete proof. This is where the PI comes in. Surveillance and hidden cameras can obtain that proof. Alternately, the PI is typically called in if or when the police fail to find any proof. Parents or their attorneys will hire the PI for peace of mind, if nothing else.

Types of Child Abuse

The basic types of child abuse are physical, emotional, and sexual. A fourth type, neglect, is not considered abuse by many people. However, most states have some type of law against child neglect. Often, the law is specific and certain tenets must be proven in order to convict, but neglect can be a serious offense.

Whether it's physical, sexual, or emotional, child abuse is ugly. Physical and sexual abuse often go hand in hand and can be accompanied by neglect. When all types are present—and they often are—the result can be catastrophic for the child. Abuse alters children in ways unimaginable to those who have not experienced or witnessed it. While some abused children are fortunate enough to spend time in therapy, more do not. These cases can exact a toll on the investigator who works them.

FACT

Sites such as Parent's Guide to New York State Child Abuse and Neglect Laws (*www.nyc.gov/html/acs/downloads/pdf/stateguide_english.pdf*) can be found in most states. Research your state's laws in order to be familiar with the state definition of abuse and neglect. The case attorney will appreciate the inclusion of any observed violations in your report.

Recognizing Physical Abuse of Children and Adolescents

There are many signs that a child is being abused or neglected. Indications include the following behaviors by the abuser:

- **Continually blames or criticizes the child**—"Can't you do anything right?"
- **Sees child as inferior to his siblings or friends**—"Can't you be more like so-and-so?"
- **Sees child as bad, a burden, or even evil**—"You're just like your idiot father."
- **Finds nothing special in child**—"I wish you'd find something you're good at doing." "You're so ordinary you almost disappear in a crowd."
- **Seems unconcerned when child is hurt**—"Is she hurt? She should be more careful." "She's so clumsy."
- **Misses appointments to speak with child's teachers, doctors, etc.**—"I'm too busy today." "I'll get his medicine when I can."
- **Uses drugs or alcohol in child's presence;** substance abuse is one of the constants in abuse cases.
- **Accuses the child,** to her face and to others, of never telling the truth.
- **Does not want to share the child nor allow her to be with others.**

The child may also exhibit signs that he is suffering from abuse:

- Obvious change in personality, temperament, appetite, or school performance.
- Appears to be overly responsive to the parent's authority, maybe even afraid.
- Either reports inappropriate physical contact or shows signs that this may have occurred, such as an early, overt interest in sexual contact with others and with himself.

Remember that just because one or two of the above warning signals are present one time, it doesn't mean that abuse is occurring or has occurred. The standard is that if one or more of these indications are present on a continuous basis, then you may suspect abuse. You can discover whether these and other abuses are taking place by talking to the child's teachers, doctors, neighbors, and even the child herself. Some investigators find a way to talk to the suspected parent or caregiver, but be very careful not to alert him. Plus, you don't want to insinuate that abuse is occurring when it might not be.

Recognizing Sexual Abuse in a Child or Adolescent

Parents may suspect sexual abuse if someone—a friend, neighbor, acquaintance—is more interested in their child than in themselves or other adults. Suspicions can be raised if an adult shows uncharacteristic interest in a child: wanting to spend time with the child; going to movies alone with the child; or watching movies alone with the child in their home. Another signal is if the adult showers the child with gifts. Also, be very sensitive to the child who no longer wants to visit a person whom he's been with in the past. Victims of sexual abuse sometimes begin to do poorly in school and become suddenly secretive and withdrawn. Although not proof of abuse, these things should be a red flag that leads to further investigation.

It's an unfortunate reality that some children show no concrete signs of sexual abuse. Therefore, it's up to the parent to know her child well enough to pick up on any subtle differences. If the abuser is a family member or someone very close to the child, she may attempt to protect him, and there may be no signs. Therefore, it's important for parents to reassure a child he can talk to them about anything. Parents must cultivate communication and never accuse their child of lying or making something up.

Hidden Cameras and Child Abuse

Child abuse is often a hidden crime. Rarely do witnesses present themselves, either because there are no witnesses or because witnesses have issues that keep them from reporting what they see or hear. Sometimes, they don't define the act as abuse, and other times they have suspicions that they can't support. Often, they feel at the mercy of the abuser themselves. Worst of all, sometimes they just don't want to become involved. A hidden camera can provide evidence that proves the crime when there are no witnesses. There are right and wrong ways to use these cameras, however.

ALERT!

It's not necessary to possess proof of child abuse to report it, but be sure you have reason to believe it's happening—an abuse charge can devastate a family. Placing a hidden camera where abuse is suspected eliminates any doubt. Without proof, it's a difficult decision, but erring on the side of the child is the best policy.

See Chapter 17 for information on investigative equipment and Chapter 18 for how to conduct surveillance. Chapter 12 provides information about working within the laws of surveillance.

Child and Adolescent Resources

The National Center for Victims of Crime, *www.ncvc.org/ncvc/Main .aspx*, lists shocking statistics about the crime of child abuse. It also provides resources, training, and help for victims and victim providers. Other sites of interest are:

- Medline Plus-Child Abuse: *www.nlm.nih.gov/medlineplus/child abuse.html*
- Prevent Abuse Now: *www.prevent-abuse-now.com/stats.htm*

- ChildStats.gov: *www.childstats.gov/americaschildren*
- Bureau of Justice Statistics: *www.ojp.usdoj.gov/bjs*
- Child Welfare.gov: *www.childwelfare.gov/systemwide/statistics/can.cfm*
- About.com, Pediatrics: *pediatrics.about.com/od/childabuse/a/05_abuse_stats.htm*
- Child Molestation Research & Prevention Institute: *www.childmolestationprevention.org*
- KidsData.org: *www.kidsdata.org*
- ChildHelp.org: *www.childhelp.org* is a new organization and will contact members when sexual offenders move into your neighborhood
- FamilyWatchdog.us: *www.familywatchdog.us* will also contact you for free if an offender moves into your neighborhood

Should You Investigate Child Abuse?

Helping clients who suspect child abuse can be a double-edged sword. There is satisfaction in either putting the abuser away or putting the client's fears to rest. However, if the abuser gets away or isn't charged or convicted, this can be hard to live with. Investigating child abuse can be as difficult and disheartening as it is rewarding. Not everyone can handle knowing the acts some adults commit against children, nor that people who commit these acts are sometimes neighbors, friends, and relatives. However, if you can deal with the bad and focus on the good—uncovering the hidden abuser—you're unlikely to find a more rewarding occupation.

Child abuse is a crime whose investigative responsibilities lie with law enforcement. Yet many people are reluctant to accuse someone of abuse when they only have suspicions. At this point, they may hire a private investigator to either set their fears to rest or gather evidence for the police. If you are hired for this purpose, remain objective. Never make a determination before all evidence is in.

Should you encounter evidence of abuse, remain as unemotional as possible. There's no end to the emotions that rage inside law enforcement officers who encounter evidence of abuse or roll up on someone abusing a child. However, they must stay cool in order to help. So must you. Of course, when evidence of abuse is obtained, it must be reported. Normally, the client will have retained an attorney who should be the police contact. Deliver any information and video to that attorney, keeping a copy of all your work. You'll probably be required to testify in court, but beyond this, your job is done.

The Pedophile

While people abuse those around them for many reasons, the pedophile is in a class all his own. He has a preference for the underaged. Don't be afraid of this subject or of discussing it with your clients or speaking of it in the community. Ignorance is the pedophile's ally. It allows him to operate under the radar, while the good folks of the world look away from his heinous activity. The truth is disturbing, but refusing to face it puts children at risk. Alternatively, knowledge is power, power that allows the good guys to fight back.

Pedophiles are usually grown men who are sexually attracted to juveniles, although 25 percent of molesters are women. Self-report studies have shown that many have a definite preference for the sex, age, and appearance of their victims, while some prey according to opportunity. Many pedophiles keep their preference for children a secret, even from family members.

FACT

The North American Man Boy Love Association (NAMBLA) has openly declared a love of young boys and what it sees as a right to choose them as sex partners. The Internet has allowed this group to become a global danger. Many hidden pedophiles also use this group to groom and meet boys.

As with other cases that require more time than most police departments can afford to spend, PIs are often hired by individuals, attorneys, or even the police to help investigate pedophiles. Social networking sites have information that can help the investigation. Sometimes pedophiles give up their information. Under pressure from parents' groups and law enforcement, networking sites like MySpace and Facebook have purged their sites of known sex offenders on several occasions and now advertise that they police themselves. The problem is that it's so very easy to be someone else on the Internet—and many abusers remain unidentified.

◀ Pedophiles remain a threat in the physical as well as the online world.

Some law enforcement and private organizations' mission is to identify and arrest pedophiles before they have a chance to hurt children. PIs who are interested in this work should be sure that they are proficient in the language people use on these social networking sites. The Urban Dictionary (*www.urbandictionary.com*) will help. This dictionary stays as up-to-date as possible on popular slang. Also, be sure to research social networking sites so that you'll be familiar with the way your targeted age group actually represents itself online. For example, when asked if she has ever had sex, a twelve-year-old would probably not answer with yes or no. She might write, "As if!" or "Hello? I'm twelve." She might use some previously established code. Developing the authentic voice of the age group whose role you plan to take online may require some study and a lot of hanging out with kids of that age. However, it's not enough to hang out. You must pay attention to how they speak and respond; taking notes might help.

Many of these organizations use people to pose as juveniles. For legal purposes, there are many rules in baiting online pedophiles. The undercover operative cannot make the first move and cannot elicit contact or make sexual innuendos. As far as keeping tabs on known or suspected abusers, nothing beats old-fashioned surveillance.

QUESTION?

How can I locate my state laws?
It's important to be familiar with state laws concerning sex offenses, electronic monitoring, and offender registration. Associates of John Walsh's National Center for Missing and Exploited Children, the FamilyWatchdog. us site lists current sex offender laws and definitions for each state. Find them at *www.familywatchdog.us/statelaws.asp*.

If you think you know a child abuser or have spotted a fugitive abuser, go to the FBI Web site, *www.fbi.gov/contact/fo/fo.htm*, locate your local field office, and report the sighting.

Spousal or Relationship Abuse

Abuse is a crime. Typically, relationship abusers threaten, verbally attack, pull hair, push, throw, pinch, choke, squeeze, and/or strike the person with whom they're in a relationship—many times the person they profess to love. Abuse often escalates, slowly conditioning the victim to accept each worsening threat or heightened attack.

Relationship Abuse

The longer one remains in an abusive relationship, the more normal it feels. If the abused has been raised in an atmosphere of violence and abuse, her past experiences strengthen the sense of familiarity and normality of her present situation. In other words, to this person the dynamics of dysfunction, while often frightening, can feel like home on some level.

Yet it's not only the person who has been abused in the past who stays in an abusive relationship; research shows that most people can be vulnerable to abuse. In addition, the longer the abused stays the more power the abuser gains and the more fear he instills. Although the abused may want to leave, leaving becomes increasingly difficult. Violence can increase so gradually that the abused can be conditioned to accept it until it rises to an unacceptable, even dangerous, level.

There are many reasons people become involved with abusers, and many reasons why they stay. Reasons are particular and unique to each person and each situation. While the investigator's responsibility doesn't extend to answering the whys, understanding the client can allow her to provide services to her client with sensitivity and respect.

FACT

Spousal or relationship abuse is not only hurtful, it's embarrassing. The abused person typically doesn't report it because of a fear of exposing his powerlessness and shame. Even close family members are often unaware until someone is arrested or hospitalized—or worse.

Males almost never report abuse to law enforcement. Self-report studies have shown that the main reason for this is because males are ashamed to report abuse at the hand of a woman. In addition, they don't feel that they'll be believed.

Because it's difficult to prove, reporting abuse doesn't always result in the offender being charged, even after she is arrested—at least until the abuse escalates to real damage. Without proof, it remains a he said-she said battle. In this situation, males and females alike will turn to a private investigator in hopes of gathering evidence to prove their claim. Some PIs use hidden cameras to catch the abuser in the act. This eliminates most of the abuser's defense, as her crime is available on screen for everyone to see. See Chapter 17 to learn about types and uses of cameras and Chapter 18 for surveillance information. Also, see the National Domestic Violence

Hotline at *www.ndvh.org*. The toll-free number is 1-800-799-SAFE (7233), and the TTY for the hearing impaired is 1-800-787-3224.

The Centers for Disease Control and Prevention Definition

The CDC defines relationship abuse in the following categories:

- Physical Abuse—pinching, hitting, shoving, kicking
- Emotional Abuse—threatening language, name-calling, teasing, bullying, belittling, and keeping the abused from family and other relationships
- Sexual Abuse—forcing sex acts, which include fondling as well as rape

The CDC defines abuse as a public health problem, and it reports the numbers are rising close to epidemic level. What this means to the PI is that he can expect to receive more of these cases, and had better know something about them. It also means that there is a grave need for professionals to work within communities providing public awareness and education about this problem.

Teen Dating Abuse

Dating abuse can happen to anyone. Teens aren't the only age group at risk, but they are the most vulnerable due to inexperience and lack of power. Alarming numbers of abuse have been reported among teens— male and female—and as with all crimes of this nature, there are bound to be many more cases that go unreported. Many adolescents possess the erroneous belief that possessiveness, jealousy and even physical abuse is proof of love.

Like those locked in spousal abuse, many teens find it difficult to determine where argument ends and abuse begins. Research has shown that alcohol is present in 40–50 percent of all abuse cases. According to research performed in March 2006 by Teenage Research Unlimited (TRU), the following numbers tell the disturbing tale:

- One in five teens in a serious relationship report being slapped, hit, or pushed
- One in three girls in a serious relationship report concern that they would be physically hurt
- One in four teens in a serious relationship report that their partner has tried to keep them from family and friends and pressured them to spend time only with the partner
- One in three girls between the ages of sixteen and eighteen report that sex is expected in a relationship
- Half of these girls experiencing sexual pressure report that they fear the relationship will end if sex isn't provided
- Nearly one in four girls reported going further sexually than they wanted because of pressure

The investigator who is hired to look into abuse must tread carefully. In the case of adolescents, he should always remember that the targets are children, although they may not look or act like it. Care must be taken to protect their rights while gathering evidence.

FACT

Liz Claiborne Inc., working with the National Domestic Violence Center, has launched the National Teen Abuse Helpline (1-866-331-9474, TTY 1-866-331-8453) and the Web site Love Is Respect (*www.loveisrespect .org*). This site provides a live chat line, newsletter, bill of rights, and pledge. The bill of rights informs teens they have the right to be treated well, and the pledge is intended to underscore the importance of treating others with respect.

Surveillance is the best method of determining how someone is treated. Follow the teen and her suspected abuser. Use covert body cameras to follow them inside a party, restaurant, movie, or club. You can get excellent footage in low-light areas with black and white cameras; color is better during the day or in well-lighted areas. Don't neglect the value of interviewing those around the suspected abused teen. Teachers, neighbors, relatives, and even friends may be so concerned that they're willing to speak with you about what they feel is demeaning and even possibly dangerous to the teen. Interviewing those close to the abuser is more difficult, but there are always people who don't approve of his actions, and you can find them.

Stationary hidden cameras can help in proving this type of abuse. If the client is a parent, suggest putting cameras in the home, in an area where the teen and her abuser may spend time. Outside cameras can be a wonderful method of catching arguments when the couple arrives. Many arguments occur in the car on the grounds before a teen enters the house. Cameras can be purchased in waterproof outdoor lights, tree stumps, plants, and other materials.

Elder Abuse

Many elder care facilities and caregivers are exactly what they seem. However, others are understaffed or are lacking in the number of qualified personnel necessary for optimum patient care. There is also a natural turnover of employees in any facility—and though it's difficult to acknowledge, some caregivers are drawn to those most vulnerable for their own twisted reasons, much as pedophiles are drawn to occupations that allow them access to children.

It just makes sense to check those who care for the elderly. Even when it appears that all is well, why take the chance? When the client knows that all is as it should be she can enjoy peace of mind.

No one doing this type of investigation should attempt to cause fear in his clients. Instead, focus on empowering them to protect those they love. When they are empowered, there's no reason for fear. They can sleep at night knowing their loved ones are safe, mainly because you are making sure of it. To accomplish this, the investigator should wear a body camera or carry a covert camera to visit the home or facility. He should document the facility's cleanliness, attention to patient needs, speed of answering calls, delivery of medication, manner of addressing the patient, and anything else that's important. Finally, interview the patient about her care. Hidden cameras in the form of plants, radios, and other items can be left in the room to film activity after the investigator leaves.

After the initial visit—and after any minor problems have been addressed with the staff and any major problems reported to authorities—

the PI can return at intervals, unannounced, and make his presence known to the staff or caregiver. When minor problems are uncovered, the staff should be made aware that someone cares enough about this patient to keep an eye on those who are responsible for her. If abuses are uncovered, the video proving them should be turned over to the client's attorney.

ALERT!

These are important investigations. Elder abuse is an unfortunate fact of our society. However, those who can no longer care for themselves should never be left unattended and unprotected. Caregivers who are forced to be accountable are forced to be trustworthy.

Often, PIs who work eldercare investigations charge different fees for different levels of investigations. They may have a minimal charge for a run-through, where they spend a few minutes dropping by the facility, making themselves known to the staff, and speaking to the patient. The more time that is involved and the more tasks performed, such as installing a hidden camera or documenting cleanliness and staff helpfulness, the higher the fee.

Elder abuses are almost unbelievable until you see irrefutable video evidence. Cameras have saved a nonverbal patient whose nurses were eating his food. They've documented an orderly turning off a call button, preventing a patient's calling for much-needed oxygen. Thankfully, these instances are rare, but the fact that they happen at all necessitates protection of the elderly.

CHAPTER 10

Working Your Case

While not all cases will end up in court, many will. If you work for attorneys it's even more probable that you'll be required to testify and present evidence to a jury. Because of this, you must be familiar with certain basic laws and aware of rules of courtroom demeanor. This chapter will provide an overview of these issues, but exposure to the process will be necessary to refine your knowledge and expertise. Other elements of casework, such as surveillance, records, reports, and testifying in court have been given chapters of their own, but will be easy to plug into this process.

How to Begin

With all missing persons, search for persons cases, or any other general investigation, you must take certain steps at the outset. These steps involve paperwork and analysis; they may seem tedious, but they are absolutely necessary for obtaining the swiftest and best possible outcome. In fact, a preliminary analysis, or subject profile, will aid in all types of investigations.

Create a Profile and Determine Motivation

Creating a profile of the skip, while time-consuming, will save you a great deal of time in the long run. With the profile in front of you, you'll be unlikely to forget a crucial piece of information. Your client is the first source of information, but you'll find that the subject's friends, associates, and coworkers can often provide information of which the client is ignorant or has incorrect or incomplete knowledge. Prepare a form or a computer template and include all the information necessary to create a profile of the skip. Include the following:

PERSONAL INFORMATION

Complete name	Eye color
Maiden name	Past and present religious affiliations
Nicknames and aliases	Present and former addresses
Place and date of birth	Present and former phone numbers
Social security number	Present and former neighbors
Height	Marks, scars, or tattoos
Weight	Identifying mannerisms or tics
Race	Glasses or contacts
Sex	Preferable type of dress
Hair color and style	

PERSONAL INFORMATION OF FRIENDS, FAMILY, POSSIBLE ACCOMPLICES, AND POSSIBLE LOVERS

Gather as much personal information as you can about friends and family

VEHICLES—CARS, WATERCRAFT, AIRCRAFT, MOTORCYCLES

Description

License number

Location

Loan/financial institution

Insurance agent

EMPLOYMENT INFORMATION

Present and past occupations

Dates of employment

Addresses of supervisors and coworkers

All training, skills, licenses, diplomas, and certificates

INTERESTS AND HABITS

Hobbies, interests, associations, and clubs

Types of movies watched

Books and magazines read

Habits of gambling, alcohol, tobacco, or drug use

Level of computer literacy

Favorite sports and sports teams

FINANCIAL INFORMATION

You can obtain this through a background check and records search

ANY RECENT CHANGES IN THE SKIP'S USUAL HABITS, BEHAVIOR, OR HEALTH

Changes in marital, family, or employment situations

Changes in relationships with friends or coworkers

Recent known financial losses or acquired debt

A missing person's motivation is often obvious, such as the avoidance of alimony or child support, but in the case of the legendary guy who goes out for a loaf of bread and never returns, motivation is crucial in locating him. Your profile may illuminate motive, should any logical motive exist.

For example, if you discover that the skip was a heavy gambler, it may lead to information proving he owed the local leg-breakers an exorbitant amount of cash. That's your motivation. However, there will be times when motivation won't be available to you.

Gather Information

Former personal and employment addresses may lead you to people who have information about the skip, and places or people to whom the skip may return. The profile is your map, but it's only the beginning. Use all possible leads.

When digging into information databases you may find that the skip has purchased property in names other than his own—perhaps aliases, children, pets, family names, or even names of hobbies or interests. If you don't know these names, you can miss what's right in front of you. Get all information at the outset—even if it seems trivial.

Knowing that your skip receives a worker's comp or SSI check at certain times of the month can help you stake out mail drops in the area to which you've traced him. Mail drops are services which provide an address for individuals to receive mail. Some offer forwarding services, but for an extra charge (in most cases). Therefore, your skip may show up to claim his mail if he hasn't purchased forwarding.

In this case, all you need to do after you narrow your search is stake out these mail drops until your skip arrives. However, if he uses forwarding services, which are more and more available, you'll not find him at the drop. Some service personnel will provide an investigator with the skip's forwarding address, but don't count on it. In this case, you'll have to find another way. The following list contains some examples of mail drops:

- **UPS Stores**—*www.theupsstore.com/products/maiandpos.html*
- **MailLink Plus** allows you to access mail online—*www.maillinkplus .com*

- **Home Sweet Home** e-mails mail to customers—*www.homesweet homemailinc.com*
- **The Mailbox Works**—*www.mailboxworks.com/CAT_DropBoxes .html*
- **Earthclass Mail** allows you to access mail online—*www.earth classmail.com*
- **PaperlessPOBox.Com** e-mails mail to customers—*www.paperless mail.com*
- **MaildropGuide.com** lists mail drops in each state—*maildropguide .com*

Directories that offer global mail drop information are also available. Maildrop-Directory claims to list all mail drops in the United States and around the world.

- **Maildrop-Directory,** *www.maildrop-directory.com*, searches are completed by country and by contacting the owner
- **Global Virtual Offices,** *www.global-virtualoffices.com*, provides worldwide mail drops plus virtual offices for doing business
- **Servcorp,** *www.servcorp.com*, has 500 offices globally and is still growing

Many of these drops offer other business services as well. Use of a mail drop in itself is not an indicator of wrongdoing or hiding, as many legitimate businesses employ them. However, drops provide a powerful cover for the illegitimate user. The relatively new service of scanning mail and either leaving it on a server for viewing or e-mailing it to the recipient has provided even more layers of cover for those who wish to hide.

Remember that skips use mail drops for receiving packages as well as regular mail. If she doesn't have forwarding, she'll eventually pick up any packages delivered. Investigators have developed relationships with clerks who've agreed to call when such has been received, so the drop can be staked out until the target arrives. The staff may even aid in sending a package to her. To prevent the clerk from violating laws and procedure by giving up the target's box number, you can bring a package to the drop and ask that it be delivered to the appropriate recipient—then wait until she shows up. For obvious reasons, this is a touchy situation, so be careful if you use this ruse.

Crime Scene and Evidence Handling

Evidence is the backbone of all investigations. However, its efficacy lies in the manner in which it's handled, collected, stored and processed—all human functions. As human functions, the processing of evidence is subject to mistakes. For instance, mistakes caused by lack of knowledge or training, sloppy handling, lack of adequate personnel, and—while rare—intentional alteration or destruction, can cause evidence to be suspect. In other words, evidence is only as reliable as the people who collect, document, process, and store it.

FACT

Evidence is not truth. The purpose of presenting evidence is to prove or confirm a fact in question. Matching fingerprints from a crime scene to a defendant may prove that the prints belong to the defendant, and that he was present at the scene at some point. It doesn't, however, prove the larger question of whether he killed the deceased. Supportive evidence is needed.

The PI's Role in the Crime Scene

PIs rarely deal with a crime scene, except under certain circumstances, and usually only after the police have abandoned it. The best action if you're the first to arrive at a crime scene is to touch nothing and call the police. However, should someone be injured and need help, or be in imminent danger of injury or death, you may be forced to enter the scene. In this case you need to know something about crime scene procedure and evidence handling.

Law enforcement officers follow a standard procedure for crime scene handling and processing. The most important rule in this procedure is protection of the scene. Only a few circumstances allow for anyone to enter a crime scene before it's been processed. The first, and most important, of these circumstances is threat of injury or death to someone inside.

Another circumstance in which police enter a crime scene before it's processed is if evidence could possibly be destroyed. For example, if drugs are known to be inside, there's a chance they will be flushed. In this case, police usually enter and prevent this destruction. Most officers advise against the PI attempting to do the same, however. The private investigator should only preserve the scene until police arrive.

Preserving the Scene

Preserving a crime scene is the most important step in gathering evidence. Anyone who enters a scene brings something with him—fibers, hairs, or soil—and takes something from the scene on his person when he leaves. This exchange contaminates the scene. If you can do so, keep it from happening, but remember that you're not the police, and aren't in the enforcement business. Don't go so far as to use force or you could be looking at an assault charge yourself. Do what you can to help and let the police deal with any unruly "looky-loos."

QUESTION?

What is a looky-loo?
Looky-loo is a term used by some law enforcement personnel to mean someone who gawks at a crime or accident scene. Although the motives of everyone who gathers at a scene can't be determined, it's believed that many who do are hoping for a glimpse of other peoples's pain. Even those absent this motive obstruct the scene, distract officers, and hinder job performance.

Some investigators keep orange construction/traffic cones and yellow caution tape in their vehicle in case they roll up on a fresh scene and want to seal it off. If you do this, the first police officer on the scene will take over for you. It's her business to keep everyone out until the arrival of detectives or forensic techs. In small departments, there isn't much division of labor, but in large ones, special crime scene investigators may be dispatched to process evidence.

Defining crime scene parameters can prove difficult, as there could be multiple scenes. For example, at a murder scene, the location of the body when discovered is usually considered the main crime scene. The body and its clothing is another scene. The victim may have been stabbed in the bedroom and crawled into the living room where he was actually killed, resulting in two more scenes. If the body has been moved, that area is the fifth scene—if transported, the vehicle is a sixth scene. The clothing and body of the suspect is the seventh scene and his home and vehicle the eighth.

You can see that in such a situation everything can be evidence—not only at the identified crime scenes, but in areas between them. If people are allowed to tramp all over these areas, valuable evidence can be lost, altered or moved, changing the story that each crime scene tells.

Documenting the Scene

The purpose of a crime scene investigation is to discover what happened, how it happened, when it happened, determine the areas that show what happened, and who did it, or who committed the crime.

In furtherance of this goal, forms are used in the documentation of scenes. Everything can't be included on every form, therefore forms vary from department to department. They're used not as substitutes for thinking, but as reminders of important steps to take in scene examination. Anything discovered that's not listed on the form can be added. Six categories of documentation are generally recognized as being applicable to any scene, however. The six follow:

- **A general worksheet**—for recording all activity at the scene that relates to when, what, where, and how evidence is collected and packaged, and possible suspects

- **Scene description worksheet**—for recording a narrative of the general, overall description of the crime scene and any impressions elicited from it
- **A diagram/sketch log**—for showing an overhead view of the entire scene, the location of physical evidence, as well as the distance of each piece of evidence from other objects in the scene
- **Photographic log**—for recording photographic views of the scene—specifically, overall or distant, medium, and closeup views of the scene and objects in it
- **Latent print lift log**—for documenting the collection, marking, and packaging of latent print lifts and the location in which they were found
- **Evidence log**—for documenting the collection, marking, and packaging of all evidence

A thorough documentation of any crime scene would include such observations as weather conditions; lighting; whether objects and furniture are out of place, disturbed, or destroyed; whether windows, curtains, and doors are open or closed; whether doors or windows are broken or display tool marks; whether emergency or medical teams have moved anything in order to work on a victim; and whether anything seems to be missing or might have been brought in and left by an offender.

Collecting, Packaging, and Storing Evidence

Investigators approach a crime scene using different methods of collecting evidence. Many of these methods are similar to methods used for searches. For example, some begin collecting evidence at the entrance and work in a pattern toward the exit. Some work in a spiral from the center (or the body if there is one) and work toward the outer edge, and some employ a grid pattern. No matter which method you prefer, be sure that you use one.

In years past, it was procedure in many departments for evidence to be stored in plastics—plastic containers and plastic bags. A good deal of crucial material was rendered useless by sitting in plastics, sometimes for years. It's now known that paper and metal are the preferred storage materials for evidence. Blood drawn from suspects is placed in vials with different colors.

The scientific examination of this type of evidence falls under the heading of forensics. The two major branches of forensics are Criminalistics and Forensic Medicine. Those trained in these branches are responsible for turning physical clues into evidence. The following list shows what each branch is responsible for examining:

Criminalistics Examines:
- Wet Chemistry
- Instrumental Chemistry
- Firearms and Tool Marks
- Photography
- Fingerprints
- Lie Detection
- Questioned Documents
- Voice Spectroscopy

Forensic Medicine Examines:
- Pathology
- Serology
- Toxicology
- Odontology
- Psychiatry

The following Web sites provide much more information about packaging and storing blood evidence should you want to know more. They also have information on other subjects related to this.

Forensic and Procedural Web sites
- Zeno's Forensic Site, *forensic.to/forensic.html*
- International Association of Forensic Nurses, *www.forensicnurse.org*
- American Academy of Forensics Sciences (AAFS), *www.aafs.org*
- Association for Crime Scene Reconstruction, *www.acsr.org*
- Reddy's Forensic Page, *www.forensicpage.com*
- Investigative Links 2000, *www.pimall.com/nais/links-forensic.html*

- D.P. Lyle M.D.'s Web site, *www.dplylemd.com/books.html*
- Lee Lofland's Web site and blog, *www.leelofland.com*

These often have links to other sites, many with specialty information. With these Web sites, you should have enough resources to satisfy the largest appetite for this kind of information. Dr. D.P. Lyle, M.D. and Lee Lofland author books in a unique new series, the Howdunit Series. The series covers the entire spectrum of criminal justice information. Originally created for writers, the Howdunit Series has become the source of information about all aspects of law enforcement, not only for writers, but for readers across the board. Books in the series follow:

- *Book of Poisons, A Guide for Writers* by Serita Stevens, RN, BSN, MA, LNC and Anne Bannon
- *Police Procedure and Crime Scene Investigation* by Lee Lofland
- *Forensics, A Guide for Writers* by D.P. Lyle M.D., to be released in 2008
- *The Book of Weapons, Surveillance and Technology* by Sheila L. Stephens, to be released in 2009

Regarding crime scenes, it's probably easier for you to understand the processing of a scene if you walk through one. The next chapter will take you through a fictional homicide scene.

CHAPTER 11

Processing a Homicide Scene

Remember that the first officer on the scene protects it, closes it off from everyone else. Other officers help protect the scene and provide security. Depending on the size of the department, different people will do the processing. Many times, detectives process the scene—in large departments, crime scene investigators do it. If you're the crime scene processor, you begin with an external inspection.

Processing the Exterior of the Scene

This inspection is performed for several reasons. One, you need to be sure the offender is not still on the premises; and two, you need to determine how many entrance and exit points exist and where they're located. The scenario used for this illustration assumes that there's a murdered victim inside, not one who needs aid. If the latter is the case, take care of those who are hurt or in danger before doing anything else. If you're the PI hired by the client or her attorney, you'll probably be processing behind the police, after they have released the scene. Yes, you're at a disadvantage because of this, but don't underestimate the fact that you might find something others have overlooked.

To begin processing, inspect the exterior and form a plan, jotting down areas which need to be worked. It could be a cut in the fence that allowed offender entry into the yard. It could also be the backdoor where the screen was cut and a glass pane broken, allowing easy access to the inside doorknob. In a case such as this, don't forget to check for pry marks on the doorframe. After the outside inspection, photograph the exterior from all angles.

If you've spotted footprints beneath the window, place a ruler next to them to establish size, and photograph them. Don't assume that police have already done this—collect what you see—all exterior evidence first. Also, don't assume that a half-smoked cigarette belonged to the homeowner or victim, or that a piece of chewed gum was thrown down by a neighborhood child. Photograph and place it all in metal evidence cans or paper packets.

When the exterior has been combed for evidence, sketch it. Using measuring tape, be sure to include measurements in the sketch. Instead of a measuring tape, you can use an optical range finder that determines the distance between objects. However, don't touch anything without disposable gloves, even when working on the exterior of the scene. This will prevent contaminating the area with your prints or DNA, and will protect you from contamination by the same. Process any door or window that appears to have been tampered with for latent (hidden or invisible) prints and pry or tool marks. Cast tool marks with a silicone rubber, or some other type of casting material. Silicone material creates an excellent cast of any marks and gouges, dries very quickly, and can be stored like other evidence.

Processing the Interior of the Scene

Inexperienced investigators often neglect to process the inside of the offender entry point—the inside of the broken or cut fence, and the inside of the door or window where the intruder entered. This is every bit as important as is the exterior, and may provide evidence not found in any other place. For instance, the intruder could've cut himself on raw edges of the fence, leaving behind blood and possibly clothing.

When entering the residence or building, be careful where you step and place your hands. Evidence is everywhere, and although you're wearing disposable gloves, you can easily disturb an important sample. Evidence isn't only important for itself, but for where it has been found.

When inside, examine pry or tool marks from the inside, cast and photograph them. Look for latent prints on areas next to point of entry and process any found. Latent prints are the result of organic and inorganic substances as well as environmental ones. When water in perspiration evaporates, these substances are deposited on surfaces touched in the pattern of each person's unique fingerprints. Substances that lead to the deposit of latent prints are:

- **Organic substances**—byproducts of food metabolism such as fats, oils and waxes contained in perspiration
- **Organic substances**—certain vitamins in perspiration allow for laser identification of prints
- **Inorganic compound**—salt in perspiration
- **Environmental substances**—matter picked up during contact with the environment, specifically plant pollen, grease, oils, dust, soot, animal hair and dander, insect material, human hair and body preparations and treatments
- **Environmental substances**—dust and foreign matter from the crime scene itself

Experienced detectives realize that fingerprints are often unavailable at a crime scene, and that what is most often available are partial prints. Still, they must search for prints, in case even one is present. Partial prints have been used, successfully, to match offenders to a weapon or crime. Yet it's definitely more difficult to match using partials than when making comparisons using a whole or entire print. By the way, unless you've been trained in lifting prints or collecting evidence, don't attempt to do it yourself. Hire a professional to walk through the scene with you and perform the tasks you can't.

The knowledgeable detective also realizes that even when prints are deposited, they're very often blurred or smudged beyond possibility of identification. He knows that it's possible to handle a weapon or an object with bare hands and never leave any prints at all—it's rare, but possible. So, a defense attorney's warning to the jury that "if there are no prints you must not convict" simply won't hold water. Other factors influencing whether prints are deposited on surfaces follow:

- Some people don't sweat sufficiently to leave prints
- The sweat of certain people doesn't produce enough necessary organic substances for prints to remain
- The nature of the surface touched, whether porous or smooth, affects whether prints remain
- Temperature, humidity and other environmental factors contribute a good bit
- The manner in which the surface was touched may have caused smudged prints

After processing the inside of the entry point, continue your search for evidence by moving through the house along the path which the offender appears to have taken. Watch the floor and walls for evidence, and the ceiling as well. If the crime was egregiously violent, evidence could be anywhere, including above you. The admonition to look up is not only to help you locate evidence, but is given for your protection from blood or body fluids which may drip from the ceiling or from lamps. This is one reason for protective clothing and goggles.

As you move through the scene, if shoeprints are visible, photograph them. You might use a crime lamp to identify faint prints, holding the light at an angle in order to illuminate foot or hand prints. If you spot one of these, a shoeprint residue lifter with adhesive on one side will lift the print pattern nicely. This pattern can be used, later, to compare with a suspect's shoe print. While there are other methods for lifting shoeprints, this is a very common and fairly inexpensive one.

FACT

Check doors and drawers the offender may have opened. If a large amount of blood contaminates the floor and areas you must touch, beware of splash back—tiny droplets of blood or fluids which splash when disturbed, and deposit on your shoes, clothes or person. To guard against this, forensic techs often wear goggles, facial coverings, aprons and blood boots: clear boot-shaped plastic coverings that protect from body fluids which may contain disease.

A forensic investigator, in a department with available funds for expensive tools, will often wear a full body suit protecting her from dangerous evidence, and protecting the scene from her own trace evidence of hair, fibers, perspiration, and blood should she be injured. In this scenario, you're wearing one too.

When reaching the body or area where the body has been, photograph the spot from all angles. It's important to keep at least one item from the previous photo in the subsequent one in order to provide perspective. For instance, if a cat bed sits at the right edge of one photo, include that bed in the left edge of the next photo, then continue around the room in the same manner, and back to the first photo.

When it's fresh, blood evidence is usually obvious, but exposure to air, sunlight, bacteria, heat, and age can alter it so much that it's difficult to recognize. Many field (presumptive) tests exist which disclose the slightest residue of blood evidence. One of these tests is performed with luminol. Luminol is only used as a last resort, however, especially if the suspected blood material is very limited. One reason is that in some cases, these types of tests can render the results of the "precipitin test" inconclusive. The precipitin test determines whether blood is from an animal, human. This test is also important because, performed on a sample that's been well-preserved and is of sufficient quantity, it can provide blood type as well.

These field tests aren't usually admissible into evidence, but they have extensive investigative value. For instance, if your field test uncovers the crime scene or scenes, the field test is worth its weight in gold, as processing of the scene can begin. DNA tests are best done in a lab, using sophisticated equipment.

You may investigate a scene where an attempt has been made to clean up evidence, as many criminals are under the mistaken impression that blood can be removed with soap, Clorox or some other chemical. The scene may look spotless. In this case, how do you know where blood may have been deposited? Field tests will alert you when blood is present once you've isolated a suspicious spot. So how can you locate the area you need to test? The following list will familiarize you with examples of suspicious areas:

- A bedspread, mattress or piece of furniture is missing—the reason for its absence cannot be adequately explained, nor its whereabouts confirmed
- There's a spotlessly clean floor or area in an otherwise dirty and unkempt home or building—or in a relatively clean home, a much cleaner, newer, area jumps out at you
- Carpet or flooring that has been recently replaced, or part of the carpet or floor boards look different, newer than that of the surrounding area, and are without use and age marks of that area
- Seat cushions have been removed, from chairs, couches or vehicles, and/or replaced
- Pieces of a set of furniture or a vehicle's seat covers have been freshly recovered
- Furniture or rug has been moved to an inappropriate or inconvenient area, leaving a lighter spot where it seems to have been more appropriately placed—it may be covering a stain
- The area has been recently painted, or the paint is limited to one or several walls, instead of all
- Some other substance appears to have been rubbed into carpet or floor material in an attempt to create a new stain to mask a blood stain

Next, make a sketch of the floor plan, the perimeter and everything in the room. This sketch is intended to include all furniture and items where they sit. It must show windows and doors, and whether doors open to the inside or outside. It must be very detailed. Many software programs are available for this purpose and some departments employ, as a special part of the forensic team, a computer crime scene reconstruction officer.

The next step is to take measurements. Indicate the distance of objects in relation to each other, and in relation to other items in the room. When moving through the crime scene, always collect any large evidence first—soda or beer cans, wine bottles and glasses, anything that may have been touched.

Processing Trace Evidence

Now, you'll look for trace evidence such as blood, hair, fibers that don't match the surroundings, and the like. Collect any you find and place in metal containers or small paper packets, labeling as instructed next, under Preserving the Chain of Custody. If you don't have containers, folded paper will work—in a pinch. Collect blood for sending to a crime lab. If an article of clothing or part of couch material is covered in wet blood or body fluids, let it dry then place it in a cardboard box or paper sack. You may need to cut the area with the sample from a large couch, chair, or rug. A blood stain on a vehicle's carpet or seat covers should be treated the same way.

Paper items should be collected and sent to the lab, where special chemicals can pick up prints. Should you collect a piece of paper with a partial shoe print visible? A tissue thrown on the floor or in the trash? Yes, anything such as this. Also, when collecting, remember that weapons do not consist of only knives and guns, but may be ice picks, letter openers, scissors, fireplace pokers, heavy vases, and other objects. Collect any object which appears to contain body fluids (the tissue) and store it in paper or metal. Place larger ones in paper sacks. Depending on the cause of death, collectible evidence may be poisons, natural or pharmaceutical, and drugs—so don't overlook these things.

Which type of evidence is found most often at crime scenes?
Trace evidence is present at many crime scenes. However, some trace, if not all, is very often overlooked and not collected at all. Of evidence that's most often collected, material such as fingerprints, firearms evidence, and blood evidence are collected more often than paper, glass, soil, wood, and body fluids such as semen, urine and stomach contents.

When finished with the main crime scene, go through the same procedure in every room of the house. This will give you the entire picture as to what happened and where it happened.

Preserving the Chain of Custody

This is the most important part of processing a crime scene. When you collect a piece of evidence, you must indicate on the package the following:

- The case number
- An identification number
- A brief description of the item
- The time, day, date, and place of collection
- The name of the person who collected it

When you collect evidence it's considered to be in your custody. When you deliver it to the crime lab, the person receiving it must indicate the same—case number, time, day, date, and place of collection—and sign it. She now has custody. This must be repeated when the sample is examined, and any time it's transferred from one person to another. This process is called the chain of custody, and is the documented history of this piece of evidence. Most importantly, evidence must reach court with the chain unbroken. If a question is raised concerning custody, suspicions will also be raised as to tampering, or accidental alteration. Either way, it throws suspicion on your evidence—and your testimony concerning it.

You'll also find yourself in possession of evidence apart from crime scenes—court records, video of subjects and the like. You must be able to account for each person who touched that evidence and where it's been stored, in order to protect the chain of custody. Breaking the chain is cause for inadmissibility of evidence.

Let's say that someone who works for you records video of a workers compensation subject, and brings it to the office. A technician downloads the recording onto a DVD and stores it in a locked file cabinet. Each one of these people must sign and date that they've had this evidence in hand. If there's ever a time when evidence can't be accounted for, the chain is broken.

Using The Scientific Method

Investigators use different methods for putting evidence together to prove facts. The scientific method is used most often.

- **State the problem**—state crimes committed and in what jurisdiction—if working for attorney or with police, match state and local law to the crimes
- **Form the hypothesis**—determine possible suspects based on information gathered from victim, witnesses, physical evidence, and possible motive
- **Collect data**—search records, locate additional witnesses—obtain physical evidence from the scene and compare it to the suspects' physical evidence if possible—interview the witnesses again based on data you've discovered
- **Interpret data to test hypothesis**—evaluate evidence and focus on the most likely suspect (police provide Miranda at this point), interrogate suspect
- **If data supports hypothesis, collect additional data**—review evidence again—seek new evidence—review whether this data supports or disproves your original hypothesis—if not alter your hypothesis (many falter at this point—they don't want to begin again)
- **With new hypothesis, go through steps again**

- **Draw conclusions**—when your data and hypothesis match as much as possible, draw a conclusion as to what, where, how, and why the crime happened
- **Develop a theory**—develop your theory as to who committed the crime from these conclusions

This is a simple example, but it provides an overview of one means of getting to conclusions and theories that can be presented in court. Investigation is an unusual profession. It exists along a continuum of art and science, and although it's still more of an art, both disciplines play a large part. Some experts insist that, with recent advancements in technology, investigation is moving farther along the continuum toward science, and will continue to do so. In this case, investigators, including PIs, will need to become much more acquainted with the scientific method.

CHAPTER 12

Working Within the Law

Being knowledgeable about the laws that apply to investigation is important for the success of a private investigator. While there's a lot more concerning this vital subject than can be covered within this section, an overview of specific laws that are likely to affect you and your business is within its scope. It's recommended that you check out the included resources for further information.

Understanding the Law

Laws applicable to investigative work are widely disparate. This section is concerned with basic laws to which law enforcement officers must adhere. Some don't apply directly to your work as a private investigator, though many will, but knowing them will mark you as a serious investigator. It will separate you from the PI on the street and garner respect from both the public and the law enforcement community.

Overview

Cornell University Law School publishes a listing of links to state laws and statutes at *www.law.cornell.edu/statutes.html*. This includes links to federal and state constitutions, statutes and codes, as well as bills, hearings, reports, and related information. It's connected with the Legal Information Institute, which provides access to numerous court opinions, directories, publications, and topics for research. Use the Cornell site as a reference when you need to research a particular law or when you want to brush up on general legal knowledge.

FACT

You don't need to be an attorney or police officer to be a good private investigator, but you do need to know something about the laws that govern law enforcement, as well as laws that apply to your profession. You must also know where your responsibility ends and law enforcement authority begins. Never allow anyone to think you are a law enforcement officer. Impersonating an officer is a criminal offense.

An individual client or attorney will often hire a PI to investigate; in some cases, this necessitates the search of a crime scene. The crime scene is law enforcement's domain, and officers don't appreciate hotshot PIs interfering with their work—so don't. Act within your responsibilities and restrictions and you may develop respectful working relationships with officers.

◀ Understanding the law is key to providing the best private investigation services you can.

Pretexting Law

Pretexting is an essential tool in the PI's box of tricks, but it's trickier than most. Read this section carefully to be sure that you understand the issues involved and the laws that govern pretexting. If you feel uncomfortable with this tool, you can get by without ever using it, but it can be most valuable in certain situations. However, if you intend to use it, do it correctly. Don't cross the line from legal to illegal for any reason.

What Is Pretexting?

The *American Heritage Dictionary* defines pretexting as: 1) an ostensible or professed purpose, an excuse; 2) an effort or strategy intending to conceal something. Basically, pretexting is lying, but not lying for personal gain or with intent to hurt another. It has become controversial because of serious misuse in the past, yet when it is properly executed, courts have upheld its use.

Lying for any reason is a moral issue, and in certain circumstances it is a crime. For some, lying is merely a means of getting what one wants. Others won't misrepresent anything in any way. The criminal justice system has struggled with how far deception should be allowed to go for years, and the issue is still presented to the courts from time to time.

FACT

Undercover work is lying—every step—from the false name and credentials to the unmarked car masking the law enforcement operative's true identity. Yet it isn't done for personal gain. While some argue against pretexting, the courts have consistently ruled it permissible if it was done without coercing the innocent into a false confession.

Civilized Ideals Versus Real-World Practicality

A problem lies in the need to balance the reality of criminal behavior with laws that protect the rights of all. The criminal doesn't abide by laws, and many prey on the average citizen's uninformed idealism and naiveté about the criminal mind and behavior. Because of this, the law enforcement officer, and by extension the PI, may feel constrained by laws protecting the rights of this person who cares nothing for the rights and safety of others. Yet commitment to the rule of law (defined basically as a universally accepted and defined group of laws) separates countries such as the United States from those ruled by totalitarianism.

Because of what's at stake, adherence to the law must be the PI's top priority, yet it must be balanced by protection of the public. Considering the real-world side of this coin—the need to provide protection—the Supreme Court has recognized this challenge. In order to balance the scale when necessary, it has given permission to certain behavior that skirts the hard-line rule of law, and it allows those with responsibility for public protection to push the truth ever so slightly when seeking information from a suspect. The line is fine, however, and must be tread carefully.

In achieving this balance, the cost of lying is weighed against the foreseeable benefits to the public and victim should this lie result in solving a crime. When placed on the scale, the moral wrong of the lie (if done correctly) isn't as weighty as achieving justice for the crime victim and protection for the public by removal of the offender—especially a violent one—from society. Unfortunately, this isn't the only situation in which legal ideals and real-world practicality clash. For every ideal a civilized society vows to uphold, there is something else to challenge the practicality of that ideal. Some of these challenges follow:

- The presumption of innocence is challenged by the knowledge that many are actually guilty.
- The ideal to protect each person's civil rights is challenged by the fact that some have abused, and will continue to abuse, the civil rights of others. When victim and offender rights conflict, the question of whose rights are more important strains the ideal.
- The ideal of the right to bail is challenged by the knowledge of the violent potential of many offenders should they be released.
- The ideal of law enforcement refraining from use of physical force is challenged by suspects who refuse to be taken into custody without a fight and by the need for the officer to protect himself and the public.

More challenges exist within the law, but this short list is intended to give you some idea of the problem of finding a balance. It also illustrates the fact that separate arms of the law sometimes line up on different sides of these challenges. For example, part of the defense counsel's job is obtaining bail for her client. The officer's or detective's job is to apprehend and put the defendant in jail until trial. He and the prosecutor may want bail denied to a violent defendant. The judge must look at both sides, thus the challenge: choosing between bail rights of the defendant and rights of protection for the victim and the public.

Permissible Deception

In light of the information about the challenges of law, the challenge of lying "correctly" can be discussed. The lie in question is called permissible deception. It means that law enforcement can lie to a suspect if the answer wouldn't harm an innocent person or coerce one into making a false confession. Instead, the aim is to reveal the guilt of an offender. Luring the suspect into falsely confessing to something he hasn't done isn't permissible. For example, an investigator can't tell a suspect that his child is in the hospital and that, upon confession, he'll be taken to this child who's barely clinging to life. Under these circumstances, many innocent people would confess for the chance to see a beloved child one last time. This type of lie is outside the parameters of legality and morality and won't hold up as permissible deception.

So what can the investigator say to elicit information? She can tell the suspect that his partner, spouse, girlfriend, or another person has given him up as the offender. This has been used so many times on cop shows you'd think it wouldn't work anymore, yet it does. The investigator can allege that some evidence from his person was found at the scene or on the victim. This ruse wouldn't hurt an innocent person because nothing of his was actually found at the scene, but it may convince a guilty person to tell the truth. There are many other aspects of permissible deception, but these form the basic tenets.

Gaining Access to Information

Using a pretext or ruse has also been upheld in the courts for the purpose of gaining entry to an otherwise unavailable person or area. Pretending to be organizing a future class reunion, masquerading as a past coworker, or acting as a person who owes her money or wants to send a package are all permissible ruses for gaining access to the suspect and those around her. Other ruses are more questionable for the PI.

ALERT!

Police pretending to be in other occupations in order to gain entry have been exonerated for using pretexting, but the PI must be more careful. If you are posing as someone you're not, be careful who you pretend to be and where you desire access. Never pretend to be someone in whom most people have automatic trust, such as a doctor or pastor—and it's illegal to claim to be law enforcement.

Not only should you carefully choose who you pretend to be, you must also be careful where you gain access using a ruse. Attempting to enter a private residence by pretending to be an inspector of some type, someone providing a free service such as cleaning carpets or giving an estimate for painting, or an employee from the alarm company checking an irregularity, be careful: This is an area that can get you into a lot of trouble.

Entering a private residence under these pretenses is not something most PIs will do. Not only is this considered a bit sleazy, but should you be found out, the subject can charge you with something you didn't do, such as stealing, breaking a valuable object, or even committing violence against him, his property, or his family. Using pretexts to talk to public employees or enter parts of public areas that aren't usually open to the public is somewhat different. The expectation of privacy in these places is not as great.

To avoid these problems, it's not necessary to pretend to be someone you're not. Instead, you can pretend to want something other than what you really want, or pretend to want the desired information for an entirely different reason. By doing this, you encourage the person to talk. When she's comfortable and answering freely, slip in your real questions.

One way to encourage people with information to talk is to scope them out and discover something you have in common. Does he work on cars? Does he like boats? Does he garden or golf? If you can't find anything you're knowledgeable about, discover what the subject is interested in and research it so you can speak intelligently with him. People love to discuss hobbies and interests, so use this knowledge. Then find a way to work in your questions. See Chapter 18 for more on expectation of privacy.

Why Do Some People Fear the Legal Pretext?

Some people fear that officers or investigators cannot tell the difference between what is permissible and what isn't permissible. Others see it as a slippery slope; they fear that a person given permission to lie and deceive in one situation won't be able to prevent herself from doing it in other situations. Anyone who cannot separate these situations shouldn't work in law enforcement or private investigation.

The small percentage of those who abuse their discretion and power do so because they choose to, not because they don't comprehend the legalities, and certainly not because they can't stop themselves from falling down the slippery slope of deception in other areas of their work and personal lives. Officers deal with complicated legal decisions on a daily basis and are familiar with the necessity of making instant choices in difficult situations.

Arrest Law

Police powers come equipped with the authority to arrest in clearly defined situations. As a private investigator, you aren't given this broad authority. Your authority to arrest is the same as any other citizen's, the parameters of which are listed later in this section. Understanding this is especially important for PIs working with attorneys and police agencies.

Police Powers of Arrest and Detention

The difference between arrest and detention can be confusing. There is, however, a definite line between the two. Many standards of proof have been set in place to justify an officer's arrest and detention of citizens while protecting the rights of those citizens. However, only an overview of the most common standards will be discussed here.

What Is an Arrest?

An arrest has taken place when someone has been deprived of his liberty, such as being placed under restraint or taken into custody. When a suspect is restrained, cuffed, and placed in the back of a police car with no handles on the inside of the door, it's pretty clear he's under arrest. Yet handcuffing isn't necessary to place someone in custody; all that's required is for an officer to inform the suspect that she cannot leave or must go with him to the station. If he does this, however, he must charge the suspect.

FACT

Because of television shows such as *CSI* and *Law and Order*, there's a misconception that officers must read a suspect the Miranda rights at the moment of arrest. This isn't true; reading of Miranda rights is not done on the street. Neither is the subject questioned on the street, unless circumstances exist in which time is of the essence, such as the need to locate a kidnap victim. Questioning the suspect in the station is the norm.

Apart from arrest, the officer cannot transport anyone for questioning unless that person agrees to go. If an officer forces a noncompliant subject, then she's placing him in custody and must charge him. Police feel it's best to question or interrogate in the station, on their own turf. Even the questioning of witnesses is best accomplished in the station if possible. Witnesses and informants are often taken there in patrol vehicles. Someone who agrees to go and is placed in the back seat of a patrol car isn't in custody. Yet sometimes, by virtue of being in the car, she begins to feel that she's under arrest. She's not; she has agreed to go.

Miranda Warning

This court decision declaring the U.S. citizen's protection against self-incrimination arose from the case *Miranda v. Arizona* in 1966. An officer need not invoke Miranda until he wants to question or interrogate. Police can ask questions without Miranda as long as the suspect isn't in custody. Remember, all that's required for someone to be in custody is for the officer to inform her that she cannot leave.

FACT

In 1963, Ernest Arthur Miranda was convicted of rape and kidnapping after the prosecution presented his confession at his trial. The Arizona Supreme Court upheld the conviction, but the U.S. Supreme Court ruled that the confession was inadmissible because it had been obtained by coercion. The ruling mandated that suspects be informed of their rights before being interrogated.

Once the suspect is in custody, an officer must read him his rights. Of course, nobody reads Miranda, it's memorized and stated. The PI doesn't need to concern herself with Miranda, but it's helpful to know the procedure when she works with attorneys and police. The Miranda waiver of rights follows:

a. You have a right to remain silent. Do you understand this right?
b. You have a right to have an attorney present at questioning. Do you understand this right?

   c. If you cannot afford an attorney, one will be provided to represent you before questioning begins. Do you understand this right?

   d. Do you understand all these rights as they've been explained to you?

   e. Understanding these rights, do you wish to talk to me (or us) now?

Should the suspect decide to talk, he signs the waiver, marking all questions as yes. If he wants his attorney, he still should sign the waiver, marking yes to all but e. The officer also signs, as does a witness; more than one witness isn't necessary, but it is preferable. Many investigators have the suspect place initials at the end of each sentence as well. The reading of rights at each subsequent questioning isn't required, but doing so has been shown to make it easier for jurors to believe that the suspect was granted every opportunity to speak with an attorney. Videotaping the entire procedure has the same effect as reading Miranda at each interview, and is highly recommended, especially if the suspect refuses to sign or initial any of the Miranda points.

ALERT!

The suspect who agrees to waive her rights and talk to officers or detectives can change her mind at any point and reclaim her right to silence and to an attorney. The officer must stop eliciting information from her immediately. Continuing to question her is illegal, and any information the officer acquires after the subject's change of mind cannot be used against her in court.

For information about interviewing, interrogation, and taking statements, see Chapter 19.

Probable Cause

An officer can arrest with or without a warrant. In either case, she must have probable cause. Probable cause is defined as a reasonable belief that a person has committed a crime. Facts and circumstances known to the arresting officer must be sufficient to lead a prudent person to believe the suspect has committed, is about to commit, or will commit a crime.

The problem with this definition is that what seems reasonable to one person may be murky or even ridiculous to another. People possess a wide range of morals and baggage, which is why cases of wrongful arrest and malicious prosecution are often brought before the court. Because of this, obtaining a warrant is the best course, if there's time to get one. The process can be complicated and lengthy, and it must be written up correctly. Most importantly, it must include enough probable cause to encourage a discriminating judge to sign off on it. Several situations exist where an officer can arrest without a warrant. Some of these are:

- An offense, misdemeanor, or felony committed within the presence or view of the officer
- When a person believed to be creditable informs the officer of a felony and there's no time to obtain a warrant
- To prevent theft, a breach of the peace, or injury
- Upon the order of a magistrate before whom a felony or breach of the peace has occurred
- Officer hears an admission of guilt or a statement made by a witness as the crime is committed or immediately after (sometimes ruled an excited utterance)
- Reasonable suspicion—officer believes suspect has done something but isn't necessarily sure what it is; officer can detain briefly and frisk (not a full search, but a pat down for weapons to protect himself); evidence found in a pat down or frisk isn't admissible, but under certain circumstances a frisk can turn into a legal search
- Probable cause—defined as facts or evidence that would lead a reasonable or prudent person to believe a crime has been, is being, or will be committed; the difference between this and reasonable suspicion is that the officer usually knows what crime he suspects the subject of committing and has evidence to support this

An example of reasonable suspicion might be when a suspect acts nervously and lies, gives inconsistent answers to police, or runs away as police approach. Why the person acts strangely or runs from police may be unknown, but her behavior leads to a reasonable suspicion that she has something to hide.

Alternatively, an officer could claim probable cause when he stops a vehicle and views, in plain sight, contraband such as drugs, burglary tools, or the like. Probable cause is strengthened in the case of burglary tools if burglaries have taken place in the area and/or the suspect or her vehicle fits the description given by witnesses.

Detention—the Stop and Frisk

Detention is the temporary interruption of someone's liberty. Police officers can detain people for several reasons. Besides reasonable suspicion, an officer can stop and detain someone who has committed a traffic infraction, such as speeding or running a red light. Although the driver has a right to protection against self-incrimination, in this situation he has no right to refuse the officer his driver's license and vehicle identification. He's in a state of detention and may not leave until the police officer views his identification, runs him through NCIC for wants and warrants, and releases him—or decides not to. If NCIC returns a warrant, he can be arrested and a full search performed pursuant to the arrest.

No matter the reason for detention, a person must show personal and vehicle identification and comply with an officer who stops her—unless, of course, the officer asks her to commit an illegal act, gives her an order outside the purview of stop and frisk, or abuses her civil rights.

In *Terry v. Ohio*, the court ruled that an officer who can articulate the reason for his suspicion can frisk a detainee for weapons in order to protect himself and others. Courts have ruled that requiring an officer to have probable cause in all situations may put the officer and the public in danger. Therefore, with reasonable suspicion, he's allowed to frisk for protection and can even require the suspect to submit to metal detectors and drug or accelerant sniffing dogs.

Citizens' Powers of Arrest

Citizens' arrests are rarely seen, but they do occur. A citizen cannot arrest except in the following cases (in most states):

1. Felonies or breach of the peace committed within her presence or view; in some states, citizens can arrest with reasonable suspicion
2. With a warrant naming the citizen as the arrester of a specific person(s)
3. Prevention of theft and its consequences
4. Aiding a law enforcement officer or someone authorized to arrest

In all cases, the arrested person must be delivered to law enforcement immediately; otherwise, these actions may be seen as kidnapping. The PI's arrest powers are the same as those of the private citizen's. If you arrest outside of these parameters, you may be arrested yourself. Some states even allow the arrestee to sue the arresting citizen for false arrest or imprisonment. However, check your state laws because many cases of citizens' arrests have been upheld.

PIs do not normally need to be concerned with arresting or detaining suspects. They are primarily information gatherers. However, if someone is in danger or if evidence is in danger of being destroyed, PIs have been known to detain or even arrest suspects. Most of the time it's better to call the police and let them do the job they're trained to do, yet in those rare cases where you may feel compelled to help someone or protect evidence, the citizen's arrest is legal.

One recent case of citizens' arrest concerned a driver weaving all over a busy freeway, barely missing several vehicles. A young man in a truck slowly eased this erratic driver toward the shoulder of the road. Another driver spotted his efforts, moved in front of the suspect vehicle, and slowed his speed. The two men stopped the car and detained the inebriated driver, claiming citizens' arrest until police arrived, at which time they were praised for possibly saving lives. Though their actions were brave, they were also dangerous, so don't try this unless you've had training. Most opportunities for citizens' arrest will prove dangerous because the citizen doesn't carry the same authority as a police officer, and they will usually face resistance. Nevertheless, many citizens have stepped in to help others, especially when violence or potential violence is involved.

The Law of Evidence

The laws of evidence are lengthy and complicated, and many books have been written on the subject. Therefore, while this overview is thorough enough for most readers, it's also intended as a guide for further research for those who want more.

Types of Evidence

Should you continue your study, you'll find that authors differ in their manner of classifying evidence. Some write that there are three types, while others list four, and still others break evidence down into many more categories. For the purpose of this book, there are four kinds of evidence: testimonial, real, documentary, and demonstrative evidence. Other types referred to in investigations and in court are usually subtypes of these four—and many of them often overlap:

- Testimonial evidence (verbal or written) can be statements, interviews, depositions, and confessions.
- Real evidence is anything whose materiality and relevance are obvious, and which is directly involved in a case. Also called physical evidence, it can be a weapon, a wrecked automobile, a bloody shirt, or forensic and trace evidence such as DNA, hairs, and fibers.
- Demonstrative evidence is anything that is the representation of an object. It can be photos; x-rays; audio and video recordings; illustrations; maps; computer simulation, animation, and reconstruction; models; and more.
- Documentary evidence is anything in the form of documents that is presented in order to examine its contents. It can be records (written, printed, on film, microfiche, etc.) such as wills, contracts, letters, invoices, and printed e-mails. It is subject to authentication, usually by testimony. Documents presented for a different purpose, such as proving that they were handled and contain prints from a victim or suspect, are real evidence, but they may be documentary as well if the contents are relevant.

Read about rules of evidence in Chapter 14, which addresses evidence as it relates to that which can be testified to. The rules, however, apply to all evidence. Some of these rules apply to every type of evidence, some only apply to one, and some apply to several types.

QUESTION?

Why do I need to know about rules of evidence?
When you are working a case, you should be aware of basic principles of evidence so you can recognize what is usually accepted into the court record and what isn't. Knowing these rules will help ensure that your work is accepted if the case goes to trial.

Putting Evidence Together for Proof

Evidence exists as the means for establishing facts. When enough facts are gathered, they prove a point in question. Standards necessary for proof are different depending on whether the case will be tried in civil or criminal court. In civil court, the standard for proving a point—and the ultimate point of the defendant's guilt—is a preponderance of evidence. In criminal court, the standard is beyond a reasonable doubt. The House Judiciary Committee uses clear and convincing evidence as the standard for proving impeachments.

- **A preponderance of evidence.** This is the lowest level of proof of guilt. It relies on jurors concluding that evidence points more toward one direction than another, or that the defendant is more likely guilty than not guilty or vice versa.
- **Beyond a reasonable doubt.** This doesn't mean there can be no doubt whatsoever; it means that guilt must be proved beyond a "reasonable" doubt, beyond that standard of doubt that would make a reasonable person hesitate.
- **Clear and convincing evidence.** The level of proof required is somewhere between the other two; it must be proved that evidence points substantially more in one direction than the other.

Standards of proof are different from burden of proof, which means the obligation to prove an allegation or allegations. In criminal cases, the prosecution, not the defense, has the burden of proof—the burden to prove charges against the defendant. Investigators use different methods for putting evidence together and proving facts. The scientific method is the one most often used. This method is outlined in Chapter 11.

CHAPTER 13

People in the PI's Life

People are the crux of the PI's business. If you dislike dealing with them, you'll have a difficult time doing private investigation. Alternatively, if you're just not very good with people, you can learn to be. Practice talking to the people you meet in the course of your day. Learn ways to engage them in conversation, and identify ways that work for you. Sometimes the soft-spoken, friendly personality appeals to people and disarms defensive postures more than the backslapping extrovert.

Working with Employees

The most interesting aspect of being your own boss is that of dealing with people, but it can also be the most exasperating. In the real world, everyone answers to someone else—at least on some level. When you open your business, you'll find that all kinds of people expect you to answer to them. Should you decide to use employees such as other investigators, secretaries, or others, they will hold definite expectations of you.

- They'll expect you to pay them as agreed.
- They'll expect your trust and loyalty when they've earned it.
- They'll expect you to provide appropriate training and guidelines within which to operate.
- They'll expect you to be available to answer questions and put out fires which routinely ignite within normal business operations.
- They'll expect you to keep them abreast of business developments that allow them to perform their job properly.
- They'll expect you to provide appropriate materials with which to do their jobs.
- They'll expect you to do what you say you'll do, to be a man or woman of your word. You can't retain respect by promising employees one thing, then doing another just because you're the boss.

Neither can you allow employees to believe that they call the shots. This is all a balancing act. Managing people is akin to riding a horse. Too heavy a hand on the reins and the horse will balk and rear up. With too light a hand, the horse becomes confused as to who's in control and will fight to get the bit in her mouth. Give the horse her head and you have no idea where you'll end up. However, with the right touch and the appropriate level of pressure on the reins, the horse goes where she's directed, doing what is required, and doing it with a proper respect for the person in the saddle.

Multiplying Yourself, Your Time, and Your Fees

Many PIs work alone. Some prefer it, and others don't have enough work to justify hiring employees. While it's not necessary to employ anyone at all, it helps. A private investigator can type his own reports or contract them out. He can hire an answering service or install a computer answering system. The downside is that he can only handle so many cases at once, and may find himself refusing cases or working cases poorly due to time constraints.

Therefore, if you want to multiply the hourly fee that you bring in by working alone, and you can endure not working each case yourself, you'll want to employ other investigators. For ease of demonstration, let's say you charge $100 an hour. You can easily pay an employee $25–$50 an hour, depending on her quality and experience, keeping the rest for yourself and for operating and advertising costs.

Don't think that headaches don't accompany the use of multiple investigators, or that there are no costs accompanying their use. However, if you can manage it, it's a lucrative business. Some investigator problems to guard against are:

- **Padding bills**—charging more hours than actually worked or charging more gas than expended
- **Fantasy reports**—PIs turning in fictitious reports on a target that has never been followed or records that were never searched—or worse, an investigation that was never worked at all
- **Switch-hitting**—an investigator who offers evidence or a surveillance recording to the target for a higher price than the client pays, thus getting paid by both sides
- **Lazy surveillance experts**—some PIs sleep, some run by the target's place then leave to do errands or other personal business on your time; many firms require the PI to film continuously to prevent this behavior

Make sure you put safeguards in place to make sure your business is fully legitimate and is doing everything to help the clients who are paying for your services.

Working with Clients

Client relationships can be the most challenging in private investigation work. Clients come with all manner of personalities, motives, needs, and pocketbooks. Many of them also come with baggage. Learning to identify the ones you can work with, and taking proper precautions against the rare ones that you'll turn away, will enable you to better help all of them.

Meeting with Your Potential Client

If you have an office with a back entrance, reticent clients will often meet you there. If you don't, most new clients prefer to meet in a public location. You might prefer it also, unless your office is well staffed. Meeting a new client in public gives you an opportunity to scope him out and determine whether you want to take his case.

Meeting for coffee or lunch can also provide the new client with a sense of security. She doesn't know you, and she is scoping you out as well. Also, meeting this way doesn't identify her as a client; depending on the type of case, she may want to avoid broadcasting the fact that she's using a PI. Meeting in a restaurant or bar gives the appearance of two friends having lunch or drinks and conversation.

FACT

Bars aren't optimum areas for meeting the opposite sex. The atmosphere can elicit feelings of intimacy, feelings you don't want to entertain toward a client and that you don't want the client to entertain toward you. Involvement with a client can interfere with objectivity, alter focus, and may elicit an association whose connection is difficult to sever. Some PI organizations prohibit such involvement.

By accepting a client's money, you're acknowledging that you work for him. You start the investigation when he says to start and end when he wants to stop. In this way, he's the boss. However, he's not in control. You're the expert, so you must guide him to the most sensible and cost-effective decisions in the case. Ultimately, there are some things you'll never do at the client's direction, such as break the law.

Be prepared for many different kinds of clients. You will love some of your clients and merely tolerate others. You'll not see many clients more than one time, but be assured that some of them will recommend you to others if they've been happy with your service. Of course, if their case is sensitive, clients will never tell anyone that they've used you, and if they mention you at all, they'll say a friend used your services. An unfortunate but universal truth is that people who are unhappy with your service may talk more about you than those who are satisfied. When people feel mis-used, they usually voice this feeling. Therefore, it's important that you put your all into every case, not only for the satisfaction of doing your best, but for the reputation you're building.

Learning from the Difficult Client

You will eventually run into the client who cannot be satisfied no matter what you do. Make reasonable efforts to mend any breach, then let it go. Don't obsess over things you can't control and people you're unable to please. Real-ize that some people are professional complainers. However, don't assume that everyone who complains falls into this category. Be open to the fact that there may be a legitimate reason for a client's complaint, and know that this reason may have caused the client to be understandably distraught.

Try to see the difficult client in a new way. Even if she isn't entirely right, there might be a kernel of truth to her complaints—something you can mine from the rubble that will help improve your service. If you can put aside your pride and preconceived notions about how things should be, you may see that some complaining clients are giving you the gift of objectivity. Taking an objective look at yourself is difficult for everyone. Allow the client with a suggestion or complaint to help you do this. Conversely, if you examine the complaint next to the service and find that nothing was done incorrectly, you'll be comfortable keeping things the way they are. That's good to know also.

Working with Police and Other Agencies

If possible, gain a working relationship with police in your community. Many police officers have little use for PIs, but if you know the law, behave in a professional manner, and are diligent in solving cases, they'll often accept you as a professional. Never get between officers or special agents and their work. Never try to take over a case or crime scene, even though you've been hired to work the case.

Know your position and work within it. Be respectful of the officer's time and expertise, and offer to help where you can. Be willing to do the grunt work. Should you arrive on a scene where a car needs to be pushed off the road, join in with the pushing. If the officer gives you a direct order, don't push it. Even PIs who are former or retired law enforcement officers are subject to obeying commissioned officers, so don't feel rained on if you're asked to step aside, and don't make a scene. Acting out is the best way to burn your bridges with these officers and others.

ALERT!

Officers know each other, and they talk. Should you get into a power struggle with one, you can be sure your name will come up one day when he's on the subject of those difficult PIs. You don't want your name on that list. Cultivate respect and cooperation.

Letting maltreatment roll off your back and treating those who are rude with respect can sometimes put a mirror in front of the face of the person acting badly. You may have caught him on a bad day. There may have been a tragedy in his family or circle of friends. You never know why someone reacts with venom for no apparent reason. Try returning kindness for bad treatment. Turning the other cheek isn't just a platitude; it often really works to defuse unreasonable anger. By giving Mr. Rude the benefit of the doubt, you may turn him into a friend. However, if he doesn't come around, this says something about him, not you, so let it go. Realize that he won't be one of your contacts, and good riddance.

Working with Informants and Contacts

Contacts are necessary for the PI to operate. Because a contact has no law enforcement badge to plop down on a counter, no police powers that encourage people to provide information, and no ability to petition for search warrants, she must rely on people for certain information. Technically, informants are contacts, but contacts aren't necessarily informants. Therefore, this section will treat them separately.

Contacts

A contact is anyone with access to information needed by the PI. Contacts can be paid or unpaid, friends, police, government workers, or private citizens. In other words, anyone in any industry or business who holds information relevant to the PI's needs can be a contact. Cultivate these people. Form some type of relationship with them so that they trust you. People in records, police, and child welfare departments are good contacts, as are those in the media, insurance, politics, real estate, and forensics or crime labs. Developing as many contacts in as many areas as possible will help, as each new case presents different information requirements. Don't wait until you need someone—cultivate relationships now.

QUESTION?

Must I pay contacts in order to receive help?
Cultivating doesn't mean paying people or spending money to keep people "in your pocket." It means taking advantage of opportunities to get to know people who have access to information you may need, and to help them where you can. Be genuinely interested in their lives and show appreciation for what they do.

If you're able, you might gift these contacts with small tokens such as sticky notepads or pens with your phone number. Become a learner—let the contact educate you about his work. Be interested in pictures of children or pets that someone may have on her desk. Remembering children's names and asking about them from time to time is a means of meeting people on a more personal level. However, don't overdo it or your interest can feel creepy. During holidays, you might bring cookies or another inexpensive edible to a department you do business with. More importantly, become a friendly face that people welcome. Be alert to peoples' needs and look for ways to help. When you need something, your contacts may reciprocate.

The main thought to keep in mind is that contacts can be anyone, so don't burn your bridges with those around you. To reiterate what's been mentioned earlier, even if someone is rude, sharp, or even hostile, with patience and a little humor, you may be able to turn that person into a contact—and maybe a friend. You may even experience the privilege of pouring the salve of kindness on someone's pain; when you can do this, it'll make your day.

Informants

Informants are also contacts, but they are usually of a different breed. Informants, more often than not, want to be paid. They're usually in professions or from cultures or communities that are difficult to reach, and they may be criminals or criminal associates. First and foremost, you must determine the informant's motive. Does he crave attention? Is he looking for revenge or to settle a score? Is he trying to make a quick buck by pulling the proverbial wool over your eyes? Is he emotionally unstable? Knowing motive will help to weed out people with real information from those whose information is false or nonexistent. Sometimes motives are mixed, but the information can still be valid.

Cab drivers, bartenders, waiters and waitresses, store clerks, and the like aren't necessarily criminals or criminal associates. You may not know them well enough to know whether they are or not—and it might not matter. For example, if your target frequents a certain restaurant or bar, you may want to cultivate the bartender or someone in wait service who can unobtrusively report on the target and glean information from and about her. These people usually want to be paid, but don't let them soak you; you don't need to pay an exorbitant price. Most will take a much lower price than the one in your head. Also, be sure you receive what you need from them before paying the entire amount. If you've paid half, don't pay the rest until you have your information.

While it's true that informants are less likely to be people with whom you want to form personal relationships, even informants perform better when there's some kind of connection between you, so treat them with respect. There's a fine line to walk here because the informant must know that you can see through any duplicity, yet they should not feel degraded. Police informants are carefully controlled. They must be recorded in a book and monitored. Even confidential informants must be known to someone.

Relationships with informants can be sticky. Even police have difficulty handling them, so don't underestimate the potential for problems. The first rule is: Never trust an informant—always check the information provided. Second rule: Never trust an informant—take someone with you or have backup watching when you meet with or use an informant.

Another source of informants for the PI is hotel and motel personnel such as maids, janitors, and front desk clerks. They could be the only ones with access to information in certain areas, and they may be persuaded to share. Also, don't overlook home workers such as nannies, landscapers, yard workers, housekeepers, and the like. This is trickier, as many of these people are intensely loyal. Yet some are not well paid or are treated poorly, and some have witnessed activities of which they disapprove. They may talk.

Working with Experts and Resources

No matter what specialty you choose, you may need experts from time to time. The PI doesn't have the luxury of taking his evidence to the state crime lab, so he must use private labs. Employees in private labs are good people to know. In fact, these labs can often return evidence much more quickly than state labs.

Try to find someone who appreciates your interest and ask if you can tour the facility to become acquainted with its services. Before you do this, brush up on your forensics so you'll be able to ask intelligent questions and come out of the experience with more knowledge than you went in with.

Discover who has the best reputation for administering lie detector tests, corporate drug tests, computer accident reconstruction and crime scene dramatization, age-progression of photos, and hidden camera installations. All of these people can be invaluable when you need experts for your cases. Again, don't wait until you need them to ask for their help or to engage their services. Get to know them now. Ask questions about how their expertise is related to the cases you work.

People are always more interested in doing a good job for someone they know and like. This doesn't mean you need to feign interest where none exists. With practice, you can become quite proficient at finding something in which you can feel real appreciation and interest in almost everyone you meet. Be sure you're genuinely interested in people and what they do. Otherwise, they may sense your insincerity. Regardless of whether they sense it, using people isn't going to get you anywhere. It's an ugly business not worthy of an honorable person.

◀ It is essential that you know where to look in your investigations.

Dealing with the Media

The media can be a help or hindrance, yet you should definitely cultivate a contact in the media. By doing so, you have access to information, and you may be able to get your client's angle and best interests into the media through your relationship with your contact.

If you don't have a relationship or at least an agreement with a reporter, it's best to say as little as possible when questioned about your case. You can never know how she intends to use your information or present your client's case.

Law enforcement officers are usually not permitted to speak to the media. In most departments, only information officers or public relations officers are trained to speak to the media. If you work for attorneys, let them handle media relations. They'll no doubt insist upon it. Should you be overheard revealing a secret or should you inadvertently mention something to a reporter, do immediate damage control. Think of the viewing audience as your client's potential jury pool. Don't contaminate it with media sound bites that may present a limited or contorted view of the situation.

CHAPTER 14

Testifying in Court

Many cases never go to court. Some are commissioned by clients who merely want information, some are settled between the client and the target, and others are settled by attorneys. How many of your cases will end up in court is also dependant on the type of investigations you work. When the courtroom is the last step in working a case, it's an extremely important one. Therefore, it's vital that you understand basic courtroom procedures and legalities.

Accepting a Subpoena

If the client is an attorney, she doesn't need to send you a subpoena for your testimony. However, if the other side wants to question you, either on the stand or in a deposition, they must send one. Be aware that your client cannot prevent you from accepting a subpoena even though you work for her.

Some firms, and even individual clients, will send the investigator out of town to avoid his acceptance of a subpoena. This is not only unprofessional, it is a blatant attempt to circumvent the judicial system, and it will be obvious to the court. A subpoena is a legal order for you to appear in court—an order, not a request. If you don't appear, you can be held in contempt.

Be professional. Don't hide. Accepting the subpoena shows respect for the person serving it and for the judicial system. You never know when you may meet her or others associated with the case. One day, you may need her help or she may need a PI. Never burn your bridges with anyone.

FACT

An investigator is entitled to payment for her time in court. Bill your client. Even when you are subpoenaed by opposing counsel, your testimony is beneficial to your client's case and plays a vital part in the investigation. Include charges for court testimony in the client agreement. Because you're unavailable to work other cases, you're entitled to payment for time spent waiting to testify, not only for time spent on the stand. Travel expenses are also billable, should they apply.

You may be subpoenaed for a deposition. These are usually held in the attorney's office or that of the court reporter. A deposition is a statement made under oath and in front of witnesses (attorneys for both sides are usually present) that becomes an official record that can be used in court. It's usually written and signed by the person being deposed as well as the witnesses. It is often videoed as well.

Because depositions are quite costly, the PI is important in this process. In addition to being interviewed, the PI is also often used to interview multiple witnesses and return reports to the attorney, who uses the information to choose the witnesses she wants to depose. In this way, she won't have to pay for depositions that won't be useful to the case. Since payment for the PI's time is usually much less than the cost of depositions, total expenses can be reduced.

Demeanor and Dress

Proper courtroom attire is stylish, but conservative. If you appear in outdated styles, some jury members, especially younger ones, may view you as a throwback from another generation. Unfortunately, this could affect the way your testimony is evaluated. Stylish doesn't mean faddish; avoid clothing that may be in one year and out the next or styles that can be acceptable in another situation but are too casual, radical, distracting, or revealing for the formality of a courtroom. Classic colors and styles with updated cuts and fabrics are the best choices, and they stamp you as someone with dignity and taste. Attire should enhance your professional image without drawing attention to what you wear.

In states where attire is spelled out for attorneys, you can use the state rules as guidelines. For example, Oklahoma County asks attorneys to abide by Local Rule 40, which outlines proper dress and demeanor. Men are required to wear suits or jackets and ties. Women must wear either dresses or professional suits with skirts or pants. Rule 40 also requires attorneys to maintain courtesy and civility with all. In jurisdictions without such rules, the PI should investigate and follow the accepted dress and demeanor of attorneys who regularly appear in court. Further rules to follow are:

- Always be on time. This cannot be overstated.
- You will be searched long before you get inside the courtroom, so don't bring weapons; they're not allowed in the building.
- The removal of hats is considered respectful, and often required, before entering a courtroom. The exception is religious attire.
- Refrain from doing anything to distract the process, such as coming in and out excessively, talking loudly, tapping your foot, or moving around in your seat too much.
- Don't eat, drink, or chew gum.

- Don't slouch, look disinterested, or roll your eyes when you disagree with a statement.
- Keep your hands away from your face and resting calmly in your lap.
- Look directly at your questioner during questioning and when answering him.
- Turn off all cell phones or paging devices; most jurisdictions also ban the use of laptops or the reading of newspapers and books in court.
- Don't bring recording devices into the courtroom without prior approval of the judge.

If you haven't testified in court or been chosen for jury duty, you may not understand the importance of these rules. If not, please understand one thing: When you are in court, you are likely to be watched and evaluated, whether you testify or not. If you testify, you'll be scrutinized.

Rules of Evidence

There are many rules of evidence, and most of the rules have exceptions. Besides the federal rules of evidence, there are also state rules, most of which are patterned after the federal rules. You won't need to memorize these—your attorney will handle that—but it's important to gain a general knowledge of the rules that are seen most often in the courtroom. It's also important to know how to research a rule when you need to. These rules play a large role in whether or not your collected evidence is admissible in court.

The Federal Rules of Evidence govern the way evidence is allowed to be introduced in Federal courts, both civil and criminal. In judging whether evidence is acceptable, most courts look first at its relevance.

Rules of Admissibility

There are three basic rules concerning the admissibility of evidence. Evidence must be relevant, material, and competent.

- Relevancy is the logical connection that one thing has to another. In most cases, fingerprints on a weapon found at the scene would be relevant to a murder case, and therefore, admissible as evidence.
- Material evidence must be proven to have bearing on the case. If it's proven to be snowing on the day a valuable artifact was stolen, that fact wouldn't be admissible unless it had some bearing on the theft. The truth of the snow has nothing to do with proving who stole the artifact, so the fact is true but immaterial.
- Competency means that evidence must meet traditional proofs of reliability. Since this section concerns testimonial evidence, the four criteria for a competent witness will be discussed. To be competent, the witness must:
  1. Take the oath and understand it
  2. Have personal knowledge about his testimony; he must have experienced it with his senses—touched, smelled, tasted, heard, or seen it
  3. Be able to remember what he has experienced
  4. Be able to communicate what he experienced

Even relevant, material, and competent evidence can be ruled inadmissible and can be excluded if, in the court's opinion, the following conditions exist:

- Evidence is prejudicial
- Evidence may confuse the jury
- Evidence is speculative—if many different conclusions can be drawn from it
- The sheer amount of the same evidence is unnecessary and wastes the court's time. Evidence can be ruled admissible for one purpose or party and not another; the jury will be instructed to consider it relevant regarding only the party or person to whom it is ruled admissible.

State courts aren't bound by federal rules, but many states have used them as a foundation for developing their own rules of evidence. While differences in civil and criminal court exist, federal rules apply to both.

What's the difference between civil and criminal trials?
Civil trials are concerned with resolution of claims by individuals or groups against other individuals or groups. In reaching a decision, the burden of proof is governed by "a preponderance (or weight) of evidence." Criminal trials deal with prosecuting those accused of violating criminal law. The burden of proof (for proving guilt) in a criminal trial is "beyond a reasonable doubt," a stricter standard.

How Rules Work in Court Procedure

Civil procedure, or courtroom conduct and etiquette during a civil case, is governed by the Federal Rules of Civil Procedure (*www.law.cornell.edu/rules/frcp/index.html*). The government's criminal code, U.S.C. Title 18 > Part II (*www.law.cornell.edu/uscode/18/pII.html*) and Federal Rules of Criminal Procedure, outline conduct and procedure in federal criminal courtrooms. These rules are designed to protect the rights of defendants.

The first attorney (usually the defense) will begin by questioning a witness during what's called direct examination. Cross-examination follows, where opposing counsel either questions the witness or passes. Only subjects brought up or introduced during direct examination can be questioned in cross-examination, unless the judge chooses to allow it. In re-direct, the original attorney can again question a witness to clear up anything that's unclear or has been introduced or distorted by cross-examination. This can be followed by re-cross. During questioning, either side can object to specific questions. Responses to objections are as follows:

- **Judge can overrule**—witness is permitted to provide the answer
- **Judge can sustain**—question must be asked again in a different way
- **Judge can ask for further information** so she can decide how to rule

When an objection is made, it's important that you stop talking immediately and wait for the judge's response. Once a ruling is made, you'll know what to do. If the question is sustained, you must answer. If it's overruled, you must wait for the next question. The most common objections you'll hear in court follow:

- **Leading the witness.** A leading question suggests the answer: Didn't you see the subject driving erratically? Nonleading: Did you see the subject driving? In your opinion, how was she handling the vehicle?
- **Hearsay.** A statement made by someone other than the testifying witness. There are many exceptions, some of which will be discussed later.
- **Relevancy.** Questions and statements may be challenged if they do not directly relate to the case.

Leading questions are allowed on cross-examination when the attorney is questioning an unfriendly witness. They aren't allowed during direct questioning, when the attorney for whom you work questions you, because leading questions suggest the answer for the witness to supply. However, when your attorney asks a leading question, knowing it'll probably be objected to and overruled by the judge, it's a clue as to where he wants you to go with your answer.

Hearsay evidence may be accepted under several conditions:

- **Dying declaration.** Although it is hearsay because the person declaring isn't in court, a person who heard a dying person's statement may repeat that statement because of the general belief that someone aware of dying doesn't have any reason to lie. For example, "I heard her say, 'John stabbed me.'"
- **Excited utterance.** It is still hearsay if the person who uttered the statement isn't in court, but this is admissible testimony because in the heat of an exciting incident, a witness may blurt out something that he refuses to testify to later. For example, "Look, that blue car ran over that little boy!"
- **Admission against interest.** A witness can testify that she heard a party in a lawsuit make a statement that runs counter to the party's case. For example, a witness can testify she heard the suspect admit he committed the crime for which he is on trial.

- **Business records.** These must be introduced by a qualified witness who can identify them and testify how they were recorded.
- **Official government records** that have been properly maintained.
- **Notes.** These must be made close to the time of an event and can be used during testimony to refresh the memory of a witness.
- **Judgments in other cases.**
- **Statement explaining a person's future plans.** For example, "I'm going to choke the life out of her and keep her from hurting anyone again." The person who heard this can testify to what was said.

There are many other exceptions to the hearsay rule. Besides these exceptions, the judge always has power to declare an exception at his discretion.

Direct Evidence

Direct evidence, sometimes called real evidence, is the evidence to which you can testify—what you know or have seen or done. Direct evidence is tangible and requires nothing to prove the truth of its existence. Examples are the production of a receipt identifying the defendant as the purchaser of a specific firearm. This doesn't prove that the defendant used it to kill anyone, but it does prove he purchased that weapon. Direct evidence is usually ruled admissible.

Hearsay or Indirect Evidence

Indirect evidence is evidence that you've heard from someone else. It can be hearsay, but not always. The most common exception is the party opponent exception. When a party to the lawsuit says something that you actually hear her say, your testimony concerning the statement is admissible. For example, the following statements are not hearsay and are admissible:

- **"He said, 'I agree to your offer.'"** Because this isn't a statement of fact that can be proven true or untrue, you can testify that you heard it; the issue is not whether the statement is true, but whether it was said.

- **"She yelled, 'Help me!'"** It's a cry for help; some say the excited utterance exception applies here.
- **"Jones told me that Smith is a thief and a liar."** If this is offered as testimony that Jones had motive to kill or assault Smith, it's acceptable as evidence. If it's offered as testimony that Smith is a thief and a liar, then it's considered hearsay.

There are many more exceptions to the hearsay rule, and you may hear them from time to time, but not as often as the ones discussed here.

Circumstantial Evidence

This type of evidence doesn't prove the existence of a fact—at least not directly. It does, however, provide logical suspicion that the fact exists, but reasoning is required to prove its existence. The general belief is that circumstantial evidence is weak, but often this type of evidence proves a case, as physical evidence isn't always available.

The compilation of inferential evidence can lead to the belief that no other conclusion is possible. For example, the defendant may have been seen in the area around the time of the murder. He may have been heard threatening the deceased and may have owned the weapon that killed her. He may also have hurt the deceased in the past. His prints may even be in the house, but they are considered circumstantial if he has been in the house before. All of these things are circumstantial, but together they begin to point to a strong conclusion. If you have enough of them, they make a case.

Audiovisual Media

Photographs or video recordings of evidence are important to your case. In order to be admissible, someone must testify that they reasonably represent the thing or person that was photographed or filmed. The person giving testimony concerning the item either must have taken it herself or been present when it was taken, so she can verify that the film or photograph accurately represents what it is purported to represent.

Charts, models, and maps, sometimes called demonstrative evidence, are not evidence in and of themselves; they must be authenticated, usually with the testimony of the person using these objects. They are used in court to make a point or to demonstrate a fact, and marks made on these items may be used to prove a fact. If so, they may be admitted into evidence. Again, admissibility is at the discretion of the judge. See Chapter 12 for information about types of evidence.

Cross Examination Response

Rookie PIs are usually nervous about being cross-examined by opposing counsel. If you are, you're in good company—almost everyone is nervous about this, at least a little. The more you testify, however, the less you'll dread cross-examination. When you understand that it's counsel's job to rattle you and there's nothing personal about it, you'll also understand that it's your job to stay cool.

Speak Clearly and Confidently

Practice speaking in a clear and modulated voice. Don't hesitate long in answering opposing counsel's questions. She can use this hesitation to insinuate that you're manufacturing an answer in the best interest of your client instead of answering truthfully. However, don't speak so quickly that it appears you're not thinking seriously about your answer. Speaking too quickly can also prevent your attorney from having time to object before the answer leaves your mouth. Never, never volunteer information. Answer only what you are asked. If your attorney wants to bring out further evidence, he can do so later.

ALERT!

Be wary of the attorney whose aim is to discredit you and who tries to cause you to react with anger, embarrassment, and/or defensiveness. Provide slow, respectful, deliberate answers to any attacks on your character or capability. Also, be careful of the overly friendly attorney who attempts to catch you off guard with a not-so-friendly question. Remember, it's not personal.

Avoid using profanity, jargon, cop-speak, or slang, unless you're directly quoting someone. The jury has a few minutes to decide what type of person you are and whether they believe you. Don't use offensive language or present an attitude that might alienate some jury members. Be respectful to both parties—speak of the defendant as Mr., Mrs., or Ms. Whoever—and don't use sarcasm or disapproval when relating the subject's actions.

Be Prepared

After receiving a subpoena, contact the attorney for whom you're working. She will want to discuss the types of questions you may be asked and prepare you for the more difficult aspects of the case.

Using Your Notes

Before you get on the stand, review all the information you have in your report and notes. You don't have to memorize everything, but refresh your memory as to important times, dates, and incidences. If the case is long or complicated, you're allowed to take your notes to the stand for the purpose of finding and confirming dates, times, or specific details that might otherwise be fuzzy in your memory. However, if you do so, know that they may be made available to the other side for inspection, and they could be placed into evidence. At the very least, the portion that is ruled to be related to the case can be entered into evidence. Talk to your attorney first.

FACT

Jurors may see you from the moment you leave home. You may be in traffic or on the bus with jurors. You may run into a convenience store or get gas at the same location, or be together in the courthouse or restroom prior to trial. They might not know you until you testify, but they'll remember an inappropriate or ugly scene, and they will judge your testimony by your behavior and attitude.

In civil cases, your notes and reports are subject to discovery anyway. Another point to remember: Accuracy is important in any case, but be aware that, when the other side gets your reports and notes, opposing counsel will comb through them looking for mistakes on which to build their case and cause doubt in the minds of jurors.

The Attorney as Client

If you interview a potential client who presents with a situation that you believe could go to trial, encourage the potential client to choose an attorney before you begin. This way, the attorney can employ you instead of the individual. This means the attorney must sign the client agreement and the attorney must pay you. Some investigators dislike having attorneys as clients because many attorneys don't want to pay in advance. Yet there are advantages to the client and to the case in some situations.

If the attorney is your client, your reports and notes won't be open to the other side in discovery. Before a case goes to trial, attorneys are required to supply each other with a list of witnesses they plan to use. Each attorney will interview or depose these witnesses to determine what they know and what evidence they possess. This is the discovery process. If your client is an individual, your investigative report is available to the other side in discovery—don't take the case until you inform the client of discovery. If your client is the individual's attorney, the report is safe under what's called the work product rule—it's safe unless the attorney decides to give it up to the other side for her own reasons.

Your Notes as Attorney Work Product

Work product is defined as any notes, documents, reports, or research materials that the attorney uses in preparing his case—anything that discloses his trial strategy. Attorney work product privilege is one of the five privileges in Exemption 5 of the Freedom of Information Act, 5 USC§ 552(b)(5). A nonattorney is said to be able to author work product and enjoy the privilege if she is acting under the direction of an attorney. Because the PI is acting under the attorney's direction, her report is part of work product. Therefore, any client who presents with a case that may go to court should be encouraged to retain an attorney. If he doesn't, your report may fall into the hands of the opposing counsel at discovery. However, your conscience is clear—you've informed your client of the possible ramifications and let him choose.

Tell the Truth

Always tell the truth. This not only allows you to live a life of integrity, it's a means of keeping you from the attorney's trap. When you're on the witness stand, opposing counsel may attempt to lure you into an argumentative posture by asking unanswerable questions. For example, concerning a workers' compensation case, you may have testified that you witnessed the subject lifting a heavy bucket from the front yard and carrying it to the backyard.

Counsel may ask how you know it was heavy. You answer that it was large, with a wide circumference, and it appeared to be full. She may counter by asking how large and wide it was, and she may continue along those lines: Did you get out and measure it? Did you attempt to lift it? No? Then how can you know it was heavy? How can you ask this jury to believe it was large when you can't even tell them how large?

What does large mean? You answer that it was full and the subject strained while carrying it. Counsel may ask how you know it was full when you couldn't see inside. How do you know it wasn't pine straw or feathers? How do you know it wasn't empty? You answer that the subject used both hands to carry it. Counsel may ask if it is possible that an injured man might need to use both hands in lifting even a light object?

FACT

Even when you tell the truth, it's the job of opposing counsel to try to confuse you and poke holes in your testimony. By misrepresenting anything, you play into her hands. Lies are difficult to keep straight, especially under the pressure of cross-examination. Tell the truth and you won't have to worry about concocting another lie to cover the one before it.

You get the picture. The opposing counsel is trying to place doubt in the mind of jurors—doubt that you saw what you saw—or worse, doubt that you haven't done your job properly. The only defense is to answer truthfully and without emotion. Being truthful will enhance your credibility and could even cause counsel to appear to be badgering you. Most jurors don't like that.

CHAPTER 15

Business/Corporate Security and Investigations

Business and corporate security offers a wider variety of opportunities for the PI than any other specialty. These opportunities include workers' compensation, accident and arson investigation, fraud (including medical and corporate fraud), theft of time or products or services, undercover investigation, product liability and wrongful injury investigation, background and pre-employment investigation, document/data analysis and forensic accounting, repossessions and collections, and process service.

Insurance Investigations

The National Insurance Crime Bureau (NICB) reports that after tax evasion, fraud is the most costly white-collar crime in the United States. It's not only costly to insurance companies and businesses, but a portion of the costs are passed along to consumers. NICB estimates that at least 10 percent of all property and casualty insurance claims are filed incorrectly with intent to defraud. Who commits insurance fraud?

- Unscrupulous repair shops, contractors, and individuals
- Dishonest attorneys, physicians, chiropractors, dentists, and other professionals
- Organized rings dedicated to sophisticated, large-scale fraud
- Individuals who add to or pad their claims

National Insurance Fraud Investigators (*www.nafraud.com*) was organized to serve a broad membership—insurance companies, law enforcement and bond enforcement officers, information services, forensic examiners, skip tracers, investigators, security specialists, and attorneys—in the United States and abroad. Membership includes access to networking opportunities, education and training, and a newsletter filled with up-to-date information on fraud investigations.

Insurance Overview

Insurance is a contract between the insured, who agrees to pay for services, and the insurer, who agrees to provide monetary reimbursement for certain losses that may be incurred by the insured. There are two very wide categories of insurance: government insurance and private insurance, each divided into industries. Government insurance can be divided into compulsory and voluntary, while private insurance is usually divided into four sectors: casualty, fire, life, and marine.

Government Compulsory Insurance can be:
- Unemployment benefits
- Social Security benefits
- Workers' compensation in many states

Government Voluntary Insurance examples:
- Savings and loans and bank depositor insurance
- Federal crop insurance
- Military personnel insurance
- Flood insurance

Private insurance is voluntary, except for the compulsory (basic collision) automobile insurance required on all drivers in most states. There are many types of private insurance, but some of the basic types are listed below.

Basic Types of Private Insurance
- Life
- Home
- Rental
- Automobile
- Health and medical
- Specialty insurance

It's important to be familiar with appropriate terms in order to work in the insurance industry. Knowing something of the most used terms will also help you when interviewing for a position investigating insurance fraud. Several Web sites offer glossaries of terms related to the industry. Some are:

- **AM Best:** *www.ambest.com/resource/glossary.html*
- **Glossarist:** *www.glossarist.com/glossaries/economy-finance/ insurance.asp*
- **Insurance Information Institute:** *www.iii.org/media/glossary*
- **Hanover Insurance Group:** *www.hanover.com/thg/tools/glossary .htm*
- **Trafalgar International LTD:** *www.trafalgar-intl.com/definitions.htm*

Personal Injury Investigations

Personal injury cases take a toll on both businesses and individuals. Legitimate injuries caused by the negligence of businesses are needless tragedies, and businesses should recompense the injured adequately. Sometimes, however, unscrupulous persons construct fake accidents and sue businesses, hoping for settlements out of court. If they can manage this, there's usually no great spotlight on the details of the accident and injury. Furthermore, many companies find it less time consuming and much less expensive to pay someone who's threatening a lawsuit than to go to court.

The Slip and Fall Artist

The fact that companies make payoffs with very little investigation into the alleged injury is unfortunate because it can encourage someone with a larcenous bent to try for her piece of the personal injury pie. One notorious type is the slip and fall artist. This person creates the pretense of falling and being injured due to negligence on behalf of a business.

For example, Mr. Slip may enter a grocery store, wait until no one is watching, break a bottle from the store's shelf, and then pretend to slip on the bottle's contents. These people have also been known to bring their own water, oil, or similar liquid, pour it onto the floor of a business, and pretend to fall in it. Unless there are witnesses, it's extremely difficult to prove this con, but stores with adequate camera systems have caught this on tape.

FACT

Most stores and businesses don't have anything near an adequate camera system. The professional slip and fall artist knows how to scope out the system, finding holes within which she can operate. This is why the visible camera system by itself is inadequate. Adding hidden cameras would cover the business and catch the artist operating where she feels unobserved.

Investigators may be hired to film the claimant's daily activity in hopes of proving the con. Also, many investigators specialize in installing hidden camera systems, a lucrative specialty whose need grows with the rise in certain types of crimes such as the slip and fall and shoplifting. Cameras are also installed to guard against employee theft and to determine whether further training is needed.

◀ Installing cameras may help business protect themselves against false lawsuits.

Medical Fraud

Doctors and other medical service providers are in a position, should they choose, to defraud insurance companies. While most do not, a large and growing number of medical professionals have chosen to make a side business of padding patients' bills. Even otherwise legitimate doctors have been known to do this occasionally in order to meet payroll or cover losses.

Most patients never scrutinize medical bills unless they're ridiculously long or more expensive than expected. Even when patients do study their bills, they're almost impossible to fully understand unless you work in the field. Medical criminals know this and count on it. Some medical service providers have learned to spread their fraudulent charges over a wide range of patients and dates. These professionals have also been known to charge for visits and services for patients who were never seen, keeping the patient from looking too closely into the transaction by having any refund sent to him. Because the patient benefits, many who realize what's going on just let it go. In this way, they're silent accomplices to fraud because they allow it to continue. Because of all these things, it's not unusual for patients to pay fraudulent medical claims for years before the deceit is discovered.

Other physicians insist that a personal injury claim be filed after an accident, even when the patient is uninjured. Another problem is that of suspect attorneys claiming that a client was injured on someone's property, when no one but witnesses she produces can verify the facts of the injury. These attorneys and cohorts have been known to deliberately stage accidents, destroy property, and fake injuries.

FACT

One of the worst problems in this area is accident-chasing attorneys. Since attorneys who appear at accident scenes have long been charged with the unflattering title of ambulance chasers, many use different tactics. One is to send cappers or runners to scenes in the guise of caring witnesses. Cappers direct injured parties to their bosses, unscrupulous doctors and/or attorneys.

Then there are the organized criminal enterprises that engage in fraudulent billing of insurance companies. Called mills, these enterprises bilk insurance companies, and by extension consumers, on a grand scale. Some of the most common mills are:

- Those who routinely inflate bills
- Those who double dip by overcharging and double charging
- Those whose operation is phony from the doctor on down, and sometimes the attorney as well

Everyone pays for this crime. Entire clinics have been set up for the purpose of filing false claims. Patients with similar criminal inclinations are often paid to participate. When you know of fraudulent medical claims being filed, report it. Otherwise, that nice, new building that won't take your insurance may take cash from someone desperate for medical treatment, then provide him fraudulent services. Most places won't do this because it ratchets them up into the far more serious crime of treating patients without a license. Yet some have gone so far as to do this, and when the heat gets to be too much, they pack up and move to another location.

The PI will often go undercover as a patient or even employee of these physicians. In this way, she can obtain firsthand information to which she can testify. Surveillance of patients is also an option. Sometimes they can be convinced to testify against the physician or his billing staff in return for immunity from prosecution. This is a tricky situation, however, and must be handled carefully.

Corporate Fraud

Corporate fraud covers a large range of investigative services, some of which will be mentioned here.

Product Liability and Wrongful Injury

This type of investigation places you, the investigator, on one side of a claim against the manufacturer and (usually) the seller of an alleged defective product. Investigators who do this work are normally former police detectives or federal special agents who've been highly trained in the special points of making a case of this type.

Accident Investigation

Accident investigation is highly specialized, and it is usually performed by PIs who are former law enforcement officials. However, this doesn't mean that you can't intern with one of these people or that an insurance company won't hire you to do so. Do your homework about this and be prepared to show yourself an excellent candidate for further training.

The Occupational Safety and Health Administration (OSHA) cautions anyone against investigating accidents without proper training. This Web site explains OSHA's position on business accident investigation and prevention: *www.osha.gov/SLTC/etools/safetyhealth/mod4_factsheets_accin vest.html*. Many businesses employ in-house investigators for this important work, but they also may use a contract investigator from time to time.

Northwestern University (*nucps.northwestern.edu/division/ai.asp*) offers an interesting accident investigation program online. It comes complete with a traffic accident reconstruction kit, and the site offers numerous links to resources for investigators of accidents. Northwestern's School of Continuing Studies offers several books and DVDs concerning this topic as well.

In accident investigation, the PI learns to use software and hardware to calculate speed and distance traveled before an auto accident. He will learn to determine at what point a driver applied that brakes—or if they were applied—by measuring any available skid marks on the road at an accident scene. Many other skills are necessary to adequately determine fault in a vehicle accident. This is not limited to vehicular accidents, but a PI will be hired to investigate these most often.

- Princeton University offers an overview of accident investigation procedure at *web.princeton.edu/sites/ehs/healthsafetyguide/A2.htm.*
- The Workplace Safety Store offers CD-ROM training programs, plus books and manuals at *safety.1800inet.com*
- Accident Investigation Training Manual, *www.amazon.com/Accident-Investigation-Training-Manual-Arnold/dp/1401869394*
- Thomas Investigative Publications, *www.pimall.com/nais/bkp.menu .html*, advertises the largest selection of books for the PI available, accident reconstruction among them

Workers' Compensation

Insurance investigation covers a large area, and these investigations are so specialized that some firms do nothing but insurance investigation. Many large insurance companies employ their own investigators, but most firms occasionally contract PI firms who specialize in this work. Smaller firms may contract all their investigations. Many states have annual conferences where PI firms can set up display booths advertising their capabilities, equipment, and personnel.

Businesses Need Investigators

According to the National Insurance Crime Bureau, an organization dedicated to investigating insurance fraud, workers' compensation fraud results in more than $5 billion in losses to the insurance industry each year. Furthermore, according to Columbus, Ohio's Bureau of Workers' Compensation Fraud Division, as of April 2007, 5–15 percent of all cases involve some element of fraud.

Businesses are required by government regulation to carry workers' compensation insurance. This insurance compensates employees who have sustained on-the-job diseases or injuries with partial wage replacement and full payment of medical and rehabilitation expenses. These are delicate investigations. The employer has an obligation to care for any employee whose injuries result from his employment. Because of this, the employer must treat the claimant as a valued employee unless this is proven otherwise. Disabled or injured workers deserve compensation. Yet when suspicion is raised, owners must investigate for the sake of the company's fiscal health. Some have such a serious problem with fraud that they spot check all claimants.

ALERT!

If you specialize in workers' compensation, you work for the insurance company. However, never allow yourself to be pressured into looking for an outcome that favors your client. Remain objective in order to be fair to the claimant as well as the employer. Report the facts, no matter what they are and whom they favor.

Workers' compensation investigations are extremely specialized. The investigator must be familiar with techniques and possess equipment specific to the solving of these cases. The PI must also be familiar with appropriate laws and statutes. For more information, see this site for workers' compensation law by individual state: *www.workerscompensation insurance.com*. Also see *www.ambest.com* for information on insurance companies—your potential clients. Chapter 17 contains information about necessary equipment.

Workers who have been injured as a result of something or someone in their workplace deserve compensation and help returning to work. If they cannot return, they deserve a percentage of their salary in order to survive. Unfortunately, there are cases where employees have faked an injury or overstated the extent of an injury. Some workers have had legitimate injuries, but haven't admitted that the injury has healed enough to return to work.

In some cases, a worker is injured away from the job but pretends it happened at work so he can make a claim against his employer's worker's compensation insurance. Many times, this is done because the employee has little or no insurance. Other times, he merely uses this injury as an excuse to stay off of work for a while—and sometimes he decides he likes it, and drags it out. In other, even more egregious cases, workers have been known to stage fraudulent injuries in order to acquire workers' compensation. Some people do this out of laziness, boredom with a job, revenge against a supervisor or employer, or a need for money.

The most extreme false claimant is the one who intentionally injures herself for the purpose of collecting workers' compensation. This is understandably difficult to prove, even when it is suspected by everyone involved, including physicians. Insurance companies don't relish charging someone with such an act, and jurors don't like watching the big business or insurance company accuse the little guy of doing herself harm for money, especially when she appears to be in pain or disabled. Therefore, companies don't often charge the claimant with this. Instead, they use private investigators to keep the person under periodic activity checks or even full-time surveillance. If enough evidence is acquired to show intentional fraud, they'll charge the claimant. Worker's compensation investigations are almost entirely performed by PIs. It can be a lucrative business for the investigator who learns to do this well.

Accepting compensation under false pretenses is stealing. Not only does this behavior take funds that could be spent on people who are really injured or incapacitated, it costs employers the expense of investigators, insurance, surveillance systems, and more—a bad situation for the employer, but an opportunity for the PI to help.

In order to qualify for an on-the-job injury, it isn't necessary that the injury occur inside the workplace or on the employer's premises. When a position requires an employee to spend some or all of his time away from the workplace, workers' compensation insurance coverage applies. However, should the employee stray from a defined route for personal reasons, coverage is nullified.

Investigative Options

When workers' comp fraud is suspected, several options are available for determining whether fraud is being committed or not. Some of these options are:

- **Records check.** It's doubtful that a claimant will work where she'll be required to pay taxes, but you might find that she has applied for a loan using her under-the-table workplace or has used that address for some other reason, such as to receive packages.
- **Activity check.** Usually a short surveillance, a day or two, of the claimant's activities. If suspicious behavior is discovered, a longer surveillance is usually authorized. Sometimes activity checks are ordered when claimants attend doctor's visits, and investigators film activity before and after the visit.
- **Extended surveillance.** Usually ordered as a result of something suspicious uncovered during an activity check and used to determine if it's a pattern of behavior or a one-time act.
- **Hidden camera surveillance.** When a claimant has very little outside activity, hidden cameras are an answer and can be set up for filming activity when it occurs; otherwise, an investigator might need to sit for days and even weeks before this person exits the residence.

PIs new to the profession are often appalled at the behavior of some claimants, but they quickly become numb to the infractions they see. For example, Mr. Smith claims to have a back injury so painful he can't lift anything, but he is seen digging up a tree with a large root ball and carrying it on his shoulder to a distant pile of trees that he's already dug up.

◄ Private investigators who specialize in workers' compensation investigations will often be asked to provide photographic or video evidence.

PIs sometimes become impatient to get something on the claimant. They've been known to stoop to such acts as letting the air out of tires or even puncturing a tire to see if the claimant will attempt to change it. This type of thing is beneath the professional and should never be done. To test someone who claims her injuries are so severe that she cannot bend over or bend down, place coins or a cheap billfold by the claimant's car door or mailbox or some area she frequents. If she bends down or bends over to get the bait, the PI is there to film it. This only works once, however. Several uses of this type must be repeated in order to prove that this isn't a onetime activity.

Inexperienced investigators don't realize that the claimant's defense will be that he did indeed bend, was incapacitated by doing so, and couldn't get out of bed for some time after. This is why it's so important to film the claimant for several days to a week after an incident such as this—or any incident when he's caught doing something he claims is impossible for him to do.

While some claims handlers encourage the coin/wallet trick, these types of things aren't always perceived as playing fair with the claimant. Many companies prohibit them, seeing these strategies as tricks that set the claimant up to do something she wouldn't do on her own. This argument alone is reason enough for refraining from this activity, because jurors might be convinced to see the situation in the same way. Therefore, the modern PI must consider all ramifications of an action before he takes it. He must look down the road to the end—the courtroom—and be sure that his techniques will not hinder his case should it go to trial.

ALERT!

An entire book can be written on workers' compensation investigations. In fact, a lot have been, but be careful who you read and emulate, as some investigators cross the line of ethics and propriety. Stay on the side of law and fair play, reporting facts as you find them.

Theft of Time, Product, or Services

Though this subject concerns the use of hidden cameras, it belongs in the business services section more than in the covert camera section. The theft of time, products, and services accounts for huge losses for businesses. The Association of National Fraud Examiners reported in 2004 that 6 percent of U.S. businesses' annual revenue is lost because of fraud. This translates to a loss of $660 billion per year when applied to the gross national product. In light of these numbers, businesses must protect themselves.

How Businesses Protect Themselves

Because of the tremendous loss of revenue, businesses are forced to protect assets. One way to do this is the installation of covert cameras. Some owners never inform their employees of the existence of these cameras. If that's her choice, she's within her rights to record video if she doesn't record audio with it.

Some owners choose to inform employees that there may be cameras watching and listening to them at any time. In this case, it's best to have the employee sign a release confirming that he's been informed of possible surveillance (using "possible" surveillance gives an owner the option of leasing cameras periodically rather than purchasing them).

By disclosing the existence of her cameras, the employer can record audio. Because the cameras are hidden—sometimes remarkably so—the employee will never be sure if he's being monitored, nor will he know the location of monitoring devices. With this strategy, one purpose for installing covert cameras can still be achieved—the employee will refrain from theft of products or services, or his theft will be disclosed. This should also increase employee productivity and quality of client or customer service.

By informing clients that they may be monitored and having them sign that they've been informed, all three problems that plague businesses most—theft of time, products, and services—can be addressed, along with the added bonus of improved customer service.

In regard to telephone monitoring, should the employer want to monitor every employee's interaction with customers as a matter of policy and for training, federal law allows her to do so. Yet, the moment the conversation changes from business to personal, monitoring must stop. This is a gray area, because business owners who monitor don't do so themselves, and automated systems cannot determine which part of a conversation is about business and which is personal. However, rulings have been made that if the owner informs the employee that monitoring will occur, or is a possibility, the recording is legal.

CHAPTER 16

Special Investigations and Investigators

Many areas related to private investigation are becoming growth industries. Some of these may not be considered private investigation to the public, but they fall under the broad heading of PI work. Several of the most popular specialties will be discussed in this chapter, but there are many more.

Background/Pre-Employment Searches

The business of providing pre-employment and background checks to businesses and the public alike is growing by leaps and bounds. Aside from cost, the most important aspect of a background/pre-employment check is accuracy and completeness. Almost anyone can apply to online systems that claim to supply full background and criminal history reports. However, there are problems with many of these. One of the weightiest is their limited access to complete records that are updated often.

Background/Pre-Employment Search Clients

If you are going to run background/pre-employment searches, it's helpful to know who purchases them.

1. An insurance company may purchase background information on someone to be sure she isn't a serial complainant and that she isn't double-dipping or receiving compensation from other departments.
2. Attorneys purchase background checks on behalf of their clients, but they may also purchase background checks on their own clients, especially those involved in divorce, personal injury, lawsuit, child custody, and criminal or civil cases.
3. Business owners purchase pre-employment checks before hiring employees.
4. Individuals often want to check backgrounds for personal reasons, most commonly for information about those they're dating, their fiancés, birth parents, siblings, or children, or for locating an old friend or high school sweetheart.

Sometimes information checks are ordered to search for new information and to verify information already in the client's possession, such as that provided on job applications.

Consent

Of course, employers and investigators who perform background checks must notify the applicant of their intent to run the check and must obtain a signed consent to do so as recommended by the Fair Credit Reporting Act (FCRA). In fact, higher-level information services require that you state the reason for running at least some parts of the background. You can run subject info such as alias, social security number verifier, addresses and phone numbers, court and business records, licenses other than driver's license, and surrounding neighborhood facilities, all without stating your purpose. The moment you request driver's license information—license, licensed drivers at residence, and vehicles registered at address—you must name your reason.

When you inquire into criminal records, sex offender records, warrants, arrests (provided by some service providers, but not all), you'll be asked to indicate your purpose from this list:

- To protect against or prevent actual or potential fraud, unauthorized transactions, claims or other liability
- For required institutional risk control or resolving consuming disputes or inquiries
- Due to holding a legal beneficial interest relating to the subject
- To effect, administer, or enforce a transaction to underwrite insurance at the consumer's request, for reinsurance purposes, or for (relating to consumer's insurance) reporting, investigating, fraud prevention, premium payment processing, benefit administration, or research projects

A consent, or release form, is standard in most companies, but if you perform searches for employers you must obtain a copy of the consent as well. Also, the consent must be worded to include permission for you to perform the search. If it doesn't include you by name, it should indicate permission for an agent of the company to do the background check.

Choosing an Information Database

The untold truth is that there are only a few fully functional systems that can really deliver what they promise, and not just anyone can become certified to use them. Passing their rigorous requirements takes time, effort, and specific qualifications—time and effort that many are unwilling or unable to expend and qualifications most don't possess. Another not-so-widely-known fact is that not only do these inferior systems lack up-to-date information, the scope of their information may not be sufficient to do proper due diligence on perspective employees.

QUESTION?

What is due diligence?
It means that an employer does everything reasonably possible to verify an applicant's true history and identity. The courts have ruled that this is essential to providing workplace safety for employees and security for clients or customers. Read more about this and negligence at: *www.safer securityinc.com/professional11.html.*

Due Diligence

Due diligence has been defined, according to the National Institute for Occupational Safety and Health (NIOSH), as having the following elements:

- Background/pre-employment checks
- Verification of references, work history, and degrees
- Periodic criminal history rechecks
- Drug testing in some positions
- Adequate employee training, observation, and management— including resolving complaints by employees against other employees in a timely and reasonable manner

One of the most important reasons that some brokers can't provide information which fulfills the due diligence requirement is that, in many states, information is not entirely accessible online because it hasn't been entered into an online database. While a system may provide certain information to its customers, there's much more that's just not available to the system, which therefore, cannot be provided to the consumer.

Because of this, the few reliable systems hire private investigators around the country to gather any information that is not yet automated. The more reliable PIs employ the best of these systems—not just one, but two or more—in an effort to ensure accuracy and completeness of reports. Keep in mind that these types of reports are returned only to licensed PIs.

Most importantly, the reason experienced investigators return the most accurate information reports is that they have the ability to decipher these reports. They can spot trouble areas and inconsistencies that can otherwise be easily missed, as well as information that's conspicuously absent, deceptive, or altered. An operator sitting in a cubicle for the purpose of running an online check cannot do this for you.

The National Crime Information Center

Be aware that no database or information system is infallible. Even the federal law enforcement database, the National Crime Information Center (NCIC), is subject to errors. One problem is that of agency reporting. Agencies from all fifty states report to NCIC—but do they report crime accurately? Certainly many do, but mistakes can be made. Do they report using the same or similar system? The answer is no. Furthermore, do all of them report? That answer is also no—some smaller departments don't report their crime statistics at all, and others don't report consistently. NCIC is also subject, as is every database, to human entry errors.

FACT

Private investigators aren't allowed direct access to NCIC, and acquiring this information from police officers or other law enforcement employees has long been illegal. Because of abuse in recent years (individuals paying law enforcement to run NCIC on citizens), those committing this crime have been searched out and even prosecuted.

This doesn't mean that NCIC isn't reliable; it's a great system that's been a boon to law enforcement since its inception. It isn't infallible, but it has been instrumental in putting many criminals in prison. Most importantly, the system undergoes continual improvements and additions. Its highest mandate is to ensure that, as far as is possible, NCIC information is accurate. At any rate, without it, information sharing between police departments would return to the dark ages. For more information, see these sites:

- NCIC—Criminal Justice Information System's overview of NCIC, how it works and its benefits, *www.fbi.gov/hq/cjisd/ncic_brochure.htm*
- FBI, *www.fas.org/irp/agency/doj/fbi/is/ncic.htm*
- Partners NCIC FAQs, *www.ice.gov/partners/faqs.htm*

Database Services

The best database services receive most of their information from state and federal records, not from middlemen. Receiving information from databases whose information has come from other databases increases the possibility of human input error. The better services also update records every few days; some do it daily. Information from middlemen services can't promise the same.

Purchasing an errors and omissions insurance policy is important to those who provide background and pre-employment searches. Though rare, even when using a capable information database, errors over which you have no control can occur. Don't risk losing everything because of failure to buy this insurance.

In light of these things, it's easier to understand how systems that are hooked into fewer national law enforcement databases and connected more distantly than the NCIC are also fallible. This means that even the best service provider is subject to errors now and then. When running reports for your clients, you should counsel them about this possibility in order to present a realistic picture of the information business. While it may be rare that the information returned from your service provider contains errors or omissions, your client should be prepared for this possibility. Otherwise, if it happens, he can feel that you've been negligent—or worse, that you've been intentionally deceitful.

Tracers Information Specialists

Founded in 1996, Tracers' user-friendly system (tracersinfo.com) is enhanced by excellent customer support (from real people!)—reports aren't difficult to run and are returned quickly. Their searches aid businesses and individuals in the following areas:

- Law enforcement
- Insurance investigations
- Risk management
- Legal research
- Vendor certification
- Due diligence
- Loss prevention
- Asset identification
- Fraud protection
- Skip tracing
- Identity verification

Tracers has access to, and provides integration of, billions of records on individuals and businesses, including criminal history, civil court records, sex offender registries, state drivers license bureaus, people searches, and more. Upon being approved to access Tracers' databases, you're assigned a representative to train you and ensure that you get the most out of the system. Visit *www.tracersinfo.com* for more information.

IRBsearch

IRBsearch (*www.irbsearch.com*) also provides training once you've been approved to use the system. It provides online seminars to which you may return to refresh your skills, and you can also take advantage of seminars and conferences in your area. IRBsearch has been a reliable system used by many PIs for years. IRB also publishes a newsletter with tips for members.

Alternatives

Don't despair if you're unable to obtain approval with one of these information service providers; others can be utilized. Just be sure to consult a PI organization, or perhaps a PI magazine, before you use a service. Consider also that if you don't want to expend the time and money involved in gaining approval for membership with information service providers, nor do you want to learn operational details of the program and various methods of running searches, you can hire them out to another investigator or agency that specializes in backgrounds.

This is actually a good idea for many PIs because searches may not be needed regularly enough to justify membership with an information service provider. You also need to consider the time it takes to run searches, evaluate them, type reports (you may need to hire someone to do this if you're investigating cases), and get them to clients. It may be more time and cost effective to have an agency do this for you.

ALERT!

If membership in an information service provider isn't cost or time effective for your business, contact SaferSecurity, Inc. (*www.safersecurityinc .com*) or another investigative service that is able to access the better, more reliable databases and provide reports—in your name and for your clients—with accurate interpretation and a professional presentation.

Check services and prices to find the one that best appeals to your needs and budget. Although there are many other services, the two discussed in this chapter are the most commonly used suppliers of quality information and are used by many PIs.

The Internet and Background Checks

Employers and investigators alike have added a strategy to the traditional background check. They are searching Google and Yahoo, as well as social networking sites such as MySpace, YouTube, and Facebook. In a recent Society for Human Resource Management survey, 15 percent of human resource professionals admitted that they routinely check social networking sites, and one in five of these professionals reported disqualifying candidates because of what was viewed on a Web site.

What many searchers find on these sites is, in many cases, disturbing and revealing. Very often, the clean-cut professional appears on his site as someone else entirely. Revealing pictures and the discussion of controversial subjects can damage job applicants. When something is posted on the Internet, the poster loses all control of it. Even years down the road, she won't know who has possession of it. For the PI performing a background search, checking these sites can throw light on a different aspect of the applicant.

Negligent Hiring and Negligent Retention

Background and pre-employment checks are important for many reasons, but they are extremely important because fraud and identity theft are relatively common today. Although an employer may be duped by a slick communicator with an even slicker resume, she can still be held accountable for the failure to authenticate the identity of her employee. She can be charged with what is usually called negligent hiring and negligent retention.

In other words, it can be charged that she negligently hired an employee if she didn't perform the due diligence required to authenticate that he was, in reality, who he represented himself to be. Furthermore, she can be deemed negligent if she kept this person on the job without performing any periodic checks that would have revealed he was bogus. If he commits an act of violence, she's guilty of negligence. According to the courts, she's been negligent toward the safety of her employees and the public, especially if the applicant has a history of violence or criminal record or any kind.

You may say that this isn't fair. It's not the employer who's done anything wrong. Yet in the eyes of the law, she has. The standards that exist to prove negligence are:

- Whether a remedy (background check) is known to be a remedy
- Whether a remedy is available (background checks are widely available)

- Whether she knew of the remedy and its availability (business owners are assumed to know)
- Whether she made any effort to apply the remedy (did she commission a background/pre-employment check on this individual?)
- Whether she's used this remedy on other applicants in the past

This employer can be charged with negligent hiring and retention. Negligent hiring theory is the basis on which claims such as this are brought. This theory argues that it doesn't matter that the employer didn't know of the applicant's past violent history; what matters is that she could have known because it was easily discoverable through a background check. It also maintains that she should have known. She should have expended the time and effort to use available resources to uncover his history.

Background/pre-employment checks uncover those who lie about their backgrounds and qualifications and those with criminal histories or other problems. Too many people think that a good background result indicates that an employee can be trusted. That's taking the power of the database search way too far. It's important to realize that just because someone passes a background check with flying colors, doesn't mean they haven't committed crimes in the past and just weren't caught. Nor does it mean they won't commit a crime in the future. Encourage your clients to be vigilant in supervising employees, even when the background check has revealed no past problems.

Perform background checks on anyone with access to your home and family. This includes housekeepers, nannies, maintenance workers, landscapers, and anyone who will work on the house, such as painters or contractors. Be sure that any company you hire for work such as carpet cleaning or appliance repair has supplied bonded employees. Again, being bonded or passing a background check doesn't place a halo around the employee's head, so don't be presumptuous about the level of anyone's trustworthiness. For comprehensive background/pre-employment checks (and other services) see: *www.safersecurityinc.com.*

Mystery Shopping

Few investigators offer mystery shopping as an area of expertise. A mystery shopper is someone who enters a store or business, makes a purchase, and later reports on customer service.

Cameras and Mystery Shopping

Businesses have been using mystery shoppers for years. Business owners rely on these shoppers' subjective opinions about what went down during the purchase. Most of the time, no issues arise, especially if the owner is interested in whether his employees are adhering to policies and procedures or whether retraining is needed.

Yet if something else is discovered, it results in a he said/she said situation. All the owner has is the shopper's word for what happened, and he could be faced with denial or a semi-plausible explanation from the employee. This puts him in the position of having to investigate further, costing time and money he cannot spare—and perhaps leaving an incompetent or unscrupulous employee on the job.

The answer to this is hidden camera mystery shopping—best performed by a private investigator. The investigator wears or carries a small covert camera. These cameras can be purchased already installed in hats, ties, buttons, watches, pens, briefcases, purses, and other objects. The price isn't inexpensive, but neither is it prohibitive, and the purchase pays for itself many times over if the service is marketed correctly and aggressively.

Many businesses, especially chains and franchises, use products and services that come from their corporate division, including mystery shoppers. The manager may not be interested in using someone outside of the network. However, if she's having trouble with employees or unexplained loss, she may jump at the chance to discover what goes on when she isn't on the premises.

You as Hidden Camera Mystery Shopper

If you've ever gone through a drive-thru and felt like pulling your hair out because of the employee's bored or hostile attitude, or stood at a counter as a clerk talked on the phone or interacted with another employee while you waited for help or the opportunity to make a purchase, you have a starting point for your business.

Return later with your camera and film. Ask questions. Attempt to get the employee to help you. Don't show the recording to the employee or even the mid-level manager, attempt an appointment with a regional manager or owner before revealing the evidence. Success with this may bring more work, as well as referrals to other business owners. Remember that some owners aren't happy with anyone who films in their establishment, though, so be careful to record only the employee's activity and not anything that could be considered proprietary.

QUESTION?

How can I advertise this service?
Arrange to speak to business clubs and organizations. Use a small monitor or television to demonstrate the camera. It's also effective to show (with owner approval) film of employee behavior in the presence of the owner/manager, then her behavior in his absence. Stress how film can reveal those in need of more training, more direct supervision, or pink slips—all without controversy because the proof is on the film.

Should you decide to invest in this specialty as part of your business, buy your camera system and practice wearing it if it's wearable. Practice using it correctly if it's in the form of a pen, purse, or carried object. It's important to get a feel for which direction your camera will point and how much of the area it will record. You also need to become comfortable using it so you don't end up with ceiling, floor, or wall footage—and so you don't move unnaturally and alert the employee to your intentions.

Sometimes, success in this area can lead to orders for hidden camera installation in the businesses you service. This won't cut into your mystery shopping much; installed cameras will catch everyday behavior, but you can market your services as a means of testing employees' reactions to specific requests for services.

For example, an employee may have been trained to respond to requests for an out-of-stock item with, "Let me check the availability of ordering that for you." If he answers with a bored or disinterested, "I don't know, it should be over there," or, "We're out of that," the employer can make a decision whether to invest in retraining or let him go. In the long run, you'll save the owner time and money; if she decides to terminate employment, you'll save her controversy over the circumstances that led to this decision because it's all on tape.

Cyber Sleuths

There's a new kind of investigator in the house—an investigator for the information and computer age—called the cyber sleuth. The cyber sleuth is trained to examine computer bytes the way G-men were trained in fingerprints. These investigators are dedicated to and effective in Internet crime fighting.

Computers and the Internet have opened the world and all it has to offer to anyone with an Internet connection, but this technology is a double-edged sword. It has made education available to those with no time or opportunity to attend regular classes, and it has given friends and family on different continents the ability to keep in touch. However, the other side of this situation is that the Internet is an ungoverned no-man's land where criminals search for—and find—opportunities to hurt others for their own gain. Crimes are showcased on YouTube, Black Planet, MySpace, Facebook, and other social information sites. Pedophiles roam the Net looking to lure children into their traps. Gangs use the Internet to send messages, advertise criminal exploits, and plan for future crimes. Con artists send offers of jackpot winnings and false investment opportunities around the planet, and terrorists use the Web to further their plans.

The answer to this, at least for now, is the cyber sleuth. Social information sites are difficult to police. Besides child pornography and pedophiles, cyber sleuths investigate insider traders, hackers, violent criminals, and terrorists.

One example of cyber detecting is the case of Thomas Murray, a Kansas State University professor charged with murdering his wife. Cyber sleuths confiscated his computer hard drive and analyzed it. When they discovered search terms such as "killing quietly and quickly," and "murder for hire," Murray tried to argue that he had been researching script concepts. The jury didn't buy it, however, and sentenced him to life in prison.

Although the FBI's cyber unit is way ahead of most players in cyber crime fighting, a nonprofit organization is ahead of the FBI. The National Cyber-Forensics and Training Alliance (NCFTA) has access to funds and equipment not even the FBI has. NCFTA is an extension of the Pittsburgh High Tech Crimes Task Force, composed of federal, state, and local law enforcement. Microsoft is a closely involved partner, donating funds and lending an analyst to the group. These investigators have the most technololgically advanced equipment on the planet, and are always looking for better equipment and more effective techniques. Private and law enforcement cyber-sleuths alike are always ready to help with cases. This is why they exist—to share their specialized skills and knowledge. PIs need to form networking relationships with these investigators.

ALERT!

Computer forensics is a fairly young discipline. It's in the state of technology that DNA was ten years ago, but it is growing fast. If you are proficient with the computer, you may want to look into further training in computer forensics. The FBI has listed cyber crime as a top priority—third in line behind terrorism and counterintelligence—so the need is strong.

Cyber sleuths are working hard to stem the rising tide of Internet crime. The problem lies in the fact that cyber laws are weak. If you are interested in monitoring online activity, you may want to take a look at the Urban Dictionary, *www.urbandictionary.com*, a compilation of words and phrases used by those who frequent the Internet. Knowing the meaning of this cyber speak, a kind of Internet code, is important in understanding what's being messaged back and forth between people. These phrases are fluid and changing, but the Urban Dictionary attempts to change with them, keeping up with the most recent language used online.

Collections and Repossessions

Collections work isn't the most popular specialty in the field of private investigation. It is also not the most enjoyable, and it can even be dangerous. Those who do this usually work with collection agencies or attorneys. For a fee or, less often, a percentage of the amount she collects, the PI searches for people who have skipped out on loans and owe money or leave bad checks in their wake.

Working these cases might involve locating the person who is in possession of the item you are to repossess or who owes the money you're paid to collect. Collecting money from someone who insists he doesn't have it is difficult, but if the investigator can locate the subject and follow him to his workplace, the creditor may obtain permission to dock his salary. This is done extensively in delinquent child support cases. If the subject has no job, he's subject to time in jail.

◀ Private investigators who specialize in repossessions are often asked to repossess vehicles.

Not every person who's in default runs away. Some can be located in the phone book or with information provided by the creditor. However, even these people may not answer telephones or open their door to you, so many investigators develop a ruse to get the target to the door. Realize that you cannot threaten, bully, or force anyone into paying debts. Since you'll probably be paid only if the debtor pays, this is a tough business.

However, nothing's tougher than repossessions. Most items such as vehicles, watercraft, and aircraft are repossessed at night, hopefully while the debtor sleeps. This exposes the investigator to danger, not only from the debtor, but from neighbors and even police until they can be made aware of your legal repossess order. While vehicles are most often subject to repossession, you may be commissioned to repossess stereo systems, appliances, and even furniture. These items are more difficult to take. Those who repossess often describe their work as stealing for a living.

Bounty Hunters

The bounty hunter's work has been highlighted on reality TV in shows that follow bounty hunters locating and arresting their skips. Viewers have demonstrated an interest in this fringe sector of the court system. While it is not an official arm of the court system, bail enforcement agents serve a purpose within the system, tracking down and bringing to justice those who try to evade responsibility for the crimes they have committed.

They usually work with bail bonds offices, locating people who have run out on their bond (sometimes called bail jumpers), then returning them for reprocessing in court. If the target isn't located, the bail bondsman loses the bond money she put up for the client.

This can be a dangerous job. Bounty hunters report being shot at, shot, knifed, and beaten, but it's not always violent. As the bounty hunter improves, he learns tricks that prevent these injuries. Remember that he, with very few exceptions, never had the opportunity to train in a police academy, so he must learn on the job or from a mentor. Schools advertise programs for becoming a bounty hunter, but most people don't find this necessary.

Bounty hunters aren't restricted in the same way as law enforcement officers. In fact, they can go anywhere and pursue any type of criminals, from embezzlers and con artists to bank robbers, kidnappers, and murderers. They aren't restricted by the necessity of obtaining a search warrant. A bounty hunter can go inside his target's workplace or residence, arrest her, and search her property without reading the target her rights.

The contract between the bail bondsman office and the client usually specifies that if the client defaults and doesn't meet his court date, the bondsman is legally allowed to find him and return him to court using any means necessary. Hunters don't need warrants because their target has signed away his rights to protection from entry and searches in exchange for bail money.

FACT

A bounty hunter isn't above the law. While her privilege is broad in that she can use any means necessary to apprehend, it's also narrow in that it extends only to a particular jumper and only during the time period that the jumper runs from his court date. Anyone else—at least, anyone without a bounty on his head—is safe from the bounty hunter's entry, searches, and arrest.

Bounty hunting isn't legal in all states, so check your state laws before beginning work in this area.

CHAPTER 17

Investigative Equipment

The private investigator is in the business of gathering and selling information. In order to do this, she relies on specific tools that are designed to uncover particular evidence. Using a computer—preferably a laptop that you can take with you on surveillance—is a given, but some of the other investigative equipment might not be so obvious. This chapter will concentrate on audio and video equipment necessary to the PI's goal of acquiring information.

Video Equipment

Video equipment is perhaps the most important of all the tools in the investigator's bag. Nothing convinces more than video. It trumps eyewitness testimony, audio recordings, and any other type of evidence as far as believability and reliability.

Electronic surveillance laws vary from state to state. On the National Conference of State Legislators Web site, *www.ncsl.org/programs/lis/CIP/surveillance.htm,* you'll find a chart of all surveillance laws by state, with links to each. It's critical to be aware of surveillance law before unwittingly doing something that's not permitted in a particular state. See Chapter 18 for more information on surveillance and Chapter 12 for information about audio and video laws.

Surveillance Camcorder

Camcorders are available in all types and sizes, and they come with many different features. New camcorders are remarkably small and easily concealed. You can pay several hundred dollars for a camera that's adequate or several thousand for an excellent camcorder. Remember that changes and updates in the technology of video surveillance equipment occur almost before you can get your product home! If you don't have a good bit of discretionary income, don't buy the top of the line and expect to keep it forever. In a few months, you may want to purchase something better. Yet you mustn't buy the cheapest product possible or you'll definitely have to replace it, whether you want to or not.

There are certain things you want in your camcorder. They may not all be possible if your budget is small, but these features will give you an idea of what's important to the work of a PI:

- **Image stabilization.** This is very important in helping keep your video steady.
- **Time/date stamp.** This is essential for film that you want to enter into evidence.
- **Zoom lens.** Some cameras have 35X–45X optical zoom—the longer the better because you won't need to get as close to your target.

- **Night vision feature.** This is a low lux feature that allows you to film at night.
- **Auto focus.** With auto focus, you can concentrate on the target instead of the camera focus; it also enables you to shoot quickly without needing to make any changes.

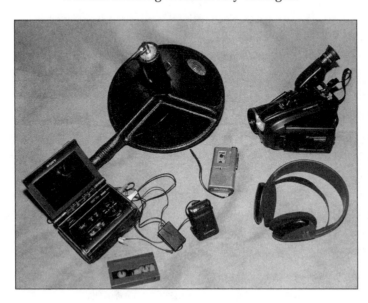

◀ It is important to purchase the correct video equipment for the type of investigations you specialize in.

A camcorder with still-picture capability is great, but only if you're going to use it—and remember that the quality won't be as good as a stand-alone camera. Many people purchase a camera with features that aren't user friendly, so the camera is never used. It's not unusual for a PI to use nothing but his camcorder, while others have multiple cameras—camcorder, 35mm or digital camera, and covert cameras for use outside the vehicle or during foot surveillance. You should use whatever works for you.

Several new camcorders have entered the market—HD or high definition, and the digital camcorder complete with a built-in hard drive. With the latter, footage can be downloaded to a computer or DVR. High definition is more costly, but it's great if it fits in your budget.

Camcorder Accessories

Accessories for your camcorder should include extra batteries and tripods of different sizes and types. Tripods are invaluable during stationary surveillance. Setting up a tripod in the rear of your van or placing a small, short one in the front of your surveillance vehicle will keep your shots steady and will stave off the fatigue of holding the camera for long periods of time.

Tripods come in different styles. You can buy one to fit on your shoulder. Tripods that fit on your dashboard are also available, as are telescoping monopods. Check out the most popular and varied tripod products at the JoEnterprises Web site: *www.joenterprises.com*. This company specializes in tripods that fit various investigative needs. They also sell hard cases for the protection of your sensitive equipment, binoculars, and some of the more unusual items. One of these is a self-contained cooling unit for those unbearably hot summer surveillances. Dry ice placed in a container is sometimes used to cool a van, but this cooling unit is infinitely more efficient and less messy.

If you have a camcorder that still uses tapes or one that records onto a DVD, keep extras nearby. It's important to keep an inverter in your vehicle for charging your technology in the cigarette lighter. Alternatively, some PIs have hooked up a marine battery for this purpose. Some cameras can be equipped with telephoto lenses and some cannot, so consider the types of investigations you plan to do and purchase accordingly.

Still Cameras

Many PIs use a camcorder to take still pictures as well. If you can afford it, get a 35mm or a digital camera with at least seven megapixel capacity. Digital cameras are smaller and easily concealed. If you decide to purchase one and you're a bit technologically challenged, take your laptop with you to the store so you can be sure that the camera will interface with your computer.

As with camcorders, be sure that your digital camera has the highest power of optical zoom that your budget can manage. It's difficult to obtain all the essentials in one camera, but zoom is one that you shouldn't sacrifice for another feature. For many reasons, optical—not digital—zoom is the important feature. An optical zoom gives you enhanced clarity and a greater ability to enlarge the picture while retaining much of that clarity.

Many cameras and camcorders come equipped with lights. Be sure you know how to turn the light off; with low lux you won't need it, and all it will do is call attention to your location. It'll also blind you for a few moments, taking away your night eyes or night vision.

This brings up an extremely important point: Any lights after dark will become a beacon to anyone within sight of you or your vehicle. Even reflective items and material have no place in a nighttime surveillance. Police departments issue dark uniforms and utility belts, and dark or black items such as handcuffs, flashlights, buttons, and even clothing trim to swat teams in order to avoid any reflection that can give away their position. It's dangerous to even light a cigarette at night. Play it safe and keep it dark; your eyes will adjust.

Binoculars

Binoculars are one of the essential pieces of surveillance equipment. They range in price and size, just as so many other items do. But, hey—a binocular is a binocular, right? Wrong! You should purchase the best set of binoculars that your budget will allow. You won't need those huge Coast Guard looking binoculars, but neither do you want a tiny pair that is inferior in quality.

Powers of 7X50 or 10X50 will be useful all around. High quality 7X and 8X binoculars work well in all terrain and environment because images are brighter when the field of view is wider. The wider field of view also ensures that you'll miss less of any quick movements made by your target. The 10X and higher will provide more detail and better viewing for longer distances and open terrain.

With a high-power, high-quality compact you'll need a steady hand or a tripod because of the sensitivity. If you wear glasses, look for binoculars with long eye relief. A popular binocular size is the midsize of 8X32, lighter and less expensive than full size. Most binoculars can stand being out in light rain, but cannot stand a downpour or being submerged in liquid. If you anticipate a lot of work in this kind of weather, purchase a waterproof set.

Covert Cameras and Security

One of the fastest-growing industries in the security field is that of camera installation, particularly covert or hidden cameras. You might suppose that alarm companies do this kind of installation more than investigators, but in most areas, this isn't true. Alarm companies usually put most of their effort into the installation of their main systems, for which they receive monthly monitoring fees.

Many alarm companies feel that there's not enough demand for covert cameras to justify paying to keep them in stock, train installers, and purchase accessories unique to these cameras. So, with only a few companies really specializing in covert cameras, there's a niche waiting to be filled in most areas. However, make sure that this is true in your area before you jump into the expense of selling and installing cameras because it's difficult for a small PI business to compete with large alarm companies.

If your area is bereft of covert camera installers, this service could be built into your business. Experienced PIs who sell and install these cameras do well because they are knowledgeable about security and criminals. It's not enough to go into someone's home or business and ask, "Where do you want these?" Sometimes the client will know exactly where she wants cameras, but an experienced investigator can always advise the client where they will be most effective. The areas chosen by the owner may not be the best locations for the purpose for which she purchased the cameras. The PI can advise from his perspective, one that's different from the home or business owner and very different from the alarm company.

Stationary Covert Cameras

Covert cameras have become smaller and are hidden in more inventive items than ever before. Prices have also been lowered. You can purchase a covert camera in almost anything—clocks, VCRs, air purifiers, sprinklers, exit signs, speakers, books, plants, and much more. Cameras in pens, eyeglasses, hats, briefcases, and the like can be used for recording by being carried on your person. Many companies will install cameras in anything you wish. The best improvement in decades is the availability of cameras and recorders with batteries to power them all contained in one unit.

In the past, investigators were forced to be very creative when installing stationary covert cameras because of the problem of hiding and powering a recording device. Now, many recorders power themselves and the camera to which they're attached, so there are no wires to camouflage. Because of this, these cameras can be moved around much more easily.

Wireless Versus Wired

You might ask about wireless cameras, thinking they have the same capabilities as wired cameras. They do, but there have always been drawbacks to wireless transmission.

Problems with Wireless Transmission
- Other wireless devices can and do interfere with wireless transmission. Devices such as portable phones, some cable connections, microwaves, and other items can render wireless cameras almost useless.
- Wireless depends, usually, on line of sight
- Transmission is limited to a fixed distance between transmitter and camera receiver. Usually, the distance is very short. Only law enforcement personnel are allowed to use wireless transmission that extends far enough for a backup team to be inconspicuous.

At any rate, stationary covert cameras can be placed in hospital rooms to monitor nursing personnel and in nurseries and other locations for checking on nannies and babysitters. They can also be used to prove spousal abuse. One woman contracted with a PI service to help prove that her husband regularly abused her. She'd never been able to prove it because his blows landed on her midsection. They didn't leave any visible bruising, but they were hard enough to require hospitalization.

The man's behavior escalated and his wife was afraid that the next beating would kill her. Worse, she was terrified that her children would be hurt. Investigators installed a covert camera inside a speaker in her living room where most of the incidents took place. PIs changed the tape when the husband was out. Three days after the camera was installed, the man arrived home intoxicated and beat his wife with both fists until she passed out on the floor. She was admitted to the hospital, this time with internal bleeding, and an investigator retrieved the recording and delivered it to police. Because of the evidence on the covert camera, the husband is in prison today. The client has returned to school and she and both her children are in counseling.

Mobile Covert Cameras

Only a few years ago, if investigators wanted to wear a covert body camera, it entailed finding a way to conceal a not-so-small video recorder on his person and inconspicuously run wires to a camera, such as a pen, pager, or glasses case, in the PI's pocket. Because of this, every shirt, jacket, and pair of jeans or slacks contained a hole for threading a line to the covert camera. Things are different today; it's much easier and much less conspicuous to wear covert technology.

Covert body cameras can be used to check someone's mate and in mystery shopping, but there are other uses for these cameras. PIs who investigate childcare or eldercare facilities and treatment centers use them when interviewing. The camera records exactly what is in front of it. It can't be accused of overstating the truth or omitting facts; the facts are exhibited for all to see.

The PI walks around filming, checking the cleanliness of the child's or elder's room, common areas, restrooms, and kitchens. The camera is unemotional when watching for the response—or lack of response—of personnel to a child's or elder's needs and requests. As in the case of the abused wife, recorded evidence in cases such as this is rarely challenged.

Covert Versus Visible Cameras

Many camera purchasers, and even investigators, believe that visible cameras are superior to hidden cameras. This may have been true in the past, but is no longer the case. Visible cameras can serve a purpose, but only when they are used correctly and in conjunction with covert cameras.

Some security experts believe that because visible cameras are so prevalent, most people forget about them. The person who enters an office or retail store with the intention of stealing is keenly aware of these cameras. Potential shoplifters scope them out to ascertain location, distance apart, and possible blind spots between them. In the very misinformed businesses where the owner or operator displays the camera views to the public on a monitor or TV, he's helping the thief locate those blind spots within which he can operate.

An example of the use of blind spots occurred in a parking garage at dusk. A young woman named Anne walked through the dim garage toward her car, feeling safe because of visible security cameras spaced equal distances apart on concrete pillars. She waved at one of them. Suddenly, she was pulled into a corner of the deck and brutally raped. After crawling into the main area of the parking garage, Anne was rescued by a distraught security guard. When she was interviewed in the hospital, she reported looking up at all those cameras and wondering why no one came to her assistance. Then it struck her: She'd been dragged into a blind spot where she and her attacker weren't visible to even one of the cameras. The attacker had obviously scoped out the area ahead of time, knowing just where to commit his crime.

Owners and managers often purchase cameras in order to deter theft. Cameras may deter the basically honest soul who experiences a momentary temptation, but nothing really deters the serious criminal. Hidden cameras are the alternative. If covert cameras were to be placed strategically among the visible ones, even if a sign were posted alerting the public of this fact, criminals may be deterred, not knowing where their actions may be documented. Hidden cameras also catch people in the act of a crime, preventing loss from habitual shoplifters as well as employees.

Questions to Ask When Choosing a Camera

When choosing a camera or camera system for yourself or your client, there are several questions you should ask up front.

How will you use the camera?
- Used to watch a nanny or caregiver?
- Used to watch housekeepers or maintenance persons?
- Used to monitor employees in a business for possible retraining?
- Used to observe suspected thieves, employees, and customers?

What do you want to record?

- How long will you need to record?
- Will you record inside or outside activity?
- Will you move the camera or keep it in one location?
- How much movement is in the room; a business will have more activity than a room in a home.
- Will you need motion-activated cameras for a slow activity area? Scheduled recording? Both?

Where will the camera be located?

- Is the location a bright or low-light area? Black and white is best for low light.
- Can a recorder and wires be hidden or would wireless be preferred?
- Will power be available for the camera?
- What type of addition to the room would not raise suspicions?
- How large is the area? How many cameras will you need?
- How many separate areas will you want to cover?
- How far away will the target likely be? This will determine the camera specs.

Would wired or wireless recording be better for your purposes?

- Are you aware of problems with wireless transmission? Microwaves, cordless phones, and other wireless products such as wireless Internet can interfere with transmission.
- Is it necessary to watch from another room or will recording alone suffice?
- Is there no way you can find to hide a wire and recorder?
- Have you looked into a camera system with recorders inside the item?

For a great array of cameras for purchase, both hidden and otherwise, see these sites:

- SaferSecurity Inc., *www.safersecurityinc.com*
- SpyTekBirmingham, *www.spytekbirmingham.com*

Audio Equipment

An array of audio equipment is available to the private investigator. Clients may come to you with requests for recording equipment. They may have no need for video, may not have the budget for it, or may not want to spend the money required to buy hidden cameras. In this case, you can suggest audio recording devices.

The size and quality of covert audio devices have increased as their costs have decreased. Audio recorders are available in such items as working pens that look no different than pens used by executives everywhere. With a pen such as this, the client can sign contracts at the very moment he records every word that's spoken. With no lights or buttons, this pen won't alert anyone to the fact that it's recording or that it can record for seven hours. Some models record as much as 564 hours. Covert recorders can also be purchased in objects such as watches.

Other clients may come to you with a request for telephone recording devices. This is a sticky subject because federal and state laws strictly govern the manner in which conversation can be recorded. These laws apply to what is sometimes called criminal eavesdropping, whether it's done in person, by leaving a device to record in your absence, or by recording someone else's telephone conversations. Therefore, know the law in your state and the manner in which it relates to federal law.

Federal law holds that recording the conversation of others is not legal unless one party to the conversation is aware of the recording. Some states adhere to this rule, but others apply a stricter standard that stipulates both parties must be aware of the recording. If you have a client who lives alone in a one-party state, you can help her install a telephone recording device on her home telephone. The client can legally record her own conversations with others because one party to these conversations—the client herself—is aware of it.

On the other hand, if your client installs a device on a telephone that he shares with his wife, there may be legal issues even if he lives in a one-party state. It's not legal anywhere to record the conversation of others when none of the parties knows the recording is taking place, so it is not legal to record his wife's conversations with other people without her knowledge.

What about recording conversations using cell phones?
When using a cell phone to record a conversation, the federal one-party consent applies. Therefore, if one party to the conversation consents, recording the conversation is legal.

Pay close attention to the parameters of recording the conversations of others, and don't become a party to the unlawful recording of conversation by another. Don't aid clients in installing recording devices when their use will be illegal.

CHAPTER 18

Surveillance

Investigators spend most of their time doing surveillance of some sort; learning to do this well is important for the success of your business. However, because of people who would use surveillance to infringe upon the rights of others, restrictions have been placed on its use. There are three basic types of surveillance: moving, stationary, and foot. However, surveillance can start out as one type and change quickly to another. Therefore, you must be prepared for any type of surveillance when you set out to watch someone.

Moving Surveillance

Moving, or rolling, surveillance is often conducted in an automobile, but other common methods include bicycles, watercraft, aircraft, or trains. It can be exciting or alarming, depending on the PI. The first rule of moving surveillance is to not put yourself or other drivers in jeopardy. If you lose the target—and everyone does at one time or another—realize that you may pick her up later. If you don't, return another day. PIs consider it a point of pride to be able to stay with the target, but you can't develop that skill overnight. It takes a lot of practice to tail successfully, so give yourself a break in the beginning. Don't run red lights or stop signs or pull out in front of other drivers in order to stay with the subject.

It's important to stay one or two car lengths behind the subject vehicle, unless you're in heavy traffic where he might turn off, leaving you unable to follow safely. Also, be alert to every possible turn off or turn around, as you may need it at a moment's notice. If you are working alone, moving surveillance will be extremely difficult, but not impossible. Use your profile so that if you lose the subject, you can check out the areas he frequents and pick him up again.

A GPS device is useful for rolling surveillance. When you are in unfamiliar areas, it will help you navigate easily; if you become completely lost, it will get you back to a known location. Tracking devices are also helpful, but they are illegal in some states, so check your laws. With real-time tracking devices, you'll need to subscribe to a service. If you are working a divorce case or one where your client is the owner or co-owner of the car you are tailing, you might allow her to attach a tracking device. It can be argued, however, that she's doing this at your direction, and it could still be illegal. At any rate, it's always best to run anything like this by your attorney.

Having the Eyeball

The ideal situation is to have several vehicles in your convoy. After a while, the lead vehicle can turn off and fall back to the end of the convoy, behind the other cars. At this point, the next in line takes "the eyeball." This is a law enforcement term, typically used by federal agents during surveillance. It means that the person with the eyeball, or the eye, has the subject in direct view.

ALERT!

Someone must have the eyeball at all times. This is much easier when more than one vehicle is involved. If you are working alone, you must always have the eye. This is very tiring, so be prepared. Get enough sleep the night before and bring coffee, tea, or snacks to keep your blood sugar up and your brain awake.

The lead driver, the one with the eyeball, also has the responsibility to inform those on the team of every movement the target makes and to relay landmarks over the radio that the team can recognize as they pass. This way, if anyone becomes separated from the convoy, he will be able to find his way to the team. The lead should continue her information even when she no longer hears confirmation from the others, because they may still be able to hear her. Use cell phones for communication backups.

Stationary Surveillance

Stationary surveillance is difficult for many PIs, mainly because of the sheer boredom that some feel when sitting for hours in a vehicle with nothing to do but stare at one location. Sometimes, however, it's the only way to obtain video of a subject who rarely exits his home.

Precautions

When you do stationary surveillance in winter, be careful of running your vehicle for warmth, as the exhaust may be apparent, much as warm breath on a cold day. Exhaust coming from a parked vehicle may draw the attention of an otherwise unsuspecting target—and the neighbors. Some neighborhoods are organized into neighborhood watch sections. If you're parked in one of these, be prepared to provide a pretext for why you're sitting there.

Investigators have used the ruse of looking for a lost dog or cat, and have even printed bogus flyers to validate being in the area. However, this isn't recommended by experienced PIs. Someone who's out looking for a lost animal will be out looking, sometimes frantically. This won't be a believable ruse to most. Besides, some of the target's neighbors may have a soft spot, should they believe you, and may waste your time and energy by insisting on searching with you for your pet.

FACT

Some investigators enjoy stationary surveillance. They report feeling energized by the knowledge that, at any moment, the target may exit, necessitating quick action in order to film her. They feel wound up, anticipating the moment when they get that difficult shot. It's a rush for them. It's what you're paid to do—so no daydreaming.

Neighborhood Issues

Stationary surveillance in neighborhoods is difficult. There are no good places to park. Sometimes, neighbors will allow you to sit in their driveway or in front of their house, usually because you've offered a plausible reason for wanting to be there. One investigator has been known to tell a female neighbor that he's watching a male cheating on his wife; he tells a male the investigation concerns a female cheating on her husband. Sometimes, the neighbor is sympathetic and will allow the surveillance vehicle in front of her house. Another investigator tells neighbors that she's received information that her spouse was seen in the neighborhood during working hours and she's waiting to see where he goes. You might not be as convincing, so choose a ruse that you can portray believably.

If police are called, don't lie to them. Tell them you're an investigator and ask for their help. Some will help, but some won't. If you know you'll be in an area ahead of time, call the station and inform them. It's not necessary to divulge the name or address of the target, however; you never know who knows whom. This is one reason it's beneficial to develop contacts in the department.

Sitting for long periods gives rise to the problem of bladder needs. Products specifically made for both males and females can be found in drug stores. In a pinch, use a jar. Always prepare for these needs because you never know how long you'll be required to sit on a case. Portable toilets can be purchased, but they're not necessary.

Foot Surveillance

Usually you won't engage in this type of surveillance unless someone you're following exits his vehicle and enters a public area or building. You'll want to jump out and follow him inside. The following are some rules for foot surveillance:

- Leave your vehicle quickly but unobtrusively
- Stay far enough behind that the target doesn't notice
- Stay close enough that you don't lose her
- Avoid making eye contact with the target, but don't hide or make sudden movements
- Don't change hats or clothing unless the change totally alters your appearance
- Don't be afraid to shoot video using a very small camera or body cam
- Don't be afraid of being burned or made
- Use store windows when available to observe target
- If in the woods or among trees, the use of a ghillie suit is helpful

A ghillie suit is a full body suit that looks as if it's made of leaves and sticks. Made of different leaf varieties and colors, it is used by PIs, hunters, the military, and some police units for concealment when on surveillance. Matching the season and the type of foliage or terrain, the investigator blends in to his surroundings. It's much more effective than camouflage. See these sites for ghillie suits:

- Ghillie Suit Source, *www.ghilliesuitsource.com*
- Ghillie Suits Plus, *www.ghilliesuitplus.com*
- Ghillie Suits.com, *www.ghilliesuits.com*
- Camo-Store.com, *www.camo-store.com/ghillie_suit_camo.htm*
- Ghillie Suit Clothing, *www.ghilliesuitclothing.com*

Many people new to the profession are terrified of being made or burned—being caught following the subject. You can be confident that this doesn't happen often. People react in different ways, but there are basically four types of people you'll follow:

- Those who never notice. These people rarely look in the rearview mirror; they just aren't suspicious.
- Those who look around but don't see the tail. They seem nervous and suspicious, but they really don't see you.
- Those who think they are being followed and use evasive action. These are the most difficult to tail; they may not see you, but they may make so many evasive moves to lose a possible tail that they may lose you, too.
- Those who actually spot you. This is a very small group, but if someone sees that you're following them, go away for a day, change vehicles or your appearance, and return later.

When you're afraid of being burned, take a deep breath and relax. The only way most people will become suspicious of you is if you act suspicious. Even if someone looks your way, so what? Don't you look at others in a crowd? Be calm and don't make sudden moves. Don't turn away quickly or hide your face. The odds are that the target won't remember seeing you, but don't give him the opportunity. Stay behind and act as if you have a reason to be where you are.

Foot surveillance is more efficient with at least two people. Techniques similar to those used in moving surveillance are also effective. When the subject turns, the lead walks straight ahead and the next PI becomes the lead as the first circles around to the rear. Different patterns, or plays, much like football plays, can be created so that each person knows which way to move depending on the actions of the target.

Insider Tips

Working PIs use many different tools to help them with surveillance. There are also many techniques you can use to increase your chances of success.

Covert Cameras

Covert cameras can be used in many ways on surveillances. They can be placed in items that sit on the dashboard or rear window of your vehicle for filming in either direction. With these in place, the investigator can leave the vehicle and allow the filming to continue unassisted. It's best to use motion-activated cameras, eliminating the need to wade through hours of nothingness to locate activity.

Cameras are available in fake rocks, tree stumps, and other items that appear unobtrusive outdoors. Many are complete with DVRs, extended battery lives, and motion activation. Use them for the subject who rarely exits his residence, or when you can't be available to film. However, if the homeowner or target is a gardener or works in the yard, be careful where you place these outdoor cameras, as the new addition might be obvious. You'll hate losing a camera system this valuable, along with all your recorded evidence.

Cameras can be worn on the investigators body or clothing. Called body cams, they're available in hats, jackets, glasses, ties, buttons, watches, jewelry, and more. They can also be carried in fanny packs, briefcases, purses, and pens. The investigator can go anywhere and film anyone using these cameras without causing suspicion.

Nighttime Surveillance

A strip of black electrical or regular masking tape placed across the subject's taillight will allow you to identify the vehicle both at night and during the day. To prevent discovery while tailing your subject at night, install a switch to turn off one of your headlights to alter what the subject sees in her rearview mirror. Be careful using this, as it can appear suspicious over a period of time. You can also configure a switch to turn off backup and brake lights to make you invisible when entering and exiting an area.

When you follow a vehicle, try to drive in the lane to his right, and attempt to stay in his blind spot. Never drive in front of the target. Though some surveillance courses teach driving in front of a subject, it's a bad move. While many drivers pay little attention to others, some notice everything and may become suspicious if they see your vehicle over and over again.

Surveillance Vehicles

It's customary for investigators to use vans or SUVs for stationary and moving surveillance, but it's not necessary. If you can afford it, having a stable of vehicles is best—not expensive vehicles that can draw too much attention, and not rattletraps that are sure to be remembered if they are spotted again, but something in the middle. Remove any stickers or conspicuous detailing that can be recognized. Color is also important; many white vans are on the roads and don't often cause suspicion when driven through neighborhoods. These can be set up as business vehicles, with magnetic signs for the sides.

FACT

You can set up your surveillance vehicle as a business vehicle, with magnetic signs listing the company's name and number for the vehicle's sides. In larger companies, someone can be prepared to answer this number with a fictitious name, verifying that one of the company's vans is in the area. If you work alone, buy a separate cell phone so you can verify yourself.

Any type of car or truck can be a surveillance vehicle. Choose colors that don't stand out, and stay away from reds, jewel, or bright colors. The color that seems best is gray for daytime and black or very dark for evening surveillance. If you don't have two cars, choose a light or medium gray, as it blends in with traffic as well as the pavement on most roads and highways.

Check the laws of your state and have the windows tinted as dark as is allowed. Remember that changing vehicles is a great tactic, especially when your surveillance goes on for several days or weeks. If you don't have access to other vehicles, rent one. Renting also ensures that the tag won't be traced back to you, except with the use of a subpoena.

Knowing When to Terminate Surveillance

It's not always easy to know when to terminate surveillance. Your client's budget will dictate when surveillance ends in some cases, but this isn't always the case. Many times, inactivity will cause your client to request that you leave and return another day. Some clients believe that surveillance is useless in the rain. They think clients won't go anywhere in the rain, but this isn't necessarily true.

Some investigators consider terminating surveillance when they think they've been made. Just because the target looks at you doesn't mean she has suspicions about you. A good rule of thumb is to continue surveillance until you experience three incidents where you feel that the subject knows she's being followed. This doesn't mean you've been made, but it's a good indication. Break off and plan to return. Alternatively, if you're definitely busted and confronted by the target, don't try to explain. The best policy is to leave, especially if she's angry.

Surveillance Attire and Disguises

All investigators need to keep a change or two of clothes in the car. You need different clothes, not only for those times when you must walk through woods, mud, trash, and other areas, but to alter your appearance. A couple of different hats will help also. Although you're not supposed to get close enough to the target to be identified, subjects looking for a tail will be lulled into a false security by your changing silhouette.

If you should happen to get too close and the subject sees your face, don't let him see you again with a different hat or shirt a few minutes later. That's a sure tipoff that you're an investigator. Only change your appearance if it's a real disguise. Real disguises are possible with a makeup kit and items such as wigs, beards, and eyeglasses.

◄ A makeup kit and an array of wigs and other accessories can help you alter your appearance.

Video Surveillance Law

Thirteen states prohibit camera installation in private areas, defined as areas in which people have an expectation of privacy. This expectation is a legal one. The following places are protected in many states:

- Private homes
- Public and private bathrooms
- Public changing rooms
- Hotel rooms
- Rental homes and apartments
- Bedrooms

There are some exceptions. For example, you have an expectation of privacy in your own home, but if you leave your drapes open, you shouldn't expect that no one will look in. You have no legal expectation in this case. Neither do you have an expectation that you won't be filmed—if the person filming is standing where it's legal for her to stand, such as on the street or sidewalk. If she's on your property, she's trespassing and the expectation stands.

PIs have climbed on trash cans or up trees and ladders on private property in order to film inside an open window. This is illegal; film obtained this way is "fruit of the poisonous tree." This means that the fruits of your investigation—the video recording—is poisoned by the manner in which it was obtained and, therefore, is inadmissible in court.

The thirteen states that prohibit cameras in areas where there's an expectation of privacy are:

- Alabama
- Arkansas
- California
- Delaware
- Georgia
- Hawaii
- Kansas
- Maine

- Michigan
- Minnesota
- New Hampshire
- South Dakota
- Utah

Laws in these states expressly prohibit the use or installation of anything that observes, photographs, or eavesdrops on the behavior or conversation of others without their knowledge or permission. Eleven of these thirteen states—all but Arkansas and California—also have laws prohibiting trespassing on private property in order to conduct surveillance; in almost all listed states, violation of these laws is a felony. Laws change, so check your state's laws to be sure.

Labor Unions

Employees and labor unions aren't as excited about covert cameras as are employers. They argue that any surveillance is an invasion of privacy. Of course, the companies argue that an employee has no expectation of privacy in the workplace—except bathrooms and changing areas. In 2005, American Management Association, along with The E-Policy Institute, conducted a survey. This survey, the 2005 Electronic Monitoring and Surveillance Survey, found that 51 percent of all employers use hidden cameras to monitor employees.

ALERT!

You can follow all state and local laws and still be in breach of union labor law. To protect yourself and your client, have a knowledgeable attorney sign off on hidden camera installations where unions are involved. No other federal law or statute prohibits the use of hidden cameras in workplaces, however.

If you install cameras and your client is involved with a union in any way, advise him to consult a competent attorney before choosing hidden cameras. The National Labor Relations Board (NLRB) has allowed hidden cameras to be installed in the workplace if the company bargains with the union before the cameras are put in place. They've also established that the camera locations don't have to be disclosed.

In 1998, Anheuser-Busch installed hidden cameras that revealed employees smoking pot, sleeping on the job, and urinating on the roof. Anheuser-Busch fired the employees who smoked pot, suspended seven others, and provided last chance warnings to the rest of the violators. Because the union, Brewers and Maltsters Local No. 6, wasn't informed of Anheuser-Busch's intention to install cameras, the NLRB and the federal appeals court found the company engaged in unfair labor practice and were in breach of federal labor laws. Read the article in Entrepreneur.com: *www.entrepreneur.com/tradejournals/article/134510370.html.* This site also has excellent advice about bargaining with unions for the use of cameras and what to do if cameras are already in place without permission.

Electronic and Audio Surveillance

The intricacies of electronic surveillance make it a specialty all its own. This section will attempt to cover the high points of this most important subject. Legality is of the utmost importance, and you need to know the laws in the states in which you work.

Bugs, Taps, and Wiretaps

The term bug usually refers to a microphone placed somewhere in a room which picks up conversations and transmits them by radio frequency, either wireless or through power lines, to a receiver outside of the room. A tap usually refers to a device that has intercepted the lines of your phone and is recording the conversations. Many taps of this kind are available online and even at Radio Shack.

A wiretap placed on your phone by law enforcement is neither of these things. When a police wiretap is instigated, the phone company runs an extension of your line to the particular law enforcement office. In other words, with a wiretap in place, when the phone rings at your house, it also rings at the detective's office or FBI, just as if it were another extension. A wiretap isn't put in place lightly. A search warrant is necessary to place a wiretap, one that cannot be obtained without probable cause. It's highly unlikely that the police or federal government is tapping a citizen's phone. If they are, the citizen is suspected of something. It's more likely that a non-police tap may be on the citizen's phone.

Title III Law

Title III, the federal wiretap statute, makes it illegal to intercept any wire, oral, or electronic communication. A business owner can use an extension phone to monitor employee conversations during the business day. Any criminal conduct found in this way is admissible in court, yet the moment the conversation becomes personal, recording must stop.

Title III also permits the recording of telephone conversations as long as one party to the conversation is aware of it. This is called one-party consent, and it means that if the investigator records conversations on her phone or uses a recorder on her person, it's a legal recording because one party to the conversation is aware of it (the investigator herself). The other party doesn't need to be informed of the recording in order for it to be legal.

QUESTION?

What is criminal eavesdropping?
Criminal eavesdropping involves the intentional use of any device to over-hear or record communications, whether the eavesdropper is present or not, without one party's consent.

All but twelve states are one-party consent states. The all-party consent states are:

- California
- Connecticut
- Delaware
- Florida
- Illinois
- Maryland

- Massachusetts
- Michigan
- Montana
- New Hampshire
- Pennsylvania
- Washington

There are some exceptions to all-party consent. In California, one-party consent applies when one party is involved in criminal activity, including extortion or blackmail. This means that if someone is blackmailing you in California, you can record that person in order to prove the criminal activity, even though the state usually requires that all parties to a recorded conversation give their assent. Another exception occurs in Arizona, where telephone conversations can be recorded by telephone service providers with no-party consent when criminal behavior is involved.

In states with all-party consent, verbal notification of the recording must be provided and a beep must alert the parties that recording continues. In the case of cell phones and wireless phones, the federal one-party consent standard applies. Scanners that can lock in on cell phone conversations are no longer legally sold, but they're still out there. Many have been sold over the years, and it's impossible to halt their use or know who uses them. Therefore, be aware that these scanners exist, and act accordingly.

Calls across state lines are tricky. Federal law normally supersedes state law, especially if the action in question crosses state lines. Yet in this case, the stricter all-party consent applies—sometimes. Judicial discretion has been different in the past. This causes a problem concerning a call made from a state with one-party consent to a state with all-party consent. Can this call be legally recorded? Judges tend to handle it differently, but it's safer to assume that the stricter law applies. When calls involve Canada and the United Kingdom, be aware that both these countries, as of now, allow one-party consent.

If you don't need to record the conversation but merely want to know the numbers dialed, you can obtain this information in a few different ways. Pin registers capture the phone numbers dialed on outgoing calls, and trap and trace devices capture numbers dialed on incoming phone calls.

Children's Tracking Device Phones

Fitting children's phones with tracking devices is a debatable strategy. All a child has to do is turn off his phone, "forget" to take it with him, leave it with a friend or in a car—you get the idea. He can even plead interference or that the phone didn't ring at all. What's worse, if the child is abducted, the first thing the abductor will discard is that phone. Realize that if you're aware of those types of phones, abductors can be also. Even if the child gets a message to the parent, he and the abductor can be far away in short order.

QUESTION?

Can I tap my children's telephone conversations?
Parents may pay the phone bill, yet they have no legal right to listen to their children's conversations. If you tap, you can't count on judicial leniency—you may get the one who's tough on these laws. Besides, most kids use cell phones!

GPS devices for locating children are promising, but they must be placed in something that cannot be discarded easily. Researchers are working on these now—bracelets and necklaces that are difficult to remove hold promise, but they are also dangerous if the abductor tries and becomes frustrated with her inability to remove them.

CHAPTER 19

Interviewing and Interrogation

Information is the business of the private investigator, and information is most often in the hands of people. For the PI, learning how to get the information you need from people is one of the most important parts of your business. Therefore, learning the techniques of interviewing and interrogation is key to success. Obtaining interviews as early as possible will prevent loss of information, and knowing how to interview a subject will ensure you will get the answers you are looking for.

To Interview or Interrogate—Know the Difference

Interviews and interrogations are two very different things. Suspects are interrogated; witnesses are interviewed. Everything that follows can be applied to all types of investigations. However, because of privacy laws, there are certain things the PI may not ask during a pre-employment screening interview. These follow:

- Age
- Children and how many times married
- Disability
- Ethnicity
- Marital status
- Political party
- Religion
- Sexual orientation

Acknowledging Differences in Perception

When interviewing witnesses, remember that men and women differ in what they remember. This is a generalization, but one that has proven true for the majority. Women look at eyes in an attempt to determine an offender's intent, so they often remember the eyes and at least part of the face. Men tend to look at build and arm length and ask, "Can I take him?"

Experts have written that, contrary to popular opinion, children can be the best witnesses. As with everything else, this is a generalization. Not all children will be good witnesses any more than all women will remember eyes and faces. When properly interviewed, children can give telling aspects of most situations. Of course, age and maturity make a difference.

The most important aspect of interviewing children as witnesses is for the child's recall to be protected. Only an investigator who is trained in interviewing children should ask the child questions or show him pictures. Most experts agree that very young children shouldn't be asked specific questions but should be allowed to speak about the incident in their own time. This very sensitive area has been the subject of books, articles and seminars. Some of them follow:

- *A Guide for Interviewing Children: Essential Skills for Counselors, Police, Lawyers and Social Workers* by J. Clare Wilson, and Martine Powell, *www.questia.com/PM.qst?a=o&d=101435106*
- *Interviewing Children and Adolescents* by James Morrison and Thomas Anders, *http://mysite.verizon.net/res7oqx1/id21.html.* While this is primarily a book concerning childhood disorders, it outlines the interview process in excellent detail
- Interviewing the Children, PBS's Frontline, *http://www.pbs.org/wgbh/pages/frontline/shows/fuster/etc/interviewing.html*
- Interviewing Children as Victims, Witnesses or Suspects, by Code 4, Non-Profit Education Association, *www.code4.org/pdf/050508children.pdf.* This organization offers conferences several times per year

Trained experts alone should interview children. However, this list will get you started learning about the subject for the part you'll play as an investigator.

Developing Rapport

One of the most interesting means of developing rapport is called mirroring or matching. The interviewer begins by mirroring the subject. As she makes small talk and attempts to gain the subject's trust, she slowly alters her posture until the subject is mirroring her. It's important to remain subtle so that you don't appear to be mimicking or mocking the subject, however.

An example of mirroring would be something like this: If the subject sits with his arms crossed, the interviewer crosses her arms. At the same time, she listens to the words the subject uses and uses them back to him, matching his pitch, speech rate, and volume. As she becomes successful in opening up the subject, she begins to open her arms and the subject will usually follow. Now the interviewer is in charge. If she wants more intimacy, she moves forward in her seat. The subject will usually follow suit.

Now she has him. First, she gets his body in sync with her, then his mind follows, and he becomes less guarded and more communicative.

FACT

The key to mirroring is to begin wherever the subject may be, then slowly bring her to your position. If you know what to look for, you'll see people subconsciously mirroring each other everywhere—people in deep conversation, lovers and friends mirroring each other when they're in agreement, and people not mirroring each other when they're not in agreement.

The basis for this interviewing technique is neuro-linguistic programming (NLP). Some critics take issue with the use of NLP as a therapeutic treatment technique, but others, psychologists and psychiatrists alike, use it in their practices. The FBI and other law enforcement agencies, federal and local, use this technique or something based on it. If you're interested, visit the NLP Information Center at *www.nlpinfo.com* for more information. There are other ways to develop rapport. You may find that your way isn't in the literature at all. If it works for you, it works.

Kinesics or Body Language

There are many types of studies and training that purport to teach others how to read someone else by their body movements. Many are too broad to really be accurate, but some hold promise. One problem with these body language techniques is that some people insist that certain traits automatically mean certain things—for instance, that rapid blinking means the subject is avoiding contact or is even lying. In reality, the subject may have dry eyes or a nervous tic, or her blinking may mean something else entirely. Of course, she may actually be lying or hiding something, although there's a difference between these two cases also. However, the investigator won't know any of this until he establishes the baseline. He must determine what eye blinking means in the case of that particular individual. Don't fall prey to broad-brush techniques; the results could be disastrous. If you're interested, the following sites have more information on the subject:

- FBI Law Enforcement Bulletin, Subtle Skills for Building Rapport-Interviewing, *www.au.af.mil/au/awc/awcgate/fbi/nlp_interviewing.htm*
- The Model-Based Mind, *www.au.af.mil/au/awc/awcgate/ornl/ model_based_mind.pdf*
- NLP Information Center, *www.nlpinfo.com*
- John E. Reid and Associates, *www.reid.com*. This firm specializes in training both law enforcement and the private sector in the art of interview and interrogation, as well as other subjects. The Reid Technique is recognized by many law enforcement officials as the way to train investigators in the area of interview and interrogation. It is outlined in Reid's Criminal Interrogations and Confessions.

Asking Questions Successfully

Never ask a question that suggests the answer. Avoid closed-ended questions, or questions that can be answered with a simple yes or no—this is the best way to halt an interview. Your questions need to be phrased in such a way that the answer is an elaboration, providing information that can lead to more questions.

Asking, "Were you at the corner of Twenty-first and Roman on the night of July 18?" will get you the answer "Yes," and dead air. If you ask, "Why were you at the corner?" you'll get information that will often lead to other questions and more information. Closed questions stop the conversation and break any rapport you've established with the subject.

Many investigators begin with questions they already know the answers to. Questions the subject will almost certainly answer truthfully are asked first. This is along the lines of the lie detector question formatting, when a base-line of truthful answers is obtained at the outset. While the investigator doesn't have the subject hooked up to a lie detector, she can watch the subject's mannerisms and judge them against any future answers. This way, she can see how the subject's body responds when he answers a truthful question.

A Test Case

For instance, when she answers simple questions she only has to recall, not create or make up, the subject may look up and to the right. Most people look up when answering with recall or creation of the answer, but they don't all look in the same direction. Perhaps your subject looks up and to the right when she tells you that the color of her house is white. She's recalling this, and it's (probably) a truthful statement. Ask a string of these to verify that looking up and to the right is her response to recall questions.

Next, ask a string of questions to which he must create answers: If you were to change the color of your house or apartment, what color would it be? The subject may look up and to the left or slightly to the middle when answering this question. Once again, ask more questions to verify that looking up and left is his habit when he creates answers. Now you can begin to ask questions connected to the case, having established that up and right is recall for this subject, and up and left is creation or making up (or lying).

There's a lot of research behind this technique, but it won't prove anything in court. It will, however, give you an idea of how truthful this subject is in response to your questions. This technique is very different from so-called body language, where an authority insists that looking to the right has a set meaning for every person. This is simply not true. You must establish what looking to the right means for that particular subject. It's been established that there is an unconscious link between the nervous system and communication (the body can communicate what the mind is thinking), yet this isn't a one-size-fits-all kind of communication. At any rate, this type of interviewing isn't an easy discipline and can be easily misused.

Interviewing Witnesses and Interrogating Suspects

It is vital that you interview both witnesses and suspects to get a clear picture of your case. Interviews and interrogations are handled differently, and it is helpful to know what to expect.

Witnesses

Witnesses are people who have information. They can testify that they've seen, heard, felt, tasted, or touched something that has importance for an investigation.

If the witness is injured and has been taken to the hospital, or must leave the scene for some reason, always ask for her identification and contact information. Be sure to record it from a driver's license or official papers, as some may give false information. Although their percentage is small, some people are afraid to get involved in someone else's accident or incident, and others don't want to.

Be sure to record the license number of your witness vehicle if he has one. The PI is often in the unfortunate position of interviewing witnesses after the fact because police have gotten to them first. It's not unusual for witnesses to be irritated at the request for further interviews. Yet it's vital that you interview witnesses as soon as possible before their memories start to fade.

FACT

In old cases, also known as cold cases, interviewing becomes much more difficult. Witnesses may have had second thoughts or may have been coerced or intimidated by the suspect or those close to him. Witnesses move, change their names, and even die.

Suspects

Interrogation is not merely questioning; it goes beyond questioning and seeks an incriminating response from someone who is considered a suspect. Because of this, it requires a Miranda warning by the questioner (law enforcement) and a waiver of rights from the suspect. As a private investigator, you're not bound by this. However, if you're employed by an attorney, you're acting on her behalf and you want the interrogation to be admissible in court, so you must abide by these legalities.

Law enforcement officers must inform the suspect's attorney of the time and date of an interrogation and allow him reasonable time to arrive.

Witnesses should be present so that there is no question about coercion of the suspect. A typist is usually present as well.

Taking Statements

Cases are won or buried on the strength of statements. Be very sure that you learn to do this most important part of the investigation. On the practical side, be sure that your audio or video equipment works. Take several pens in case one doesn't work, and prepare your questions ahead of time.

Statements can be taken from witnesses or defendants. If taking statements at the behest of an attorney, you'll usually do so in the court recorder's office and she'll take it all down. If you are doing the interview yourself, take your secretary or another investigator with a laptop to type the statement as it's being recorded. Recording your statement is a must. You have no axe to grind. You're looking for facts not railroading anyone, so nothing can be said that shouldn't be recorded. A PI may be afraid of recording because answers may be a surprise or he may make mistakes. Everyone makes mistakes, especially in early work. Yet a recording protects you from witnesses or defendants who decide to change their minds, who blame you for leading them in a certain direction, or who cry coercion or any other defense a good attorney can dream up.

When you take statements, remember that you're neither defense nor prosecution. No matter which side hires you, you're not trying to prove either side's point. The moment you begin to elicit information that leans toward a conclusion for either side, you've compromised your finest tool—objectivity. You are an information gatherer. Let the attorneys slug it out using that information.

The fact that you need to remain objective doesn't mean that you're not trying to find out who is guilty, and that you won't use strategy to discover information that may lead to a confession by the guilty party. Objectivity prevents you from being so sure that someone is "the guy" that you use these strategies to coerce an innocent person to confess. Innocent people confess all the time. The motives of some are still a mystery, as there are "professional confessors" known to all investigators. Professional investigators aren't looking to get a confession at all costs; they're looking to find the actual offender, not just another cleared case.

When you arrange to take a statement from someone who is identified as a suspect, inform her counsel of the statement date and time. Law enforcement officers must do this, and it is in the private investigator's best interest to do it as well. Keep length in mind; you do not want the statement to be too long. This will guard against charges that you've placed the subject under undue duress. For the same reason, be sensitive to the subject's thirst or requests to go to the restroom. If you try to withhold these very basic needs in an attempt to encourage her to divulge further information, the information may not be admissible in court.

Most PIs use audio to record statements, but if you want to be able to go back and study the subject's reaction to your questions, use video to record the statement. Should the case end up in court, video allows these reactions to be visible to the jury as well. The following information should be included at the beginning of any statement you take:

- State the date, time, day, and place
- State your name, occupation, and name of your agency
- Name everyone in the room—an attorney, another investigator, police, court recorder—the fewer people in your interview, the better
- Ask the subject to speak her full name
- Ask the subject to speak her address
- Ask the subject to speak her phone number
- Ask the subject to speak her social security number
- Ask the subject to speak her occupation and name and place of employment

Add any information you need. Speak clearly, and should anyone else speak identify them immediately. Be polite and respectful. If your interviewee refers or points to something, identify it and have her confirm it. If she nods or shakes her head, ask her to speak her answer. If she mumbles, have her repeat it. Your questions should be asked from a prepared list, but let the answers lead you to others. If she mentions names, ask her to clarify who these people are and spell the names if she's able.

At the end of the statement, let the typist quickly review the tape and add anything you missed. Get the interviewee some coffee and ask incidental questions until the statement is printed. Next, the statement should be read by the interviewee, who initials each page and signs the last page. If he finds a mistake, he should correct it, and initial the alteration. It's very important to intentionally include several small mistakes in the printed copy. This will allow the subject to correct them, proving to the court that the opportunity to make corrections was afforded the interviewee. As a result, anything that he doesn't correct will stand, and will be difficult for his attorney to argue against later. Finally, you should sign the statement, along with a witness.

ALERT!

Statements should include the following elements above the subject's signature line: "Without coercion or promises of gain, monetary or otherwise, I attest that all information on all____ pages of the above statement is true and correct to the best of my knowledge. I have read the statement and initialed changes I have made." Make sure you have an audio recording of the subject reading the statement or a video recording of her reading and signing it.

If you do not have access to a computer, have the interviewee write out her statement. Many investigators have her write it anyway, and sign or initial it along with the typed version. It's the recommended way to do it, but some people feel that it takes too much time. If, for any reason, she can't—if she's injured, sick, or emotionally distraught—be sure to record her admittance of this. If someone close to the subject is in the area, let that person write the statement. Don't write the statement yourself unless there's no other way. If you must write for her, as a protection, record the subject telling you what to write, as well as her signature of the results.

When the statement has been signed and initialed, put it out of sight and never return it to the subject. It's not uncommon for her to become panicky at the possible consequences of her statement and attempt to take it back from you. If she wants a copy, make one. If no machine is near, tell her you'll send one. Follow through and send the copy in case you must speak to this person again, but never put the original back in her hands.

Obtaining Confessions

If you think confessions are obtained by officers standing over a suspect who cowers and sweats under a bare bulb, you'd be surprised to witness a professional interrogation. Law enforcement has learned a thing or two about interrogation over the years, and it's rarely conducted like that anymore. Intelligent officers use finesse and sometimes even charm to convince a suspect to confess.

According to Michael R. Napier and Susan H. Adams, M.A., there are several magic words or phrases that can induce suspects to confess. Some of these are, "anyone in your situation might have," "accidents happen," and "everybody makes mistakes." By listening to the suspect during the initial interview, an investigator can ascertain the defense mechanism this person might have used to justify her crimes—rationalization, projection, or minimization. By using these RPMs as the basis of magic phrases, the investigator allows the suspect to save face by speaking her own rationalizations back to her. Using phrases such as these, investigators need to do one or more of these four things in order to obtain confessions:

- **Rationalize subject's actions**—"I can understand how you might . . . "
- **Project the blame to others**—"Somebody like that can be difficult to deal with."
- **Minimize the crime**—"Accidents can happen . . . "
- **Provide reasons for telling the truth**—"You're the only one who can tell your side of the story."

No one benefits from a false confession. The innocent pay the price for the guilty, who go free, perhaps to offend again. If you have any idea that there's something amiss with the confession, investigate further. Trust your instincts.

You might have trouble believing that innocent people confess to crimes, but they do. There are all kinds of reasons people confess: Some do it to protect someone they love; some who do it are mentally disturbed; some are guilty of another crime or perceived crime and want to be punished; and some confessors have no discernible motive.

Investigators can become hardened to the possibility that confessions are false. The reason is that almost everyone recants a confession as soon as an attorney explains the consequences and provides a possible defense. Very few offenders actually admit to their crimes, so it's easier to view a recanting as false rather than entertain the possibility that the confession might have been false. The investigator doesn't have x-ray vision into anyone's mind, but as long as he uses good judgment and abides by the law, he's done his job in an imperfect system.

Paranoid Suspects

Sometimes, offenders become so paranoid that they must find out what the police or investigators know. It's not unusual for them to report as witnesses about the very crime they committed. In this way, they try to accomplish several things. First, they want to find out what information is already known concerning the crime; second, they attempt to provide false information they believe will take the investigation in a different direction; and third, they hope their presence as a witness will keep the investigation away from them.

Sometimes, offenders are fascinated by the fact that they're the star of it all. It's all about them, and they delight in their secret knowledge. Many of these won't be able to keep it secret, however; they long for the spotlight and will often make mistakes that result in arrest. At this point, the entire world knows who they are and what they were able to do. Sometimes, they'll even talk if it serves their purpose of gaining stardom. Others toy with investigators, enjoying their sense of power over the authorities.

APPENDIX A

Research Tools and Resources

The theme that runs through this book is that the private investigator's job is locating information. However, there are so many information sources that it can be confusing even to seasoned private investigators. Not everyone is cut out to search for information. If you're that person, hire your searches out to someone else—just be sure this person or agency knows the ins and outs of searching, and be prepared to pay the costs. On the other hand, if you are interested in doing your own searches, there are many resources you can use.

Information Access Law

In a free society, everything is not free. The freedom to view records must be balanced with the right to privacy. Therefore, some information is readily available and some isn't available at all. Some information is available under certain circumstances.

Freedom of Information Act (FOIA)

The Freedom of Information Act was put in place to provide access to specific government records. Enacted in 1966, it allows for federal government records to be reasonably available to the public. Conditions exist under which certain laws are not available, however. Federal records that are available follow:

- Military or Defense Records
- FBI Records
- Social Security Administration Records
- Veteran's Administration Records

Records that are held by state and local government agencies, Congress and the court system are not made available to the public by FOIA. Before the enactment of the FOIA, the standard for accessing most government records was the "need to know" standard. After FOIA, the standard became the "right to know." The act also determined the standards for which records must be made available to the public and which records can be withheld. For more information, read *usinfo.state.gov/infousa/government/overview/docs/citizen.pdf.*

Privacy Act of 1974

The Privacy Act protects certain records with sensitive information belonging to and about individuals from unauthorized disclosure. The key word is unauthorized. Citizens may see their own records, and with certain permissible reasons, others can view this information as well. For instance, when you receive permission to run record searches through one of the large information database services, you receive permission to obtain sensitive information—but only if you possess a permissible reason for wanting the information, reasons detailed in prior chapters.

The FOIA and Privacy Act can be seen as two sides of the same coin. Together, they create a balance which must be maintained in a free society which also seeks to protect the privacy of its citizens. Read more about this act at *www.usdoj.gov/oip/04_7_1.html*.

Fair Credit Reporting Act (FCRA)

FCRA ensures that certain information regarding citizens is both accurate and protected. This protects employment applicants, causing certain information desired for pre-employment screening to be inaccessible to the general public. You must have permissible reasons for acquiring this information. You can find more information at *www.ftc.gov/os/statutes/fcrajump.shtm*.

Internet Web Sites and Database Services

There's a danger in using free Internet search sites; many of them aren't really free. They allow you to input information, but to get answers, you must pay money. It's a scam, and the worst part is that some of these sites go on to feed you bits of information, charging you again and again until you've paid quite a bit and have very little to show for it. The following are truly free sites or sites that have at least some areas that are free with upfront information about any costs (which most don't charge) for specialty searches:

- **Anywho.com:** *www.anywho.com/tf.html*
- **Blackbook Online:** *www.blackbookonline.info*
- **Infospace.com:** *www.infospace.com*
- **Switchboard.com:** *www.switchboard.com*
- **PhoneValidator.com:** *www.phonevalidator.com*
- **Superpages.com:** *www.superpages.com*
- **MSN.com:** *www.msn.com*
- **Whitepages.com:** *www.whitepages.com*
- **Canada411.com:** *www.canada411.ca*

- **Argali White and Yellow:** *www.argali.com*
- **Dex Online:** *www.dexknows.com*

You'll like some of these more than others. Some will take time to figure out how to use, and none will provide everything you'll want.

One mention about Blackbook Online. It's the online version of *The Investigator's Little Black Book 3*, by Robert Scott, an invaluable resource for just about anything you could ever want to search. No investigator should be without it.

Understanding Databases

In the past, private investigators were forced to search records by hand. Sometimes, it's still necessary, but now information databases can perform nationwide or state-by-state searches. This is something you could not feasibly do in the days before these databases. However, this is both good and bad. Many investigators rely on these databases alone, even when only a hand search will locate the information they need. The solution is to use the databases—the good ones are wonderful—but analyze your returns and be sure that there isn't something you need to research in person at the courthouse. Sometimes, you'll need to search several courthouses in several counties, but don't be lazy about this important task. Neglect to verify your data and you can end up with egg on your face. You're the investigator, so investigate. That means searching as far and as wide as you need to.

If it's necessary to search the courthouse, don't fear the task. Most of the time, attendants will show you where to search and help you find what you need, especially if you inform them that you're new to the job. Throw yourself on their mercy. Become a learner, and you can usually find willing help.

Remember that some states don't have all records online yet. Others may have all categories online, but only for a number of years back. Accessing records from databases requires a bit of training as well. There are tips and tricks that will save time and money, while providing the optimum amount of information; but remember that no information database is infallible.

Possessing a private investigator's license allows for access to several proprietary information databases that aren't available to the general public. Some of these are:

- *www.irbsearch.com*
- *www.tracersinfo.com*
- *www.merlindata.com*
- *www.locateplus.com*
- *www.choicepoint.com*

These sites charge for your services and you may have to be screened in order to gain access to them. They contain information about addresses, criminal records, phone records, property records, and other searchable areas.

Legal Resources

The following resources are reliable for researching legal definitions and information. While you'll find other good Web sites, be very careful of the sites you choose, as some may only provide partial information. Others may even steer you wrong.

- Public Resources: *public.resource.org*
- AltLaw: *www.altlaw.org*
- American Bar Association: *www.abanet.org*
- Justia.com: *www.justia.com*
- Cornell University Law School: *www.law.cornell.edu*
- NOLO: *www.nolo.com*
- Washlaw Legal Research: *www.washlaw.edu*

- Law.com: *www.law.com*
- LLRX.com: *www.llrx.com*
- Westlaw: *www.westlaw.com*

A resource specific to law and court rulings for the private investigator is Dalman Investigations, whose homepage can be found at *www.dalman investigations.com/index.html*. It has an interesting section on laws in relation to the PI, at *www.dalmaninvestigations.com/id7.html*.

Also, check out *PI Magazine's* site at *www.pimagazine.com/* for lots of information for private investigators. The site also offers sales of equipment.

APPENDIX B

Police Codes and Abbreviations

Ten-codes are used for quick and surreptitious communication. There will be some differences from jurisdiction to jurisdiction, but these are the basic codes. Some organizations and municipalities also use other codes in addition to the ten-codes. An example is the California Highway Patrol's use of eleven-codes, and the New York/New Jersey Port Authority Police Department's use of eight codes.

10-0	Use Caution	10-26	Driver's license check by number or name
10-1	You are being received poorly		
10-2	You are being received clearly	10-27	Check for wants or warrants
10-3	Stop transmitting	10-28	Check registration on vehicle
10-4	Okay	10-29	Check for stolen
10-5	Relay message	10-29A	Check wants, subject (PIN)
10-6	Busy with call	10-29R	Check wants and record, subject (PIN, CJIC)
10-7	Out of service, (completely)		
10-7b	Out of service (personal)	10-29C	Check complete, subject (NCIC)
10-7c	Out of service (court)	10-30	Does not conform to rules or regulations
10-7od	Out of service (off duty)		
10-8	In service	10-31	Is lie detector available?
10-8ot	In service (over time)	10-32	Is intoxilizer available?
10-9	Repeat last message	10-33	Emergency traffic/Don't transmit unless necessary
10-10	Out of service, radio on		
10-11	Give F.C.C. call sign/Dispatching too fast	10-33	Alarm (type: audible, silent)
10-12	Visitors or officials present	10-34	Clear for local dispatch or Open door
10-13	Advise weather and road conditions	10-35	Confidential information or Open window
10-14	Convoy or escort detail		
10-15	Prisoner in custody	10-36	Correct time
10-15m	Prisoner in custody (mental case)	10-37	Give me name of operator on duty
10-16	Pick up prisoner	10-38	Your destination
10-17	Pick up papers	10-39	Your message is delivered/Requested unit en route
10-18	Complete present assignment ASAP/ Get there quick/ASAP		
		10-40	Advise if officer _____ available for phone call
10-19	Return to office		
10-20	Your location	10-41	Call the station on alternate frequency
10-21	Call by telephone		
10-21A	Phone home, my ETA is _____	10-42	Officer now at his home
10-21B	Call your home	10-43	Have _____ call his/her residence
10-22	Cancel last message/Take no further action		
		10-44	Station _____ is calling your residence
10-23	Stand by until channel clears		
10-24	Emergency at station/All units return	10-45	Give name of officer in charge or injured person
10-25	Do you have contact with _____		

10-46	Advise if _____ available at phone		10-74	Civil defense clear
10-47	Officer _____ is available at _____		10-75	Severe weather statement
			10-76	Give daily traffic
			10-77	Give mileage for your unit
10-48	Not available for assignment		10-78	Send ambulance
10-49	Pick up passenger at _____		10-79	Send wrecker
10-50	No traffic for you/Resume patrol		10-80	Tower lights out/Explosion/Lightening
10-51	Message for delivery by telephone		10-80a	Assist radio dispatcher
10-52	Message for delivery in writing		10-81	Officer _____ will be at your station
10-53	Do you have traffic for this station?			
10-54	Unit and officer have left the parish		10-82	Reserve room for officer
10-54d	Possible dead body		10-83	Have _____ call station by phone
10-55	Unit and officer have returned to parish			
10-55d	Send coroner		10-84	Advise _____ officer will return this date
10-56	Teletype busy			
10-57	Teletype broken or Firearms discharged		10-85	Officer _____ on special detail or Meet with agent
10-58	Teletype in service		10-86	Advise phone number of your location
10-59	Tape for repeat message			
10-60	What is next for message # _____		10-87	Give call letters of your station
			10-88	Advise phone number of officer
10-61	Stand by for teletype message		10-89	Request radio servicemen be sent
10-62	Unable to copy radio, use teletype, or meet in person		10-90	Request teletype servicemen
			10-91	Prepare for inspection of _____ by _____
10-63	Net in use, stand by, will advise when clear			
			10-91B	Noisy animal (Barking)
10-64	Net clear, go ahead with traffic		10-91D	Dead animal
10-65	Clear for assignment		10-91H	Stray horse
10-66	Clear for cancellation		10-92	Your quality is poor
10-67	All stations retransmit following		10-93	Your quality is good
10-68	Repeat dispatch		10-94	Call station by teletype
10-69	Have you dispatched _____?		10-95	Advise telephone call this station
10-70	Net message for all stations		10-96	Give test count
10-71	Proceed with traffic		10-97	Arrived at scene
10-72	Stand by for civil defense test		10-98	Last detail completed
10-73	Stand by for civil defense traffic		10-99	Unable to receive your message

10-100	Out using restroom
10-102	Cruelty to animals
10-103	Disturbance
10-103f	Disturbance by fight
10-103m	Disturbance by mental person
10-106	Obscenity
10-107	Suspicious person
10-108	Officer down/needs assistance
10-112	Impersonating an officer

APPENDIX C

Phonetic Alphabets and Special Symbols

Police and NATO phonetic alphabets have long been used to prevent spelled words or letters from being misunderstood over radio transmissions. While the chart indicates that the second listing is a police alphabet, more and more police, emergency response units, and federal agencies use the NATO alphabet. Be aware that there are slight variations across jurisdictions, and other variations around the world. If you're interested, see the mother of all alphabets here: *http://morsecode.scphillips.com/alphabet.html*.

Basic Phonetic Alphabets

Letter	NATO	Police
A	Alpha	Adam
B	Bravo	Boy
C	Charlie	Charlie
D	Delta	David
E	Echo	Edward
F	Foxtrot	Frank
G	Golf	George
H	Hotel	Henry
I	India	Ida
J	Juliet	John
K	Kilo	King
L	Lima	Lincoln
M	Mike	Mary
N	November	Nora
O	Oscar	Ocean
P	Papa	Paul
Q	Quebec	Queen
R	Romeo	Robert
S	Sierra	Sam
T	Tango	Tom
U	Uniform	Union
V	Victor	Victor
W	Whiskey	William
X	X-ray	X-ray
Y	Yankee	Young
Z	Zulu	Zebra

Index

THE EVERYTHING SERIES!

BUSINESS & PERSONAL FINANCE

Everything® Accounting Book
Everything® Budgeting Book, 2nd Ed.
Everything® Business Planning Book
Everything® Coaching and Mentoring Book, 2nd Ed.
Everything® Fundraising Book
Everything® Get Out of Debt Book
Everything® Grant Writing Book, 2nd Ed.
Everything® Guide to Buying Foreclosures
Everything® Guide to Mortgages
Everything® Guide to Personal Finance for Single Mothers
Everything® Home-Based Business Book, 2nd Ed.
Everything® Homebuying Book, 2nd Ed.
Everything® Homeselling Book, 2nd Ed.
Everything® Human Resource Management Book
Everything® Improve Your Credit Book
Everything® Investing Book, 2nd Ed.
Everything® Landlording Book
Everything® Leadership Book, 2nd Ed.
Everything® Managing People Book, 2nd Ed.
Everything® Negotiating Book
Everything® Online Auctions Book
Everything® Online Business Book
Everything® Personal Finance Book
Everything® Personal Finance in Your 20s & 30s Book, 2nd Ed.
Everything® Project Management Book, 2nd Ed.
Everything® Real Estate Investing Book
Everything® Retirement Planning Book
Everything® Robert's Rules Book, $7.95
Everything® Selling Book
Everything® Start Your Own Business Book, 2nd Ed.
Everything® Wills & Estate Planning Book

COOKING

Everything® Barbecue Cookbook
Everything® Bartender's Book, 2nd Ed., $9.95
Everything® Calorie Counting Cookbook
Everything® Cheese Book
Everything® Chinese Cookbook
Everything® Classic Recipes Book
Everything® Cocktail Parties & Drinks Book
Everything® College Cookbook
Everything® Cooking for Baby and Toddler Book
Everything® Cooking for Two Cookbook
Everything® Diabetes Cookbook
Everything® Easy Gourmet Cookbook
Everything® Fondue Cookbook
Everything® Fondue Party Book
Everything® Gluten-Free Cookbook
Everything® Glycemic Index Cookbook
Everything® Grilling Cookbook
Everything® Healthy Meals in Minutes Cookbook
Everything® Holiday Cookbook
Everything® Indian Cookbook
Everything® Italian Cookbook

Everything® Lactose-Free Cookbook
Everything® Low-Carb Cookbook
Everything® Low-Cholesterol Cookbook
Everything® Low-Fat High-Flavor Cookbook
Everything® Low-Salt Cookbook
Everything® Meals for a Month Cookbook
Everything® Meals on a Budget Cookbook
Everything® Mediterranean Cookbook
Everything® Mexican Cookbook
Everything® No Trans Fat Cookbook
Everything® One-Pot Cookbook
Everything® Pizza Cookbook
Everything® Quick and Easy 30-Minute, 5-Ingredient Cookbook
Everything® Quick Meals Cookbook
Everything® Slow Cooker Cookbook
Everything® Slow Cooking for a Crowd Cookbook
Everything® Soup Cookbook
Everything® Stir-Fry Cookbook
Everything® Sugar-Free Cookbook
Everything® Tapas and Small Plates Cookbook
Everything® Tex-Mex Cookbook
Everything® Thai Cookbook
Everything® Vegetarian Cookbook
Everything® Whole-Grain, High-Fiber Cookbook
Everything® Wild Game Cookbook
Everything® Wine Book, 2nd Ed.

GAMES

Everything® 15-Minute Sudoku Book, $9.95
Everything® 30-Minute Sudoku Book, $9.95
Everything® Bible Crosswords Book, $9.95
Everything® Blackjack Strategy Book
Everything® Brain Strain Book, $9.95
Everything® Bridge Book
Everything® Card Games Book
Everything® Card Tricks Book, $9.95
Everything® Casino Gambling Book, 2nd Ed.
Everything® Chess Basics Book
Everything® Craps Strategy Book
Everything® Crossword and Puzzle Book
Everything® Crossword Challenge Book
Everything® Crosswords for the Beach Book, $9.95
Everything® Cryptic Crosswords Book, $9.95
Everything® Cryptograms Book, $9.95
Everything® Easy Crosswords Book
Everything® Easy Kakuro Book, $9.95
Everything® Easy Large-Print Crosswords Book
Everything® Games Book, 2nd Ed.
Everything® Giant Sudoku Book, $9.95
Everything® Giant Word Search Book
Everything® Kakuro Challenge Book, $9.95
Everything® Large-Print Crossword Challenge Book
Everything® Large-Print Crosswords Book
Everything® Lateral Thinking Puzzles Book, $9.95
Everything® Literary Crosswords Book, $9.95
Everything® Mazes Book
Everything® Memory Booster Puzzles Book, $9.95
Everything® Movie Crosswords Book, $9.95

Everything® Music Crosswords Book, $9.95
Everything® Online Poker Book
Everything® Pencil Puzzles Book, $9.95
Everything® Poker Strategy Book
Everything® Pool & Billiards Book
Everything® Puzzles for Commuters Book, $9.95
Everything® Puzzles for Dog Lovers Book, $9.95
Everything® Sports Crosswords Book, $9.95
Everything® Test Your IQ Book, $9.95
Everything® Texas Hold 'Em Book, $9.95
Everything® Travel Crosswords Book, $9.95
Everything® TV Crosswords Book, $9.95
Everything® Word Games Challenge Book
Everything® Word Scramble Book
Everything® Word Search Book

HEALTH

Everything® Alzheimer's Book
Everything® Diabetes Book
Everything® First Aid Book, $9.95
Everything® Health Guide to Adult Bipolar Disorder
Everything® Health Guide to Arthritis
Everything® Health Guide to Controlling Anxiety
Everything® Health Guide to Depression
Everything® Health Guide to Fibromyalgia
Everything® Health Guide to Menopause, 2nd Ed.
Everything® Health Guide to Migraines
Everything® Health Guide to OCD
Everything® Health Guide to PMS
Everything® Health Guide to Postpartum Care
Everything® Health Guide to Thyroid Disease
Everything® Hypnosis Book
Everything® Low Cholesterol Book
Everything® Menopause Book
Everything® Nutrition Book
Everything® Reflexology Book
Everything® Stress Management Book

HISTORY

Everything® American Government Book
Everything® American History Book, 2nd Ed.
Everything® Civil War Book
Everything® Freemasons Book
Everything® Irish History & Heritage Book
Everything® Middle East Book
Everything® World War II Book, 2nd Ed.

HOBBIES

Everything® Candlemaking Book
Everything® Cartooning Book
Everything® Coin Collecting Book
Everything® Digital Photography Book, 2nd Ed.
Everything® Drawing Book
Everything® Family Tree Book, 2nd Ed.
Everything® Knitting Book
Everything® Knots Book
Everything® Photography Book
Everything® Quilting Book

Everything® Sewing Book
Everything® Soapmaking Book, 2nd Ed.
Everything® Woodworking Book

HOME IMPROVEMENT

Everything® Feng Shui Book
Everything® Feng Shui Decluttering Book, $9.95
Everything® Fix-It Book
Everything® Green Living Book
Everything® Home Decorating Book
Everything® Home Storage Solutions Book
Everything® Homebuilding Book
Everything® Organize Your Home Book, 2nd Ed.

KIDS' BOOKS

All titles are $7.95
Everything® Fairy Tales Book, $14.95
Everything® Kids' Animal Puzzle & Activity Book
Everything® Kids' Astronomy Book
Everything® Kids' Baseball Book, 5th Ed.
Everything® Kids' Bible Trivia Book
Everything® Kids' Bugs Book
Everything® Kids' Cars and Trucks Puzzle and Activity Book
Everything® Kids' Christmas Puzzle & Activity Book
Everything® Kids' Connect the Dots
Puzzle and Activity Book
Everything® Kids' Cookbook
Everything® Kids' Crazy Puzzles Book
Everything® Kids' Dinosaurs Book
Everything® Kids' Environment Book
Everything® Kids' Fairies Puzzle and Activity Book
Everything® Kids' First Spanish Puzzle and Activity Book
Everything® Kids' Football Book
Everything® Kids' Gross Cookbook
Everything® Kids' Gross Hidden Pictures Book
Everything® Kids' Gross Jokes Book
Everything® Kids' Gross Mazes Book
Everything® Kids' Gross Puzzle & Activity Book
Everything® Kids' Halloween Puzzle & Activity Book
Everything® Kids' Hidden Pictures Book
Everything® Kids' Horses Book
Everything® Kids' Joke Book
Everything® Kids' Knock Knock Book
Everything® Kids' Learning French Book
Everything® Kids' Learning Spanish Book
Everything® Kids' Magical Science Experiments Book
Everything® Kids' Math Puzzles Book
Everything® Kids' Mazes Book
Everything® Kids' Money Book
Everything® Kids' Nature Book
Everything® Kids' Pirates Puzzle and Activity Book
Everything® Kids' Presidents Book
Everything® Kids' Princess Puzzle and Activity Book
Everything® Kids' Puzzle Book
Everything® Kids' Racecars Puzzle and Activity Book
Everything® Kids' Riddles & Brain Teasers Book
Everything® Kids' Science Experiments Book
Everything® Kids' Sharks Book
Everything® Kids' Soccer Book
Everything® Kids' Spies Puzzle and Activity Book
Everything® Kids' States Book
Everything® Kids' Travel Activity Book
Everything® Kids' Word Search Puzzle and Activity Book

LANGUAGE

Everything® Conversational Japanese Book with CD, $19.95
Everything® French Grammar Book
Everything® French Phrase Book, $9.95
Everything® French Verb Book, $9.95
Everything® German Practice Book with CD, $19.95
Everything® Inglés Book
Everything® Intermediate Spanish Book with CD, $19.95
Everything® Italian Practice Book with CD, $19.95
Everything® Learning Brazilian Portuguese Book with CD, $19.95
Everything® Learning French Book with CD, 2nd Ed., $19.95
Everything® Learning German Book
Everything® Learning Italian Book
Everything® Learning Latin Book
Everything® Learning Russian Book with CD, $19.95
Everything® Learning Spanish Book
Everything® Learning Spanish Book with CD, 2nd Ed., $19.95
Everything® Russian Practice Book with CD, $19.95
Everything® Sign Language Book
Everything® Spanish Grammar Book
Everything® Spanish Phrase Book, $9.95
Everything® Spanish Practice Book with CD, $19.95
Everything® Spanish Verb Book, $9.95
Everything® Speaking Mandarin Chinese Book with CD, $19.95

MUSIC

Everything® Bass Guitar Book with CD, $19.95
Everything® Drums Book with CD, $19.95
Everything® Guitar Book with CD, 2nd Ed., $19.95
Everything® Guitar Chords Book with CD, $19.95
Everything® Harmonica Book with CD, $15.95
Everything® Home Recording Book
Everything® Music Theory Book with CD, $19.95
Everything® Reading Music Book with CD, $19.95
Everything® Rock & Blues Guitar Book with CD, $19.95
Everything® Rock & Blues Piano Book with CD, $19.95
Everything® Songwriting Book

NEW AGE

Everything® Astrology Book, 2nd Ed.
Everything® Birthday Personology Book
Everything® Dreams Book, 2nd Ed.
Everything® Love Signs Book, $9.95
Everything® Love Spells Book, $9.95
Everything® Paganism Book
Everything® Palmistry Book
Everything® Psychic Book
Everything® Reiki Book
Everything® Sex Signs Book, $9.95
Everything® Spells & Charms Book, 2nd Ed.
Everything® Tarot Book, 2nd Ed.
Everything® Toltec Wisdom Book
Everything® Wicca & Witchcraft Book, 2nd Ed.

PARENTING

Everything® Baby Names Book, 2nd Ed.
Everything® Baby Shower Book, 2nd Ed.
Everything® Baby Sign Language Book with DVD
Everything® Baby's First Year Book
Everything® Birthing Book

Everything® Breastfeeding Book
Everything® Father-to-Be Book
Everything® Father's First Year Book
Everything® Get Ready for Baby Book, 2nd Ed.
Everything® Get Your Baby to Sleep Book, $9.95
Everything® Getting Pregnant Book
Everything® Guide to Pregnancy Over 35
Everything® Guide to Raising a One-Year-Old
Everything® Guide to Raising a Two-Year-Old
Everything® Guide to Raising Adolescent Boys
Everything® Guide to Raising Adolescent Girls
Everything® Mother's First Year Book
Everything® Parent's Guide to Childhood Illnesses
Everything® Parent's Guide to Children and Divorce
Everything® Parent's Guide to Children with ADD/ADHD
Everything® Parent's Guide to Children with Asperger's Syndrome
Everything® Parent's Guide to Children with Asthma
Everything® Parent's Guide to Children with Autism
Everything® Parent's Guide to Children with Bipolar Disorder
Everything® Parent's Guide to Children with Depression
Everything® Parent's Guide to Children with Dyslexia
Everything® Parent's Guide to Children with Juvenile Diabetes
Everything® Parent's Guide to Positive Discipline
Everything® Parent's Guide to Raising a Successful Child
Everything® Parent's Guide to Raising Boys
Everything® Parent's Guide to Raising Girls
Everything® Parent's Guide to Raising Siblings
Everything® Parent's Guide to Sensory Integration Disorder
Everything® Parent's Guide to Tantrums
Everything® Parent's Guide to the Strong-Willed Child
Everything® Parenting a Teenager Book
Everything® Potty Training Book, $9.95
Everything® Pregnancy Book, 3rd Ed.
Everything® Pregnancy Fitness Book
Everything® Pregnancy Nutrition Book
Everything® Pregnancy Organizer, 2nd Ed., $16.95
Everything® Toddler Activities Book
Everything® Toddler Book
Everything® Tween Book
Everything® Twins, Triplets, and More Book

PETS

Everything® Aquarium Book
Everything® Boxer Book
Everything® Cat Book, 2nd Ed.
Everything® Chihuahua Book
Everything® Cooking for Dogs Book
Everything® Dachshund Book
Everything® Dog Book, 2nd Ed.
Everything® Dog Grooming Book
Everything® Dog Health Book
Everything® Dog Obedience Book
Everything® Dog Owner's Organizer, $16.95
Everything® Dog Training and Tricks Book
Everything® German Shepherd Book
Everything® Golden Retriever Book
Everything® Horse Book
Everything® Horse Care Book
Everything® Horseback Riding Book
Everything® Labrador Retriever Book
Everything® Poodle Book
Everything® Pug Book

Everything® Puppy Book
Everything® Rottweiler Book
Everything® Small Dogs Book
Everything® Tropical Fish Book
Everything® Yorkshire Terrier Book

REFERENCE

Everything® American Presidents Book
Everything® Blogging Book
Everything® Build Your Vocabulary Book, $9.95
Everything® Car Care Book
Everything® Classical Mythology Book
Everything® Da Vinci Book
Everything® Divorce Book
Everything® Einstein Book
Everything® Enneagram Book
Everything® Etiquette Book, 2nd Ed.
Everything® Guide to C. S. Lewis & Narnia
Everything® Guide to Edgar Allan Poe
Everything® Guide to Understanding Philosophy
Everything® Inventions and Patents Book
Everything® Jacqueline Kennedy Onassis Book
Everything® John F. Kennedy Book
Everything® Mafia Book
Everything® Martin Luther King Jr. Book
Everything® Philosophy Book
Everything® Pirates Book
Everything® Private Investigation Book
Everything® Psychology Book
Everything® Public Speaking Book, $9.95
Everything® Shakespeare Book, 2nd Ed.

RELIGION

Everything® Angels Book
Everything® Bible Book
Everything® Bible Study Book with CD, $19.95
Everything® Buddhism Book
Everything® Catholicism Book
Everything® Christianity Book
Everything® Gnostic Gospels Book
Everything® History of the Bible Book
Everything® Jesus Book
Everything® Jewish History & Heritage Book
Everything® Judaism Book
Everything® Kabbalah Book
Everything® Koran Book
Everything® Mary Book
Everything® Mary Magdalene Book
Everything® Prayer Book
Everything® Saints Book, 2nd Ed.
Everything® Torah Book
Everything® Understanding Islam Book
Everything® Women of the Bible Book
Everything® World's Religions Book

Everything® Guide to Being a Paralegal
Everything® Guide to Being a Personal Trainer
Everything® Guide to Being a Real Estate Agent
Everything® Guide to Being a Sales Rep
Everything® Guide to Being an Event Planner
Everything® Guide to Careers in Health Care
Everything® Guide to Careers in Law Enforcement
Everything® Guide to Government Jobs
Everything® Guide to Starting and Running a Catering Business
Everything® Guide to Starting and Running a Restaurant
Everything® Job Interview Book, 2nd Ed.
Everything® New Nurse Book
Everything® New Teacher Book
Everything® Paying for College Book
Everything® Practice Interview Book
Everything® Resume Book, 3rd Ed.
Everything® Study Book

SELF-HELP

Everything® Body Language Book
Everything® Dating Book, 2nd Ed.
Everything® Great Sex Book
Everything® Self-Esteem Book
Everything® Tantric Sex Book

SPORTS & FITNESS

Everything® Easy Fitness Book
Everything® Fishing Book
Everything® Krav Maga for Fitness Book
Everything® Running Book, 2nd Ed.

TRAVEL

Everything® Family Guide to Coastal Florida
Everything® Family Guide to Cruise Vacations
Everything® Family Guide to Hawaii
Everything® Family Guide to Las Vegas, 2nd Ed.
Everything® Family Guide to Mexico
Everything® Family Guide to New England, 2nd Ed.
Everything® Family Guide to New York City, 3rd Ed.
Everything® Family Guide to RV Travel & Campgrounds
Everything® Family Guide to the Caribbean
Everything® Family Guide to the Disneyland® Resort, California Adventure®, Universal Studios®, and the Anaheim Area, 2nd Ed.
Everything® Family Guide to the Walt Disney World Resort®, Universal Studios®, and Greater Orlando, 5th Ed.
Everything® Family Guide to Timeshares
Everything® Family Guide to Washington D.C., 2nd Ed.

WEDDINGS

Everything® Bachelorette Party Book, $9.95
Everything® Bridesmaid Book, $9.95
Everything® Destination Wedding Book
Everything® Father of the Bride Book, $9.95
Everything® Groom Book, $9.95
Everything® Mother of the Bride Book, $9.95
Everything® Outdoor Wedding Book
Everything® Wedding Book, 3rd Ed.
Everything® Wedding Checklist, $9.95
Everything® Wedding Etiquette Book, $9.95
Everything® Wedding Organizer, 2nd Ed., $16.95
Everything® Wedding Shower Book, $9.95
Everything® Wedding Vows Book, $9.95
Everything® Wedding Workout Book
Everything® Weddings on a Budget Book, 2nd Ed., $9.95

WRITING

Everything® Creative Writing Book
Everything® Get Published Book, 2nd Ed.
Everything® Grammar and Style Book, 2nd Ed.
Everything® Guide to Magazine Writing
Everything® Guide to Writing a Book Proposal
Everything® Guide to Writing a Novel
Everything® Guide to Writing Children's Books
Everything® Guide to Writing Copy
Everything® Guide to Writing Graphic Novels
Everything® Guide to Writing Research Papers
Everything® Improve Your Writing Book, 2nd Ed.
Everything® Writing Poetry Book

Available wherever books are sold! To order, call 800-258-0929, or visit us at *www.adamsmedia.com*.
Everything® and everything.com® are registered trademarks of F+W Publications, Inc.
Bolded titles are new additions to the series.
All Everything® books are priced at $12.95 or $14.95, unless otherwise stated. Prices subject to change without notice.